Robert Bruce

Our Most Valiant Prince,
King and Lord

Colm McNamee

BIRLINN

For John

This edition first published in 2018 by
Birlinn Limited
West Newington House
10 Newington Road
Edinburgh
EH9 1QS

www.birlinn.co.uk

First published in 2006

ISBN 978 1 78027 594 9

British Library Cataloguing in Publication Data
A catalogue record for this book is available from
the British Library

Typset by Geethik Technologies, India
Printed and bound in Great Britain by Clays Ltd, Elcograf S.p.A.

Colm McNamee works for the Northern Ireland Assembly. He studied at Queen's University, Belfast, and Worcester College, Oxford. His previous publications include *The Wars of the Bruces*, published by Tuckwell Press in 1997 and reprinted by John Donald in 2005.

Stories are enjoyable
Even if they are only fables
So stories that are true
If told entertainingly
Give double pleasure in the hearing.

John Barbour, *The Bruce, c.* 1375

Contents

List of Plates

List of Maps

Preface

This book is intended as a work of popular history; a distillation of secondary sources, providing a reliable and – one hopes – entertaining biography for general readers. The original idea for such a book was John Tuckwell's, and I am grateful to him for asking me to write it. It is important to me that people who read this book enjoy it, and I have tried to put into the writing some of the enthusiasm I feel for the subject. I love this story, of a hero whose humanity comes across so strongly; of a genius who made some terrible errors, but who was vindicated; of burning ambition realised, but at a terrible cost.

It is important to commemorate one who had a profound impact upon developments right across these islands; one who, from whatever mixture of motives, has inspired generations to stand up to insult, tyranny and aggression.

As the book is intended for the general reader, rather than the scholar, I have chosen not to pepper the text with references. Rather, notes detailing sources and acknowledging the insights of other authors have been provided on a chapter-by-chapter basis in the endmatter. I have also forsaken strictly accurate rendering of proper names for their popular equivalents.

Belfast

Preface to the New Edition

I can't keep up with the scholars. I leave Robert Bruce alone for a decade to earn an honest crust and come back to him to find that, though he has been dead for 700 years, he has changed dramatically. He might be an Essex man. He might well have premeditated the murder of poor John Comyn in that church in Dumfries (isn't it what we suspected all along?). Most shocking of all, the bones dug up in 1819 mightn't even be his. And where does *that* leave us with the question of whether he died of leprosy? Many of these particular shocks come courtesy of the new scholarly biography by Michael Penman, *Robert the Bruce: King of the Scots* (Yale University Press, 2014). Other shocks have been delivered by other scholars: the Monymusk Reliquary is no longer regarded as the *Breccbennach* of Colmcille; Sir Robert Keith is unlikely to have ridden down the English archers at Bannockburn; and the voyage of John MacSweeny to Knapdale, which in the past might have been dismissed altogether as a figment of the poetic imagination, now has its place in history confirmed. Much new scholarship was prompted by anticipation of the septcentenaries of Robert's enthronement in 1306 and of his victory at Bannockburn in 1314. Many of the old unknowns remain. Despite the best efforts of Fiona Watson and others, no consensus has emerged as to exactly where the battle of Bannockburn was fought.

A popular biography of Robert Bruce should strive to keep up to date with such fast-flowing historiography. Through television and the internet, people are informed, as never before, about their favourite historical subjects. In this new edition, mistakes have been corrected and revisions incorporated with due acknowledgement to the hard work of historians. Maps and tables have been improved. Nevertheless, I am painfully aware of a few shortcomings even in this reworking. I regret that the constraints of time have prevented me from using new editions of *Scalachronica* and the *Vita Edwardi Secundi*. Should the opportunity arise in the future, I will endeavour to reconsider both the raiding of England, which Andy King has revised anew, and the Scottish interventions in Ireland, both of which are topics dear to my heart but which, with the remarkable historiographical advances in the Scottish aspects of Robert's career, will have to await my attention. Strictly speaking, neither subject is central or germane to a popular biography of Robert I. Given the pace of historiography over the last decade, I fear I will always lag behind the academics.

I am deeply saddened by the deaths in recent years of Professor Archie Duncan, who advised me in the production of *The Wars of the Bruces* and in his criticism of this book; and of Professor G.W.S Barrow who first inspired my interest in the subject and corresponded with me. For decades their scholarly dialogue formed the basis on which research into Robert Bruce proceeded. It is to the credit of these great historians, writers and teachers that so many are inspired to set off in pursuit of Robert Bruce.

August 2018
Belfast

Acknowledgements

It is a pleasure to acknowledge my great debt to learned academic historians. Had this book been 'properly' referenced, there would have been an endless repetitive reference to the works of Professor G.W.S. Barrow, and in particular to his scholarly biography, *Robert Bruce and the Community of the Realm of Scotland* (4th edition, Edinburgh University Press, 2005). This applies equally to the works of Professor A.A.M. Duncan, and in particular to his wonderful edition and translation of John Barbour's *The Bruce* (Cannongate, 1998). To put pen to paper on this subject without constant reference to these works would be to produce fiction, not history. I am most grateful to Professor Duncan for permission to use his translation of Barbour's *The Bruce,* and to Professor Barrow for permission to use his translation of documents cited in *Robert Bruce,* and to the respective publishers.

There are many other eminent historians engaged in studying aspects of Robert I's life to whom I am indebted, among them Professor Ranald Nicholson, Professor Seán Duffy and Professor Michael Prestwich.

I was fortunate enough to attend the seven-hundredth anniversary conference of historians at Stirling University in March 2006, where I listened to and learnt from all of the speakers. I was inspired and enthused. I must mention in particular Professor Duncan, Professor Alexander Grant, Dr David Caldwell, Dr Michael

Penman and Professor Michael Kaufman. I am grateful to them all for inspiration, stimulating discussions and many a good read.

My maps of Bannockburn are based on those drawn by Jean Munro and Don Pottinger in 1974, though I have changed aspects of them in line with recent thinking.

I am very grateful to Hugh Andrew at Birlinn for his guidance, encouragement and understanding; to all at Birlinn, especially Andrew Simmons, Deborah Warner and Laura Esslemont; and to Aline Hill who made a number of helpful criticisms and suggestions and edited the manuscript. I am also grateful to the following people who assisted at various stages in the writing of this book: Professor Graham Walker made important books available to me; Professor Christopher Whately gave advice on post-medieval aspects of the subject; Philip Winterbottom, Deputy Group Archivist at the Royal Bank of Scotland gave advice on coinage. I am also very indebted to the staff at the various libraries which I used: the Main Library at Queens University, the Union Theological College and the Northern Ireland Assembly Library. Thanks too to my friends and colleagues: Crawford McIlveen and Niki McKeown who proof-read for me when time became short; Carolyn Fullerton and John Fisher who assisted in other ways. I am grateful also to Gerry McNamee for help with a translation of an awkward passage.

I am also indebted to my friends at the Northern Ireland Assembly for their assistance with the present offering. I will always be immensely grateful to Judith Green and John Maddicott, who each did their best to educate me in the ways of historians with great kindness and perseverance.

Finally, thanks, as ever, to my effervescent son John who showed some patience while I wrote, to my friend Ronan for entertaining John when his patience gave out and to the wonderful Dorothy and the remarkable Kathleen for living with me and Robert Bruce for most of our lives.

I am sorry if I have forgotten anyone.

Chronology

Wallace and Andrew Moray defeat the English at
    battle of Stirling

Wallace invades Northumberland and Cumberland

1298   Second invasion of Scotland by Edward I

Edward I defeats Wallace at Battle of Falkirk

Robert and John Comyn appointed joint Guardians
    of Scotland

1299   Scots take Stirling Castle

1300   Robert resigns or is expelled as Guardian

Third invasion of Scotland by Edward I

1301   Fourth invasion of Scotland by Edward I

1302   Robert submits to Edward I

Edward I rewards Robert with hand in marriage of
    Elisabeth de Burgh.

1303   Fifth invasion of Scotland by Edward I

John Comyn defeats English at Roslin

1304   Death of Robert Bruce VI (Robert's father)

Agreement between Robert and Bishop Lamberton

Possibly an agreement between Robert and John Comyn

1305   Wallace captured and executed

1306   Robert kills, John Comyn in the Greyfriars church,
    Dumfries

Robert enthroned at Scone as Robert I, King of Scots

Robert defeated at Methven, Strathtay and Dalry

Neil Bruce captured and killed

Robert flees to Rathlin and/or Islay, and thence to
    Western Isles

1307   Robert returns to mainland Scotland

Robert's brothers Thomas and Alexander return, and
    are defeated and executed

Robert 'on the run' in Galloway

Death of Edward I

Robert defeats English at Glen Trool, Loudon Hill

1316   Edward Bruce campaigns in Ireland
        Moray and Douglas invade England
        Peace between Flanders and France: open co-operation
            between Flemings and Scots on the North Sea ceases
1317   Robert and Edward Bruce campaign in Ireland
        Moray recaptures Isle of Man for the Scots
        Robbery of the Cardinals in Northumberland
        Pope tries to impose a truce
1318   Robert takes Berwick
        Edward Bruce dies at battle of Faughart
        Moray and Douglas invade England
1319   Edward II invades Scotland
        Siege of Berwick
        Moray and Douglas invade England as a diversion
        Battle of Myton
        Destruction of Western March by Moray and Douglas
1320   Two-year truce with England
        Declaration of Arbroath sent to pope
        Soules conspiracy against Robert
        Black Parliament, trial of conspirators
1322   Truce expires
        Robert, Moray and Douglas destroy Durham,
            Western March
        Edward II invades Scotland
        Robert invades England, defeats earl of Richmond at
        battle of Bylands and puts Edward II to flight
1323   Agreement between Robert and Andrew Harclay
        Truce of Bishopsthorpe: a thirteen-year truce with
            England
1324   Papal recognition of Robert's kingship
        Birth of John and David
        John dies; David survives as heir
1326   Treaty of Corbeil between Scotland and France

Introduction

Brushing off the cobwebs

On Wednesday, 10 February 1306 a group of perhaps half a dozen men stood about in Greyfriars churchyard at Dumfries, cloaks wrapped about them, stamping their feet against the bitter wind. Out of the winter gloom two horsemen rode up. Formal greetings were exchanged as the horses clattered across the cobbles and the riders dismounted, the forced friendliness betraying a hint of tension. All present bore 'casual' weaponry. To break the ice the leader of the waiting group strode towards the newcomers, hand outstretched, and greeted the younger of them with handshake and kiss on the cheek. Setting an example for his men, Robert Bruce, the 32-year-old earl of Carrick and lord of Annandale, put an arm round John Comyn of Badenoch and together they led the way into the kirk, stooping to enter the low doorway and crossing themselves. Comyn had ridden the six miles from his castle at Dalswinton escorted by his uncle Sir Robert Comyn. Robert Bruce was accompanied by his brother-in-law Christopher Seton and others unnamed. But the principals maintained their distance from their associates by walking up the aisle to the altar. In the confidential darkness of the chapel, Bruce's chat switched to earnest solicitation. The old king was dying … together they had the resources … it was now or never. Comyn had heard it all before and was weary of listening to Bruce's scheme: Bruce *knew* that Comyn could never assent to enthronement of anyone else as King of Scots while his uncle by marriage, King John Balliol, lived in exile. Carelessly Comyn let slip some banter, some coarse flippancy – and instantly regretted it. By the candlelight he registered Bruce's face, suddenly incandescent with rage. Comyn excused himself, apologised even, but too late. Bruce began shouting that Comyn had damaged his standing at court, that he had betrayed him to the English king. Comyn countered with bitter accusations of his own, but Bruce roared that Comyn was a liar and suddenly lashed out with a kick that brought him to the ground. Sir Robert Comyn rushed to his nephew's assistance but found his way blocked by Seton, who unsheathed his sword and struck him on the head. Such a rage had stoked up in him that Bruce entirely forgot himself and drew his own sword, heedless of the sanctity of his surroundings. He brought a clumsy blow down on the prostrate Comyn. Turning his back on the wounded man, as though in disgust, Bruce walked out into the fading daylight, leaving his men to finish off the Comyns. His men followed him out, and stood about for several minutes, respecting their chief's silence. Bruce struggled to take in the drastic implications of what had just happened, and wished he could relive those last few minutes. But, realising that there could be no going back, no explanations for what had happened, no excuses, he announced to his men his intention to seize the kingship of Scotland.

Although this is a plausible reconstruction of events, we do not really know the details of that fateful encounter in the friars' church. We cannot be sure Bruce did not set out to assassinate Comyn. However, with this impulsive act of murder, treachery and sacrilege Robert Bruce launched his bid for the throne of Scotland. It was a course fraught with danger, that would cost him dear in the lives of loved ones, and personal injury, yet would safeguard the Scottish identity, then in danger of extinction, and carry him into legend as Robert I of Scotland, a hero-king unsurpassed in the history of these islands.

Few have lived as fully, adventurously and heroically; indeed, Bruce's rollercoaster career prompts searching questions. How true are the tales told of Robert Bruce? How much can one man cram into a life? How many times, and in how many ways can a man be a hero? For Robert Bruce was at once a valiant knight and a great lord, a clever politician, a murderer, or at least an accomplice to murder, a fugitive, an inspirational charismatic guerrilla chief, a military genius, a wise statesman, a self-declared hero and finally, in the eyes of Scots through the ages, the saviour of a nation. Tricks, ruses and hair-raising escapes; high politics, grim sieges and bloody battles; assassination plots; single combat to the death, Bruce lived it all. Even debilitating illness at the end of his life – was it leprosy? – did not prevent Bruce waging war in Ireland and England simultaneously, while being carried about on a litter. He was a colossus among men, and even now Scotland lives deep in his shadow.

Seven hundred years ago Robert Bruce seized the kingship of Scotland as his birthright and, defeated in battle, fled overseas, preserving in his own person the kingship of Scotland from extirpation by Edward I of England's precocious united kingdom of the Middle Ages. He may have saved the 'idea of Scotland' for future generations. Unusually for someone who lived in the Middle Ages, we know a great deal about this Robert Bruce, and whatever else may be unclear about this still controversial figure, he was a remarkable man. The antithesis of an armchair general who sends others into dangers which he does not himself share, Bruce led from the front, risking everything in pursuit of his goal. His skull – or his supposed skull – exhumed five hundred years after his death, still bears marks of the serious head injuries he sustained. Undoubtedly he did terrible things: he presided over the butchering of at least one garrison; he inflicted a decade of cruel war on a virtually defenceless civilian population in northern England; and he was personally involved in the murder of John Comyn, as we have seen. He endured deprivation and lost heavily along the way: his four brothers lost their lives in his cause; his sister and his putative lover endured years of humiliation for their association with him. And at the end of it all Robert died in his bed, confident that he had succeeded in his ambitions for himself, his family and Scotland, and he passed into history as 'the ultimate hero and defender of Scottish nationhood against English imperialism while other Scottish patriots were most unfairly vilified by historians'.

Robert's life has always made compelling reading, and it is entirely appropriate that he is compared by medieval writers to Odysseus the fabled wanderer, Aenaeas the legendary founder of Rome and the biblical heroes Joshua the Israelite general and Judas Maccabeus, who led the Jewish revolt against the Seleucid Empire. His adventures were a match for any of them. He revived the kingship of Scotland, and liberated her from English domination; forced northern England to pay tribute; and, aspiring to pan-Celtic leadership, sent his brother to conquer Ireland and threaten Wales. In the history of the British Isles, Robert I stands for more than just a brief Scottish hegemony: he represents one of history's great 'What ifs?', an alternative path of development, an alternative to English domination not just for Scotland, but for Ireland and Wales as well.

Even as things turned out, history has been kind to Robert Bruce; too kind, perhaps, since the medieval propagandists for his dynasty have successfully airbrushed over his faults. Yet he has not always been a popular figure. Over the centuries his popularity has waxed and, in recent times, waned. In his lifetime Robert spared no efforts to have posterity regard him as he is portrayed by the image on his own royal seal: the very personification of divine order in the world and the impassive symbol of divine justice. In the later Middle Ages, the Bruce legend of miraculous survival from catastrophe to vindicate a just claim provided for Scotland a necessary mythology for resistance and survival during her life-or-death struggle with her powerful southern neighbour. Then the legend lost its importance as war with England abated; and after the union of English and Scottish crowns in 1707 it potentially had the power to inspire secession and treachery. In the late Georgian era the Bruce legend was 'rediscovered' in time to take advantage of the growth of tourism, and Bruce was packaged, along with tartan, kilts and Highland clans, for mass marketing. The exhumation of Bruce's bones in 1819 and subsequently Sir Walter Scott's rendition of his life in *Tales of a Grandfather* did much to remind the nation of the debt it owed to its hero-king; but that image was not refreshed, and in the twentieth century acquired a stuffy and shop-worn aspect, an image without mystery or humanity, that belonged to a distant and irrelevant past.

Robert Bruce changed sides repeatedly in the decade 1296 to 1306 for a variety of reasons: because he wished and was expected to defend the dynastic and legal interests of his family; because, insofar as there was a 'national cause', contemporaries perceived it only as equal to or exceeded in importance by sworn personal loyalties; because he was faced with a choice between a foreign king for whom he had no love, and a Scottish king (Robert saw him as a usurper) who would destroy him; and finally, because his peers and rivals were all acting in defence of their own family and dynastic interests. This past hundred years or so, Scotland has not embraced the memory of Robert Bruce with the same warmth as hitherto. Perhaps, true to her Celtic nature, Scotland prefers her heroes in the tragic mould, and Robert has been too successful for sympathy.

Despite centuries of popular myth and misunderstanding, and centuries of propaganda generated both by the Bruces themselves and by their enemies, recent historical endeavour has brushed away these cobwebs. By patient work in archives and libraries Professors Barron, Barrow and Duncan (and many others too numerous to mention here) have revised Robert's whole career and shed new light upon the historical figure. Through their work, a dull and sombre oil painting is daringly restored to reveal hidden complexities and characteristics.

Sources are crucial to accurate history, and it helps one's understanding to know a little of the nature of the sources that underpin the accurate modern accounts. For Scotland in this period there are not the detailed household records that exist for the contemporary English kings, Edwards I, II and III. But we do have Archdeacon John Barbour's superb 'romance' *The Bruce*. Completed in 1375 or the following year, it is a verse chronicle of Robert's life – some thirteen thousand lines of rhyming couplets in the medieval Scots tongue – startlingly accurate in many details when checked against administrative sources and devoted to the chivalrous exploits of the hero-king. Barbour is not interested in dates, administrative matters or politics: he writes of war, concentrating on Bruce's valour, his martial prowess and, occasionally, on his other chivalric virtues – magnanimity, generosity and wisdom. Prominent in the story (rather to the detriment of Bruce's main lieutenant, Thomas Randolph, earl of Moray) are Bruce's companions Sir James Douglas ('Good Sir James') and Walter, the hereditary Steward of Scotland, founder of the Stewart dynasty. Barbour concentrates on these individuals with good reason: Barbour was writing for Walter's son, Robert II of Scotland, and he seems to have possessed a verse account of Douglas's chivalric deeds. *The Bruce* is a unique record of a life in the Middle Ages; nothing quite comparable exists elsewhere.

Other narrative sources also throw light on the life of Robert Bruce: the *Annals* of John of Fordun, which existed in draft in 1363, and the *Scotichronicon* of Walter Bower, written in the mid fifteenth century, which drew upon materials collected by Fordun. These and other Scottish authors of the later Middle Ages were keen to present Bruce and his offspring as the legitimate and God-given kings of Scotland, and during their lifetimes the dynasty was locked in intermittent war with England. While their works contain a wealth of historical detail, these authors were also Bruce's apologists and propagandists. For Fordun, Bruce was a saviour on a par with Christ himself:

The English nation lorded it in all parts of the kingdom of Scotland ruthlessly harrying the Scots in sundry and manifold ways ... But God in His mercy, as is the wont of his fatherly goodness, had compassion ...; so He raised up a saviour and champion unto them – one of their own fellows to wit, named Robert Bruce. The man ... putting forth his hand unto force, underwent the countless and unbearable toils of the heat of the day ... for the sake of freeing his brethren.

These are heavily partisan accounts, written by supporters of the Bruce monarchy. Here indeed is history written by the winners, not all of it inaccurate, but, as in this excerpt from Bower, heavily biased and effusive in praise of the hero-king:

whoever has learnt to recount [Bruce's] individual conflicts and particular triumphs – the victories and battles in which with the help of the Lord, by his own strength and his energetic valour as a man, he forced his way through the ranks of the enemy without fear, now powerfully laying them low, now powerfully turning them aside as he avoided the penalty of death – he will find, I think, that he will judge none in the regions of the world to be his equals in his own times in the art of fighting and in physical strength.

Evidence offered by these propagandists in support of Bruce is balanced by that of the English narrative sources, heavily biased against him: the *Scalachronica* or 'Ladder Chronicle' written in the mid fourteenth century by a Northumberland knight, Sir Thomas Gray; the near-contemporary *Lanercost* chronicle, a more balanced and informative narrative of the period, and the other near-contemporary chronicle written by Walter of Guisborough, along with many other monastic writers who contribute from the English point of view. Manx, Irish and French contemporary authors also help illuminate aspects of Bruce's remarkable career. All lend their particular slant to the story, and most have an axe to grind in the telling, but, along with quantities of misinformation, all bear aspects of that elusive quality, historical truth.

Administrative sources carry less propaganda. Not much survives from the Scottish government's bureaucracy, except for invaluable Exchequer Rolls for the latter part of Robert's reign. There are no records of royal or private estates in Scotland from this period; administrative evidence from Scotland mostly takes the form of charters or title-deeds to land, which tend to be retained in families. Enormous strides have been made in scholarship lately, and Professor Duncan has edited and assembled the extant deeds of King Robert I. We are unlikely ever to have the king's complete *acta* – all his charters, deeds and letters – but we do have a much clearer picture than ever before. By contrast, the English government of the period produced a vast archive, which is still largely intact. Research in the Public Record Office continues to throw up documents illuminating events in those parts of Scotland subject to English rule and the English king's war effort against the 'patriot' Scots. Rolls of parchment – the *Rotuli Scotiae* or Scotch Rolls, the Patent Rolls, Close Rolls, Pipe Rolls and Memoranda Rolls – contain thousands of copies of individual documents with a bearing on the situation in Scotland and on the management of a war which stretched the impressive Edwardian administrative machine to the limit of its capacity. To avoid using the cumbersome Westminster-based exchequer, the 'Three Edwards' used a department of the royal household, the royal wardrobe, as a mobile war finance office, dedicated to the funding of their campaigns. Wardrobe Books, often beautiful in their calligraphy, provide annual records of payments from the English royal household for campaigns against the Scots – expenditure on castle garrisons, all manner of supply, payments to infantry and cavalry, royal gifts and messengers – in detail that provides valuable insight into what was happening in Scotland and other theatres of war. There are other administrative sources too. Some records of the Irish government have survived the catastrophic fire of 1922, and there is a wealth of material accumulated by monastic houses and other religious institutions in northern England: bishops' registers, collections of charters and occasional estate records. A particularly well-preserved source is the monastic archive at Durham, which provides insights into Robert's exaction of tribute from the north of England and how the monastery's estates fared during his destructive raids.

The sources then are fuller than one might expect, yet they only take us so far on our journey to understand the character of Robert Bruce. With hindsight we may judge that Bruce made some appalling blunders: his murder of Comyn and certain of his interventions in Ireland may qualify in this respect. But we perceive the energy with which, in defiance of the greatest military power of the day, Bruce pursued his burning ambition; his frustration as he sides first with the patriots against the might of the foreign occupying power, then submits to Edward I to protect vital interests, and then alienates both sides in his lunge for the throne. We can sense his despair at defeat and his humiliation at being hounded out of a realm to whose kingship he aspired. There are also indications of the personal grief he suffered at the brutal executions of his brothers and the public humiliation of those dear to him.

The most telling illustration of Robert's character however may lie not in true history, but in anecdote, misattributed to him long after his death. The strength of character required to claw back from three crushing defeats is aptly represented by the tired image of Robert Bruce and the spider. Destitute, the would-be king sits alone and dejected on Rathlin Island (or Jura, or Arran, or at Kirkpatrick, or at Uamh-an-Righ, or a host of other places for which claims are staked in the tourist brochures), idly watching a spider trying to spin a web. Time and again the spider fails, yet eventually through blind determination it succeeds, inspiring Bruce to try once more to regain the throne of Scotland. As most people know, the spider story is a late fabrication. It was related by Sir Walter Scott in the *Tales of a Grandfather*, but originally invented by David Hume of Godscroft in his *Historie of the House of Douglas* (1633), where it is Sir James Douglas who witnesses the spider's doings and relates them to Bruce. The tale may not be history, but the point is well made: that Bruce, though long dead, compels our admiration through his determination and tenacity, through his heroic effort to rebuild from catastrophe his own dynastic fortunes and those of Scotland herself. Through the work of scholars the figure of Robert Bruce has emerged from the dark cave of legend and myth into the half-light of history, and it is time to reassess this crucially important figure and accord him his due place in popular culture.

1

A man of his time, a man of his place

Scotland in the late thirteenth century

The Robert Bruce who became king was born on 11 July 1274. His aristocratic family had extensive holdings in south-west Scotland, where they had been lords of Annandale for generations and great estates in England as well which had been acquired more recently. The future king is referred to in most modern works as Robert Bruce VII, to distinguish him from his forefathers. The numeral refers however to his place in succession to the lordship of Annandale; he was in fact the sixth Robert Bruce of the name. We do not know for sure where he was born. Turnberry Castle, the head of his mother's earldom of Carrick, is traditionally held to be his birthplace, though recent scholarship seems to favour the family's manor of Writtle in Essex where his father spent a lot of time. Which kingdom he was born in will not have mattered greatly to Robert or his contemporaries. Much more important to him were ties of kinship, custom and sworn allegiance. The Bruces were of more than just lordly rank: they were great magnates, the social equals of earls. Indeed, by marrying his mother, his father had acquired the title of earl of Carrick in right of his wife. The development of the Bruce dynasty will be discussed in the next chapter; for the present

Robert's early life will be discussed, together with the contexts into which Robert was born.

Life in the Middle Ages was dominated by ideas and assumptions that no longer exist in quite the same way, and common misunderstandings of Robert Bruce are often rooted in failures to understand how a man of Bruce's time and social class comprehended life, relationships and the world. 'The past is another country' and one should not go there without a guide, however brief, however sketchy. To do otherwise is to risk infecting the past with the assumptions of the present age, creating anachronisms and investing historical personalities with attitudes and assumptions that they could never have embraced. The period we are dealing with is the late thirteenth and early fourteenth century, and the backdrop to Robert's early life is known as the High Middle Ages. This was before gunpowder was commonly used in Western Europe (though great lords were beginning to explore the potential of primitive explosives). It was before the Black Death wiped out a third of Europe's population. It was a time when economic growth and agrarian expansion was levelling off, or perhaps just beginning to recede in many parts of the British Isles. Economic trends were not of course evident to Robert or his contemporaries. Perhaps because technology had not changed significantly in a thousand years, people in the Middle Ages did not usually conceive of society as dynamic or evolving. It has been said, with justification, that medieval people had no concept of evolution. It would be incorrect however to say that they did not introduce new ideas and inventions; rather they showed a tendency to represent innovation as a return to an earlier state of affairs. Medieval people were much more respectful of the past than we are, and looked to tradition, custom and lineage to provide justification for decisions or actions. To them, society and economy were as they always had been, time out of mind.

The marriage of Robert's father, Robert Bruce, the sixth lord of Annandale, around 1272, is the subject of an engaging vignette in

Fordun's chronicle, in which, during a chance encounter while she was out hunting, the lady, Marjorie, Countess of Carrick, vamps her man:

> When greetings and kisses had been given on each side, as is the wont of courtiers, she besought him to stay and hunt and walk about; and seeing that he was rather unwilling to do so, she by force, so to speak, with her own hand, made him pull up and brought the knight, although very loath, with her to her castle of Turnberry. After dallying there with his followers for the space of fifteen days or more, he secretly took the countess as his wife. Friends and well-wishers of both knew nothing about it, nor had the king's consent in the matter been at all obtained.

Whatever the chronicle says, Robert's father is unlikely to have been browbeaten or forced into marriage with a rich widow and a countess in her own right. Rather, Fordun is protecting the father of his hero from accusation of abducting Marjorie. Enraged, King Alexander III, whose right it was to approve marriages between his tenants-in-chief, took Turnberry and all the countess's possessions into his own hand; but a gift of money soon placated him. The marriage was a very fruitful union and may have been a love match, quite unusual for the Middle Ages when marriage was predominantly viewed as a property contract, to be negotiated between two families, often while the principals were still very young.

With respect to Robert's early family life we have no firm evidence, but we can hazard some generalisations. Robert Bruce VI, has been characterised as 'spineless' and 'colourless' by Professor Barrow, but this is by comparison with Robert's colourful crusader grandfather, Robert Bruce V, known to contemporaries as Robert the Noble, and to history as 'Bruce the Competitor', because he competed with others for the throne of Scotland at the hearings known as the Great Cause in 1290–91. This grandfather seems to have been an immense influence on Robert. That is evident not only from his conviction of the justice of his claim to the throne, a claim pioneered by Robert Bruce V, but also from his death-bed crusading aspirations, derived from the example of his grandfather. Robert the Noble inherited extensive lands in England and played a significant role in the affairs of that realm and the service of the king of England. Thus the Bruces became true cross-border aristocracy and young Robert Bruce VII will have travelled between all the family's properties.

Marjorie, the mother of Robert, the future king, being the daughter of Neil, the last Gaelic earl of Carrick, was a Gaelic noblewoman. Her marriage to Robert Bruce of Annandale brought that lord the earldom of Carrick as we have seen, and so it was that Robert the king-to-be inherited the title earl of Carrick. Recently Seán Duffy has suggested that Robert's maternal grandmother, the wife of Neil, earl of Carrick, may have been a daughter of an O'Neill king of Tyrone. It may therefore be no accident that the Christian name Neil occurs in the Bruce family. The O'Neills of Tyrone harboured pretensions to the kingship of Ireland, and if it were the case that the Bruces were connected by blood with the O'Neills it would have profound implications for the Bruce claim to be of royal blood. It is possible too that from Neil of Carrick the Bruces inherited a claim to lands in County Antrim in Ireland, granted in the twelfth century to Neil's father, Duncan of Carrick. Be that as it may, ties with the *Gaidhealtachd*, the Gaelic-speaking crescent that extended along the west and north of the British Isles, were close, and Gaelic was quite literally Robert Bruce's mother tongue. We may be certain that all the children spoke French and Gaelic; a little Latin, the language of prayer; and Scots, the English dialect used by the Lowland peasantry. The family will have moved between the castles of the lordship: Lochmaben, the main castle of the lordship of Annandale; Turnberry and Loch Doon of the earldom of Carrick. Much time will also have been spent on the English estates, Tottenham, Hatfield and Writtle.

Robert had eight or nine siblings, but since his father married a second wife (presumably on the death of Marjorie) some of the younger children may have been half brothers and half sisters. The boys, at least Robert and Edward, were fostered according to Gaelic tradition, spending a substantial part of their youth at the courts of other noblemen. The foster-brother of Robert is referred to by Barbour as sharing Robert's precarious existence as an outlaw in Carrick during the years 1307 and 1308, while Edward was, according to one source, invited to Ireland by 'a certain Irish magnate with whom he had been educated in his youth'. It is possible then that they were fostered to Gaelic Irish magnates. Tales of Finn MacCool are referred to in *The Bruce* and perhaps the children absorbed the traditional Gaelic stories at their mother's knee. Elsewhere in the poem Robert is said to have recited the tale of 'Ferambrace' ('Iron Arm'), the Charlemagnian hero, to raise the spirits of his men; this illustrates the family's dominant francophone, chivalric background. The children could well have been taught to read in some of their languages, though those destined for knighthood (Robert, Neil, Edward and Thomas) may have considered that writing was best left to clerks. One of the younger brothers, Alexander, was groomed for a career in holy orders. As heir, Robert will have been schooled by specialist tutors in all the refinements of courtly etiquette – manners, elocution, music perhaps, and dancing – and he will have waited as a page at his father's and grandfather's tables. Periods of service with friendly aristocratic families will have been the norm, and Penman has shown that our Robert, in the company of his father, was in service from 1290 to 1292 at the truly splendid court of Edward I. He will have received some schooling in law. Special attention will have been paid to the martial arts of horsemanship, swordsmanship and jousting. Leisure activities included a prodigious amount of hunting and falconry. A love of ships and sea travel that emerges in Robert's later life may have been instilled in his youth.

The importance of piety will have received great stress. Medieval Christianity is said to have been akin to polytheism in that every day, every locality and every situation had its own particular saint. Saints

could be jealous of their due devotions and wrathful. St Malachy, as
we shall see, may have been perceived by the family as an entity to be
appeased. There are indications that devotion to St Thomas Becket
was important in Robert's life. The children will have been taught
to revere certain saints above others: Columcille, and also Andrew,
whose cult had grown over the past hundred years at the expense
of the Celtic saints. Relics and pilgrimages featured prominently.
St Ninian may have been the principal local saint, and it was to St
Ninian's cave that Robert made his final pilgrimage. His charters also
suggest devotion to St Fillan, whose shrine was maintained in the
Abbey of Inchaffray, and to St Kentigern, the patron of the bishopric
of Glasgow. Also, in later life, Robert showed some partiality towards
St Kessog, who founded the community of Inchtavannach, on the
Isle of the Monks in Loch Lomond.

It is easier to generalise about Robert's early life than to describe
the world he was born into. In Scotland there was a consciousness
of being a small and relatively poor kingdom on the very edge of
Christendom; the Declaration of Arbroath refers to 'Poor little
Scotland, beyond which there is no dwelling place at all'. The vast
majority of her half a million inhabitants were peasant farmers
living off cattle and the land. Outside the core areas of medieval
farming – such as Lothian, the eastern coastal plain and the Lowlands
generally – medieval population was either at its height or, perhaps,
just beginning to decline. In regions such as south-west Scotland,
where the Bruce lordship was centred, grain farmers were beginning
to abandon unprofitable soils and pastures as the demand for food,
and hence the price the farmer could expect, was not quite as high as
it had been. Farmers in south-west Scotland were fortunate in that
they had extensive areas of high moorland which provided seasonal
pasture on which cattle might graze. Cattle were more important
than tillage in such parts of Scotland, and this was reflected in the
social organisation of Gaelic Scotland, where the population moved
with the cattle between seasonal pastures. Over a large part of the

British Isles, Robert Bruce's wars helped to accelerate the downturn in grain farming and, viewed in the long term, to terminate many features that typified the High Middle Ages.

If tillage was beginning perhaps to falter, trade was flourishing, though it was all on a fairly small scale. There were not many towns or 'burghs' in the Scotland of Robert's day and those that existed were small and often situated on the coast. Kings and lords had realised that towns generated income through concentrating the population and creating markets, and so the development of burghs had been encouraged by the great lords through grants of privileges: rights to take tolls, and hold fairs and markets. Scottish kings had created thirty-six royal burghs, many of which developed urban characteristics. The main towns were Berwick, Edinburgh, Roxburgh and Stirling. Most of the larger towns were on the east coast where there was a growing export trade in wool, leather, hides, fish and timber. Wool in particular was sold to Flemish and Italian merchants who supplied the great cloth-manufacturing centres. The other goods were exported to England and also farther afield to Flanders, the Netherlands and the German-speaking towns of the Baltic. There was considerable Flemish interest and settlement in the leading ports of Aberdeen, Perth and Berwick – where the Flemings had a headquarters (probably something of a community centre and plant for processing exports) at the Red Hall, while the merchants of Cologne maintained a similar presence at the White Hall.

The sort of society that Robert grew up in can perhaps be most briefly explained by looking at some of the cleavages that existed. Social divisions at the time of Robert Bruce were fine, many and complex; but it will help if we look first at that between the small aristocratic elite and the great majority who were accounted as churlish, and secondly that between the Gaelic and the Anglo-Norman.

Gentillesse or nobility could only be conferred by breeding; one had to be born a gentleman, noble or aristocrat to possess the appropriate manner, speech and air. Gentillesse also implied

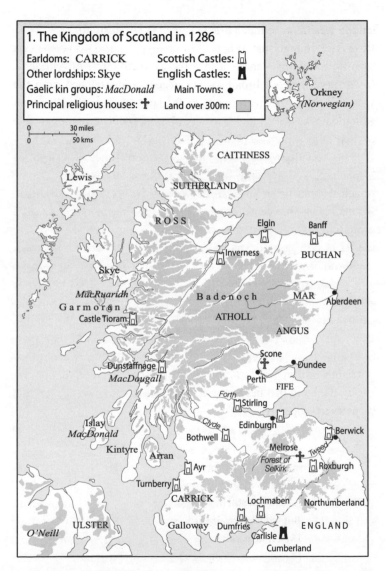

1. The Kingdom of Scotland in 1286

Earldoms: CARRICK
Other lordships: Skye
Gaelic kin groups: *MacDonald*
Principal religious houses: ✝

Scottish Castles: 🏰
English Castles: 🏰
Main Towns: ●
Land over 300m: ▓

Orkney
(Norwegian)

0   30 miles
0   50 kms

CAITHNESS

Lewis

SUTHERLAND

R O S S

Elgin   Banff

Inverness   BUCHAN

Skye

MacRuaridh   B a d e n o c h   MAR
G a r m o r a n   Aberdeen
Castle Tioram   ATHOLL
                                        ANGUS
Dunstaffnage   Scone   Dundee
MacDougall   Perth   FIFE

                    Forth   Stirling

                    Clyde   Edinburgh   Berwick
Islay   Bothwell
MacDonald
Kintyre   Arran   Melrose
                    Forest of   *Tweed*
                    Ayr   *Selkirk*   Roxburgh
Turnberry

CARRICK   Lochmaben
                                Northumberland
ULSTER   Galloway   Dumfries   ENGLAND
O'Neill   Carlisle
                    Cumberland

The Kingdom of Scotland also included the Isle of Man, which is not shown on this map.

landed wealth, an estate sufficient to maintain a noble household. It was not enough just to have money; at this period very few rich townsfolk – if any – made it into the charmed circle of *gentillesse*. It was nevertheless a broad social category, and stretched from the king and the highest aristocrats in the land (such as the Bruces of Annandale) to poor knights and squires with only a manor or two to their names, such the family of William Wallace.

The relationship between nobles is sometimes described as hierarchical, and certainly there were different degrees of rank, the principal ranks being king (at the apex of the social pyramid), earls, barons, knights and gentlemen. Everyone had to have a lord, a patron, a protector, of whom he held his fief of land, and to whom he performed the act of homage and fealty. This was a solemn occasion. The vassal knelt with hands joined before the lord in the presence of witnesses; the lord, standing up, clasped the vassal's joined hands, and the vassal recited a formula of words promising undying loyalty. The act was sealed by the gift of a fief of land, for which the vassal completed some noble service. knight service, ship service, or even a nominal service such as gifting a rose at midsummer or a pair of sparrowhawks. The bond of homage was not lightly broken. In *The Bruce* Barbour waxes lyrical on the virtue of loyalty, the bond that ties a man to his lord, and the social cement that keeps society together:

> Loyalty is to love wholeheartedly
> By loyalty men live righteously.
> With loyalty and but one other virtue
> A man can still be adequate,
> But without loyalty he is worthless
> Even if he is valiant or wise.
> For where loyalty is lacking
> No virtue is of sufficient price
> To make a man good
> So that he can be called simply a 'good man'.

There is a great irony here for, despite the social taboo, the war between the kingdoms forced nobles to break their oaths of fealty. Robert Bruce, who broke his oath to Edward I at least twice, including an oath sworn on a relic of a favourite saint, may have a reputation for breaking oaths. Malise, earl of Strathearn, is said to have scorned to come over to Bruce's side, declaring that *his* oath of loyalty was not 'fragile like glass'.

Besides the interplay of lords and vassals, there were other dimensions to noble society. The market in land allowed an earl to hold land of a knight where it was desirable, knights to rent royal demesne from the king, and monasteries to let out their lands to nobles of all ranks for profit. Noble relations then resembled a network, rather than the familiar feudal pyramid of the school history books. Rival networks of magnate interest sprang up and vied with one another for influence in localities or at court: for most of the thirteenth century the influence of the Bruces had been eclipsed at court by the dominance of their great rivals the Comyns, who had controlled most of the high offices in the land for the best part of the thirteenth century, and had built up a powerful network of castles, estates and interests across the kingdom.

The francophone, chivalric society of northern Europe provided the main cultural input to the Bruce family. As aristocrats they considered themselves natural leaders and displayed that arrogant disdain of the lower 'churlish' social orders and pride in their own ancestry common to all aristocracies. From their position near the top of the social hierarchy, as magnates or tenants-in-chief of the king, they controlled lesser baronial or knightly families through grants of land and other bestowals of patronage. As the king demanded taxation and knight service from the Bruces, so they in turn demanded food or money rents and (in time of war) knight service, ship service, castle-guard and other assistance from their noble dependents. Ecclesiastical livings such as parishes and vicarages, were also used as patronage, to be dispensed to social inferiors in return for their loyalty and their services. Perhaps unusually for a magnate family of such high standing, the Bruces had not founded a monastery in Scotland; rather, they continued to patronise the monastery of Guisborough in Yorkshire, which held the tombs of their ancestors. When Robert became king he patronised many Scottish religious houses and several English ones, but he was especially generous to the Cistercian foundation at Melrose, where his heart now lies buried.

It was expected of all magnate families to display their wealth and privileged status in a variety of ways. The Bruces lived ostentatiously; diet, dress and manners were distinct from and superior to those of social inferiors. Their main seat was at Lochmaben, but they will have maintained several grand houses and moved between them periodically, accompanied by a large group of noble retainers, known as a retinue or *meinie*. In common with aristocracies right across northern Europe at this time, they displayed armorial devices illustrating their pedigree. The Bruces flaunted their martial valour in tournaments, listened to troubadour ballads on the themes of courtly love, and enjoyed Arthurian literature, all of which were in vogue during this, the golden age of chivalry.

The churls on the other hand, were the vast majority of the people, excluded from *gentil* society and each bound to a lord by economic and social obligations of a baser kind: chiefly the payment of rents and dues, and the performance of labour services (including military service in time of war). This social category included men of greatly varying legal status, from prosperous freeholders, through bondmen to natives, bound to the soil and burdened with all sorts of services, payments and obligations. The corollary of the churl's submission was that the lord would provide protection in times of danger, settlement of disputes, justice for the aggrieved and the distribution of largesse: rewards, grants, gifts and charity. The lord's officials, the stewards, baillies or reeves, dispensed justice in the lord's court, enforced social bonds, punished evil-doers and those who defied society's taboos, and provided protection. Robert Bruce, William Wallace and their peers in the lordly class, took virtually no account of the opinions or needs of the common people. There are examples, as we shall see, of Robert acting charitably and humanely towards churls, as he was obliged to by Christianity, but beyond that he will have had little interest in the welfare or opinions of common people. A number of his acts as king show Robert to have been socially conservative, keen that bondmen should remain on their lords' estates and not desert them for the towns, and keen generally that individuals should know their place and not aspire to rise above their rank.

The second principal division in society was linguistic and cultural. Scotland at the end of the thirteenth century was far from culturally homogeneous. Until about 1200, the principal culture and language of Scotland had been Gaelic, and, though slowly on retreat before Scots English, Gaelic was still spoken widely in the west and north, in the Highlands and Islands. In the north and in the recently acquired territories of Man and the Western Isles, there had for centuries been extensive Norwegian influence and Norse language and customs will have persisted in places. In Lothian, on the coastal plains, and around the larger east-coast towns the Scots dialect of English predominated, and it was slowly gaining ground at the expense of other languages. Flemings and some Germans had settled in the large towns of the east, attracted by the prosperity of Scottish trade. Finally, everywhere, the lordly class spoke Anglo-Norman French and this was the language of the Scottish court; it was also common to most of the courts of western Christendom. Only in the west did Gaelic lords continue to use their traditional tongue.

Gaelic culture absorbed Anglo-Norman elements, such as knight service and homage and fealty, but it retained distinctive features such as living in kinship groups or clans, fosterage, and the maintenance of strong social ties with the Gaelic kingdoms of northern and western Ireland. The Gaelic lords of the Western Isles and Argyll were often referred to as 'kings' in their own language, but as 'barons of the Scottish realm' in French. The MacDougalls, MacDonalds and

MacRuaridhs were the three most powerful kin groups of the west and, though all claimed descent from a single ancestor, warfare and rivalry between them was constant. Their mercenaries from the Western Isles, known as 'galloglass', traversed the northern sea lanes, seeking seasonal employment in the endless wars of the Irish kings. These axe-wielding warriors of the Western Isles were to become extremely important in establishing the Bruce dynasty.

Robert Bruce, however, was primarily an Anglo-Norman magnate, and his family had been installed in the twelfth century on the borders of the kingdom of Scotland to protect it from raids by the Gaelic people of Galloway, who were resisting absorption into Scotland. Situated on an interface between two cultures, the Bruces did not remain unaffected by social interchange with their peers of the other culture, and consequently by 1274 the family had long been exposed to Gaelic manners and customs. Through living cheek by jowl with Gaelic forms and traditions for hundreds of years, with occasional intermarriage and development of social and economic interchange, acculturation set in, and the Bruces of Annandale absorbed aspects of Gaelic life and manners, just as crusaders living a long time in the Holy Land showed a tendency to pick up Arabic and even Islamic traits. Similarities between Gaelic and Anglo-Norman culture were much more marked than the differences: both societies tolerated considerable violence, and both put enormous stock on loyalty to one's lord as the most fundamental of social bonds.

With such a polyglot, diverse population, one may be excused for asking how far Scotland was a single entity. But the question has to be answered in the affirmative: Scotland was very definitely a single kingdom in 1274. There were many Scottish cultures and tongues – a point that makes nonsense of the allegation that Robert Bruce was somehow less Scottish because he spoke French – yet Scotland was a political entity, a kingdom. The image of the nation of Scotland being welded together by war with England, forged under the blows of Edward I, the Hammer of the Scots, is quite false. Rather, by the late thirteenth century Scottish kings had already forged for their territories an identity sufficiently strong for it to be able to exist without a king, as it did during the interregnum of 1286–92. The succession crises that occurred in 1286 and 1292, when first King Alexander III and then his only heir died, demonstrated that the combined efforts of previous monarchs had been successful in creating a political identity or nationhood, 'the community of the realm', which was capable of authoritative decision-making during interregnum and commanded the loyalty of the great majority of Scots. Constantly augmented by war and diplomacy, the kingdom of Scotland by this period had virtually attained its modern frontiers; Orkney and Shetland alone remained Norwegian territory in 1274.

Scotland was as much a unity as any medieval kingdom, yet all such kingdoms were assemblages of diverse regions linked to a monarchy by personal bond of lordship. The territories ruled over by the Scottish king were inhabited by peoples of English, Gaelic, Norse, Manx, Flemish, and Norman descent. It was to unite these disparate peoples that the monarchy began carefully to cultivate ideas of 'Scottishness' that fully embraced all its loyal adherents. During the course of the thirteenth century the royal genealogy, solemnly recited in Gaelic at the enthroning of each successive monarch, was revised to embrace Pictish as well as Scottish ancestors. Though regional differences persisted, it is fair to say that by the close of the thirteenth century the monarchy had achieved its goal of political unity. Scottish kings had previously addressed charters to the different peoples by name, as French, Scots, English and (rarely) as Gallovidians, but this had ceased by 1190. Nevertheless, the men of Galloway had their own unique relationship to the Scottish throne, completely different to that of the men of Lothian or Fife. This was bound to be the case, since the formation of the kingdom had been a far from inexorable or even process. Galloway, for example, had never quite been absorbed into the kingdom as fully as other provinces. Galloway's subjugation began around 1164; it was long, bloody and not entirely completed even by the time of Robert's birth. Galloway retained separatist tendencies. Scottish claims to Cumbria and territories in Northumbria proved unsustainable, and these territories were ceded to England. The Western Isles and Man were obtained from Norway by the Treaty of Perth as late as 1266. Magnus, the last king of Man, submitted to Alexander III only in 1264. Even then the islanders revolted against Scottish rule in 1275, and Scots and Gallovidians together ruthlessly suppressed the rebellion. The separatisms of Man and Galloway were subsequently encouraged by England when it suited her to do so. Many Scottish nobles held lands in England and in other kingdoms, illustrating that the bonds of lordship cut across the frontiers of kingdoms. Furthermore, while customs, laws, privileges and traditions were jealously preserved, such customs were often highly localised. Law was not a single point of reference; there existed a wide diversity of laws, which included: the Law of the Marches that prevailed on the borders, the Laws of Galloway, peculiar to that region, the Forest Law that applied in the extensive royal hunting preserves; the Law of 'the Four Burghs' of Berwick, Roxburgh, Edinburgh and Stirling; and Brehon Law that prevailed in Gaelic-speaking regions.

It was the monarchy, then, and the network of loyalties and obligations that flowed from monarchy, that defined Scotland. The throne descended by male primogeniture, that is, to the eldest son of each successive king. So long as the king had capable male children the arrangement worked; but if, as occurred in 1286, the king died without children, the precise rules of descent were open to some dispute. Professor Duncan has recently examined the Scottish tradition of king-making. The ceremony was very solemn, and we are fortunate to have a depiction of it on the seal of Scone Abbey. Central to the inauguration ceremony (as with all Gaelic king-making) was the setting of the king-to-be on a special stone throne, at a special location. Scottish kings were neither ceremonially crowned nor anointed at this date, but they did aspire to both and tried unsuccessfully to obtain from the papacy the right to incorporate them into the ceremony. The absence of these rituals gave credence to the English claim that the Scottish monarchy was subordinate. The ceremony began with the candidate being acclaimed as king in the church of Scone Abbey. He took oaths on the gospels to defend the church, maintain right and justice and keep good laws, and he was girded with a sword. For the open-air ceremony of enthronement, the candidate was then led to a cross in the churchyard, where stood a wooden bench-throne containing the Stone of Scone. The earl of Fife or his representative led the candidate to the throne. Once enthroned, the king would receive a symbol of authority, an elaborate sceptre. He was also ceremonially cloaked with a mantle and stole by the abbot of Scone and another cleric, symbolising endorsement by the church. He may have worn a crown all along, but it was certainly not a central part of the ceremony. Robert Bruce had to do without the Stone of Destiny when he was enthroned; perhaps for that reason, when in 1328 he was offered it back, he did not make strenuous efforts to recover it. Finally, the new king's genealogy was read out by a Gaelic historian, demonstrating that the new king was descended from the Pictish and Gaelic kings of old, right back to Iber Scot, the first Scotsman. A feast followed, and fealties were taken.

The king was lord of the royal estates (or royal demesne), but he had to factor into all his decisions the opinions and interests of the aristocracy. This was led by great landowners, the magnates. Primogeniture was the inheritance custom commonly followed by all the nobility: the first-born son would inherit the whole of the estate. If there were no son, the property would be equally divided among his daughters. Chief among the magnates were the thirteen earldoms: Fife (which was the most prestigious of the earldoms, and whose earl assisted at the enthronement of the monarch), Mar, Angus, Buchan (held by the Comyns), Strathearn, Atholl, Ross, Sutherland, Caithness (which was held jointly with the Norwegian earldom of Orkney), Menteith, Lennox, Carrick (which Bruce himself inherited), and March. Besides earldoms, there were other great lordships comparable to earldoms, including the lordship of Annandale (held by the Bruces), Garmoran (by the MacRuaridhs) and the lordship of Galloway (by the Balliols). As we have seen, there were, in addition, three great Gaelic kin groups which existed in the west, besides a myriad of lesser Gaelic kin groups.

On special occasions, when a king wanted to focus the attention of the whole realm on business of particular importance – a royal marriage, a demand for special taxation, or an important set of decrees – a parliament would be summoned. Parliament was a specially enlarged council which all the leading nobles and prelates were obliged to attend. There was no question at this date of mere knights attending, as already occurred at some English parliaments, but parliaments did formally concede grants of taxation (in the form of levies on assessed moveable property) to the monarch. The powers of medieval monarchy could depend very much upon the personality and character of the king. In general however it was agreed that, on the death of a tenant-in-chief, a king would take custody of the estate until the heir was of age to inherit. Usually an under-age heir would become a royal ward, and on inheriting his property the heir would pay a large sum to the king, known as a relief. Should a tenant-in-chief betray his oaths of homage and fealty, he forfeited his inheritance. The king had a say in the marriages of the children of his tenants-in-chief and of their widows, as we have seen with respect to the marriage of Robert Bruce VI and Marjorie, countess of Carrick. Custom decreed however that no king should disparage a widow, that is, marry her off to someone of lower rank.

By the late thirteenth century the Scottish monarchy had developed a specialised officialdom to help it run the kingdom. Royal justice was dispensed through three justiciars: of Scotia (in the north); Lothian (in the prosperous south-east); and Galloway (in the west). Sheriffs were the principal agents of royal authority in the localities. Twenty-eight sheriffs, some of them hereditary, many controlled by the great magnates, supervised royal demesne and served as chief accounting officers for royal income and expenditure. They held courts wherein they insisted on royal rights and collected the profits of justice: fines, and forfeitures. Sheriffs paid royal income to the king's chamberlain, a single officer who centrally managed the king's finances, and whose first duty was to provide for the royal household, the most lavish of all the lordly establishments. The royal household was organised along the classic Carolingian model, according to which it was divided into three main departments: the 'chapel' or chancery, staffed by clerks, functioned as the king's bureaucracy; the 'chamber' functioned as the treasury; and the 'hall' looked after provisioning and daily necessities of the large, itinerant royal household. From the chancery the king issued writs, orders and grants bearing his great seal, the stamp of royal authority. It was presided over by the royal chancellor, chief of the king's council. The chancellor and the chamberlain probably both also sat on the exchequer (an addition to the original household), which was essentially a court of audit. Royal officials were called before the exchequer annually to answer for debts owing to the king, and there they claimed what allowances they could to set against that debt.

A word about the currency and monetary values in general will be helpful at this point. The main unit of currency in use throughout the British Isles was the silver penny, which was counted in pounds, shillings and pence (£ s d). The mark however was also used as a unit of account. This was two-thirds of a pound, or 13s 4d. There is no point in suggesting a factor or multiplier which would allow one to express medieval values in terms of today's prices. Relative values of commodities have changed beyond recognition. In the Middle Ages food prices especially fluctuated greatly according to harvest, and such fluctuations affected other prices too. However the following examples might serve as a rough guide to monetary values: an earl's income could amount to £5,000 per annum; a warhorse would cost

£30 to £40; in wartime a knight earned 2s per day from royal service; and a footsoldier collected a daily wage of 2d.

No medieval kingdom could conduct its affairs in isolation from its neighbours, and, although it had diplomatic relations with all the kingdoms touching the North Sea, the neighbour with which Scotland shared a land border was of pre-eminent importance. When we ask how independent of England Scotland had been up to this point, we must bear in mind that 'independence', like 'nationality', is another modern concept that sits uneasily when imposed upon the medieval world. The kingdoms of western Christendom were not independent of one another, but interdependent. All paid lip service to the theory that a supra-national papacy was supreme in matters relating to religion (a large slice of life in the Middle Ages), and all the royal families of Europe intermarried, causing kingdoms to interfere often in one another's affairs.

Since the two kingdoms already had a history of five hundred years of sharing 'one poor island', it is barely surprising that the relationship between Scotland and England was complex. There had been peace between the kingdoms for seventy years, and many Scottish aristocrats, including the King of Scots himself, held estates in England as well as Scotland. The Bruces held substantial estates in Essex, Middlesex and in the bishopric of Durham. John Balliol held manors in seventeen English shires. Besides being much larger than Scotland, England was much more populous and wealthy. England might have sustained two and a half million people at this date; Scotland would scarcely have had a population of half a million. Wool exports (the only economic data available for comparison) suggests the same sort of proportion: Scotland exported 5,000 sacks in 1327, and England roughly five times that.

Given this order of dominance, it is barely surprising that, as soon as one could reasonably speak of an English kingdom, that kingdom claimed a 'superior lordship' over the whole of Britain. In the twelfth century certain Scottish kings had accepted the lordship of Henry I and later of Henry II, both particularly powerful kings of England, but resisted attempts by less powerful English monarchs to impose upon Scotland. By the thirteenth century the custom had developed whereby, shortly after the coronation of each king of England, the King of Scots would visit him to perform a ceremony of homage and fealty, where the vassal knelt before the lord and acknowledged his lordship. Was this done in return for the kingdom of Scotland itself, or merely for the lands which the Scottish king held in England: the lordships of Tynedale and Penrith? The interpretation placed upon this ceremony by the participants appears to have depended largely upon the personalities involved and upon the ebb and flow of the power relationships between the kingdoms and between the kings themselves. Alexander III is said to have insisted categorically that he held his kingdom from God alone; other Scottish monarchs might not have been in a position to be so unequivocal. The sources on this ceremony are either vague, or were intended as propaganda for one side or the other. The vagueness surrounding the ceremony allowed each king to interpret the act of homage as he pleased, and it facilitated the peaceful co-existence of the kingdoms for most of the thirteenth century. Edward I's insistence upon clarity and definition, which spoiled this comfortable fudge, is one of the factors that led to war in 1296.

Medieval people did not conceive of society as divided into religious and secular realms; rather the Scottish Church and religious belief generally informed every aspect of life. The clergy represented a high percentage of the population: perhaps a tenth of all the men and women in Scotland were in clerical orders of some kind. There were regular clergy (orders of monks and nuns who lived by the Rule of St Benedict) and secular, or diocesan clergy. The most powerful regular order was the Cistercians, whose abbeys (Melrose, Arbroath, Paisley, Kelso and Holyrood) maintained vast herds of sheep in the uplands and sold the wool to Italian and Flemish merchants. In addition there were friars, regular clergy who lived not in monasteries but in the community; the Dominican and Franciscan friars were well represented in the larger towns.

The kingdom of Scotland had also to maintain relations with the papacy. However, the Church was firmly under the control of the king, who could almost always have his servants appointed to key bishoprics, abbacies and other ecclesiastical offices, and he could call upon the church for subsidies and financial aids. The papacy could only tax the Scottish Church with the king's agreement, and it almost always had to share the proceeds with the monarch. Whereas the co-operation and good offices of the papacy were much to be desired, the power of the papacy was not such that a pope could impose his will on an unwilling monarch or an unco-operative kingdom. Robert Bruce himself ruled for many years as king while ignoring successive excommunications. For their loyalty to Bruce, the Scots themselves suffered the full force of papal displeasure, including a variety of harsh ecclesiastical penalties: excommunication, a general interdict imposed upon all of Scotland, prohibition from holding ecclesiastical office for themselves and their relatives. They were all ignored by the Scottish hierarchy. As in most of the kingdoms of Christendom, the papacy had influence but not power.

Nevertheless the Church of Bruce's day aspired to and usually enjoyed an especially close relationship with the papacy. With the help of the papacy the pretensions of the archiepiscopal see of York to control the Scottish Church had been resisted. Those pretensions had left Scottish churchmen with a sense of group solidarity, and from time to time the national Church assembled in Provincial Council to approve Rome's demands for greater centralisation and ecclesiastical taxation. Although Scotland lacked an archbishop, leadership was provided by the two premier bishoprics of Glasgow and St Andrews. The absence of an archbishop was considered an advantage: a papal bull of 1192 had established the Scottish Church as the 'special daughter of Rome', there being no intermediary between the pope and the Scottish bishops. This fostered effective channels of communication between the Church and the papacy, for Scottish churchmen became skilled in lobbying at the Roman curia. Both its sense of solidarity as a 'national' church, and its close ties with the papal curia, made the Scottish Church a formidable opponent of Edward I's attempts to integrate Scotland into his kingdom and a valuable expression of Scottish identity which Robert Bruce utilised to the full.

Such was the Scotland of the late thirteenth century: a polyglot and highly diverse territory and people, yet conscious of itself as a unity, even if only begrudgingly so in the cases of Man and Galloway. Society was deeply conservative, tradition-bound and resistant to change. Scarcely peaceful in any quarter, since violence was endemic in a society dominated by quarrelsome lords and rivals, Scotland had nevertheless been at peace with its neighbouring kingdom for seventy years. Such was the country and society in which Robert Bruce VII reached adolescence, mercifully oblivious to the catastrophe that waited around the corner.

2

An inheritance, a grandfather's ambition and a 'coveytous' king (1286–96)

Robert Bruce VII first surfaces in the contemporary record as his father's son, a witness to an undated charter of Alexander MacDonald of Islay, a long-time ally of the Bruces. The MacDonalds were a powerful kinship group in south-west Scotland which looked to the Bruces for leadership; other allies included the MacRuaridhs, the Stewarts and the earls of Atholl, Mar and March. As a young man (and probably before his investiture as earl) Robert was knighted. Knighthood could be bestowed by king or earl, but we do not know who knighted Robert Bruce. The knighting of the heir involved the family in huge expense, with the new knight kitted out with armour, horses, servants with specialised abilities (from noble squires to grooms and stableboys) and more prosaic equipment for an independent household. A 'feudal aid' or seigneurial tax could be levied from the tenants to assist with the expense. Knighthood was an honourable and exclusive status to which all noblemen, whether kings or mere gentry, aspired: on the death of Robert Bruce as King Robert I of Scotland in 1329 one Scottish chronicler could think of nothing finer to say of the dead hero than that 'he was, beyond all living men of his day, a valiant knight'.

As a young knight Robert would be well aware that his family had rivals and enemies as well as allies. Chief among these rivals were the powerful Comyns, who had dominated life at the Scottish royal court for two generations. There were three principal lineages bearing the surname Comyn, for, early in the thirteenth century, Walter Comyn had married twice, producing two sets of offspring. The offspring of his first marriage became known as the Comyns of Badenoch (or the Red Comyns), that of his second marriage, to Marjorie, countess of Buchan, became the Comyn earls of Buchan (the Black Comyns). The third lineage of Comyns, a cadet branch of the Comyns of Badenoch, was known as the Comyns of Kilbride. All three branches operated politically as a unit, and together they had built up a powerful alliance with extensive lands, widespread patronage and a formidable network of castles. In alliance with the Comyns were the Balliol lords of Galloway and the MacDougall lords of Argyll, traditional enemies of the MacDonalds.

However, before we examine young Robert's active role in the affairs of the kingdom, it is necessary to consider the legacy of aspirations, property, lands and traditions bequeathed to him by his ancestors. His inheritance included not only sprawling estates, considerable monetary wealth, and legal privileges and rights but also, from his mother an interest in the Gaelic world, and from his grandfather, a burning ambition that embraced aspirations to kingship. The scion of a proud aristocratic lineage, 'our' Robert Bruce was only the latest in a succession of nobles bearing that name. The family name, rendered in Norman-French as *de Brus* or *de Bruys*, derives from Brix near Cherbourg in Normandy. Robert Bruce I was a protégé of Henry I of England (1100–35) who had rewarded him for his services with the lordship of Cleveland in north Yorkshire. There the first Robert Bruce founded the Augustinian Priory of Guisborough and endowed it with vast estates so that the monks would exert spiritual influence on behalf of him and his family. From early in his career that Robert associated with another of Henry I's protégés, David, the son of Malcolm III, King of Scots, who held the English earldom of Huntingdon. On several of David's charters Robert's name is listed among those witnessing the deed. This is a strong indication that Robert served David as his vassal, or at any rate was closely associated with him. In 1124 David became king of Scotland, and it was probably on the occasion of his enthronement in that year that he granted Robert the lordship of Annandale with its castle. David was actively pursuing a policy of bestowing upon dependable warlike Norman families estates situated on marcher territories of his kingdom. Such grants were made to Norman families because Normans could provide 'knight service', which meant supplying mounted, armoured knights for the royal host. Annandale bordered both England, a potentially hostile but usually friendly neighbour, and Galloway, a Celtic region at that time unsubdued by the kings of Scotland. The Bruces were then honour-bound to defend the borders (or 'marches' as they are usually termed) of the Scottish kingdom on the monarch's behalf.

The first Robert's friendship with King David did not survive the Scottish invasion of England in 1138, and Robert made a solemn renunciation of his homage to David, a very rare and drastic step in medieval society. He fought with distinction against the Scots at the Battle of the Standard. However, before this breach occurred, the first Robert seems to have passed the lordship of Annandale on to his second son, a supporter of David. Thus Robert, a 'cross-border baron' with lands on each side of the Anglo-Scottish border, skilfully minimized the effects of war between the kingdoms on the fortunes of his family. Annandale was saved from forfeiture by the King of Scots on this occasion. Robert died in 1142, and was buried at Guisborough Priory. His first son, Adam, inherited the great estates in Yorkshire; his second, Robert, retained the lesser fief of Annandale.

From a charter of this period we learn that Robert Bruce II held Annandale by service of ten knights; that is, he had to contribute ten knights to the royal host in time of war. During his time however there occurred an incident that cast a shadow over the fortunes of the Bruces. In 1148 the great Irish saint, archbishop and ecclesiastical reformer St Malachy O'More, passing through Scotland on his way to Rome, favoured the second lord of Annandale by staying at his castle. During the visit Malachy interceded on behalf of a thief whom Robert had sentenced to hang. Magnanimously the lord gave way to the pleading of the holy man and declared that the thief's life would be spared. In return Malachy blessed the lord and his family. But the following morning, as he set out, Malachy saw the body of the thief swaying on the gallows and realised that Robert had hanged the man regardless. He revoked his blessing and laid instead a terrible curse upon the lord and his offspring, and on the town. The curse of a holy man of St Malachy's stature was a serious impediment to fortunes of any medieval dynasty. The *Lanercost* chronicle relates that 'three of his heirs perished in succession' and indeed Robert Bruce II granted a house in Lochmaben to St Peter's Hospital in York for the souls of (among others) 'his infants'. Furthermore, a misfortune appears to have occurred around the year 1200 at Annan forcing the family to move to Lochmaben. It has been suggested that the River Annan washed away a part of Annan Castle, forcing the family to move the head of the lordship from Annan to Lochmaben. That misfortune may also have been attributed to the curse of St Malachy. Whatever the historical truth of these troubles, the Bruces themselves, including King Robert, appear to have believed in the curse. Robert Bruce II faced misfortune of another sort: war between the kingdoms flared up again in 1173–74, forcing him to choose between allegiances. Robert had considerable property in England: Hartness in the bishopric of Durham, and the manor of Edenhall in Cumberland. He chose to support Henry II of England against King William the Lion, bringing immediate confiscation of Annandale. The Bruce patrimony was, however, restored after the conflict, and relations with the Scottish court improved to the extent that William the Lion married his illegitimate daughter to Robert Bruce II's son and heir, Robert. Unfortunately this Robert predeceased his father, who died in 1194.

The third lord of Annandale was therefore a younger son, William, but of William there is little to tell. He died in 1211 or 1212.

His son and heir, Robert Bruce, the fourth lord made a very successful match by marrying into the Scottish royal family. His bride was Isabel, second daughter of David, Earl of Huntingdon. This was definitely an advance on marriage to a king's illegitimate daughter, and represented a considerable increase in the family's fortunes. Imbued both with a keen sense of service to the monarchy and, naturally, to its own long-term interest, the family carried on collecting estates through the bestowal of royal patronage and astute marriages. Within Scotland they acquired one third of the lordship of Garioch and the burgh of Dundee; they also enlarged their holdings in England through marriage. By the time of our Robert's birth their English estates included the manors of Writtle and Hatfield Broadoak in Essex, one third of the manor of Tottenham in Middlesex, and Hartness in the bishopric of Durham. They seem also to have claimed territories in Ulster as we have seen: the 'Galloway lands' in County Antrim granted to Duncan of Carrick. Claims to land and titles were guarded jealously and pursued wherever possible in appropriate courts, for it was a most litigious age and no claim, however distant or far-fetched, could be allowed to lapse.

The family was acutely aware of its position vis-à-vis the monarchies upon which its fortunes depended. It was Robert Bruce V, the grandfather of the future king, who first aspired to royal dignity in Scotland. This Robert, whom contemporaries called Robert the Noble, was a most colourful and energetic magnate. The *Lanercost* chronicle records in a brief obituary that 'He was of handsome appearance, a gifted speaker, remarkable for his influence … as noble a baron in England as in Scotland.'

No doubt he had charisma, but he was also a schemer, a chancer and a very devious character. Born around the year 1225, he married into the family of the English earls of Gloucester; and south of the border he participated in the bitter struggles between Henry III of England and his magnates. He fought on Henry III's side at the Battle of Lewes in 1264. King Henry lost that battle to his over-

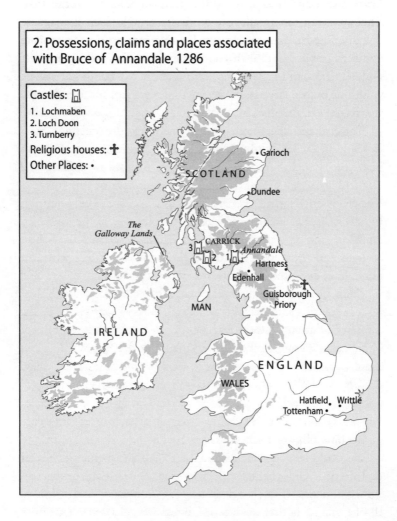

2. Possessions, claims and places associated with Bruce of Annandale, 1286

Castles:
1. Lochmaben
2. Loch Doon
3. Turnberry

Religious houses: ✝
Other Places: •

Garioch

SCOTLAND

Dundee

The
Galloway Lands

CARRICK   *Annandale*

3   2   1

Hartness

Edenhall

MAN

Guisborough
Priory

IRELAND

ENGLAND

WALES

Hatfield   Writtle
Tottenham

mighty subject Simon de Montfort and, as a consequence, Robert was captured and had to appeal to his son to arrange a ransom for his release. Capture in battle was a catastrophe often greater than death, for ransoms could economically cripple even a magnate dynasty. Robert, however, was well resourced: besides Annandale and Hartness, he had inherited on the death of his mother in 1251 or 1252 her estates in Essex and the Garioch. With this accession of wealth he built a large stone castle at Lochmaben, and the dynasty survived the payment of his ransom.

The Bruces' aspiration to the Scottish throne originated in an incident which, Robert the Noble alleged, occurred during the reign of Alexander II. Robert claimed that, at a time when King Alexander was still childless and was preparing to lead an expedition to the Western Isles, the king had recognised him as his heir presumptive. The incident, if it occurred at all, appears to belong to the year 1238. The king had just suffered the death of his queen, Joan; he had as yet no male heir and Robert Bruce V was his closest male kinsman out of infancy. Robert's contemporaries may have known of it, but there is no historical evidence beyond Robert's word that this recognition was ever made. Professor Duncan is deeply sceptical about the claim.

The historicity of these events however only became of critical importance when the throne of Scotland depended upon it. For the present Robert the Noble pursued other means of self-promotion. Even in the small, distant and impoverished kingdom of Scotland, noble families felt part of the francophone, chivalric society of Europe; testimony to this is the participation of Robert the Noble in that ambitious but inglorious enterprise of medieval Europe, the crusade to preserve the Holy Land from Islamic control. Along with Bretons and men of the Low Countries, he joined the expedition led by Edmund 'Crouchback' of Lancaster, younger son of Henry III of England. Robert was already fifty years old. They sailed in the autumn of 1271, to reinforce a previous expedition led by Edmund's elder brother, Prince Edward of England.

This Edward was to become a figure of towering importance in the lives of the Bruces. He was to become Edward I 'the Hammer of the Scots', and he bore the nickname 'Longshanks' because his lanky stature (he stood an impressive six foot two inches in height) enabled him to stay in the saddle when other men would have been toppled. The character of this king has been variously interpreted, and Scottish historians have, not surprisingly, tended to be rather harsher in their assessment of him than others. But there is agreement on many aspects of the man. Edward was brilliant in many ways: a skilled reformer of law, a courageous general and a leader of men. He demanded clarity and definition in law; and he strikes one as having been crisp and decisive in manner. It was this quest for definition that led him to disturb the convenient vagueness over Anglo-Scottish relations that had preserved peace between the kingdoms for seventy years. Edward had a short fuse, and displays of his violent ill temper are well documented. He would mercilessly browbeat those who opposed his will; the combination of his overbearing rage and his height could reduce a man to a nervous wreck. Much of his grievance against the Scots who opposed his will was founded on his perception of them as disloyal, or having broken oaths of fealty. Conventional in most respects, and much admired as a king, there was undoubtedly a streak of cruelty in Edward's character.

The crusaders sailed first to Tunis, then wintered in Sicily before setting off again, via Cyprus, to Acre, the capital of the crusader state in Palestine, known as Outremer. They enjoyed little military success, but Edward managed to shore up the beleaguered Christian state by negotiating a truce for it. Significantly, on the return journey Robert visited the monastery at Clairvaux, where St Malachy is buried, presumably to seek the saint's forgiveness for his family; furthermore, on his return, he granted land to the Abbey of Clairvaux to provide three candles at St Malachy's shrine to placate the angry saint.

Edward of England returned to a throne, since his father had died in his absence, and Robert Bruce the Noble continued to serve him, holding office in England as sheriff of Cumberland from 1283 to 1285. Robert made a second marriage. His new bride, though not as high-born as his first, was already twice a widow and therefore brought into the family two dower portions from previous alliances, all lands in Cumberland.

The fateful year 1286 probably marked the birth of serious Bruce pretensions to the throne of Scotland; indeed the events of that year generated similar aspirations and ambitions in many aristocratic hearts in Scotland and further afield. For on 18 March 1286 King Alexander III died as the result of a fall from his horse, leaving as his only descendant a sickly three-year-old girl, resident in Norway, Margaret 'the Maid of Norway'. Any medieval kingdom would have been shaken by such a calamity, for it threw into doubt the future of the royal succession and jeopardised the security and tranquillity of the realm. Although the throne was not actually vacant, the event must have inspired clerks and lawyers all over Scotland, and further afield, to research old deeds, genealogies and chronicles on behalf of noble families to discover, resurrect, or if necessary manufacture a claim to the throne of Scotland. Any claim might have a value, if it were considered worth buying off by more serious contenders.

For the two leading magnate dynasties in Scotland the event opened up the real possibility of absolute power. These were the Bruces themselves who, as we have seen, led a wide alliance of magnate families in the south-west of Scotland, and the Comyns, who for most of the thirteenth century had controlled the government of Scotland. John Balliol, lord of Galloway and of Barnard Castle, was the candidate for kingship backed by the Comyns and their allies. At the king's funeral on 29 March the magnates attending decided to send an embassy to Edward I of England. They recognised in Edward, the monarch of a friendly neighbouring kingdom, a potential ally whose enormous military and financial resources might be useful in preserving order in Scotland and warding off the distant but troubling prospect of a civil war. He was perhaps the only power capable of controlling the simmering ambitions of the rival magnate alliances. It is not known whether this embassy reached Edward (who was in France from 13 May 1286) or whether it was subsequently recalled.

The kingdom of Scotland was sufficiently robust to function for a time without a king, and the institutions of state continued to operate in the name of 'the community of the realm'. In official documents this kingdom-without-a-king referred to itself as 'the community of the realm', and the phrase may be variously interpreted as 'the governing elite', 'the nobles' or 'those who had a stake in the kingdom'. A parliament was summoned to Scone for 2 April 1286, where the magnates of the realm swore fealty to Margaret of Norway and undertook to keep the peace. At this parliament Robert the Noble flung down the gauntlet to his adversaries and boldly stated his claim to the Scottish throne, based upon a theory (or perhaps it was merely an opinion) that a female could not succeed in Scotland. At once the tension increased. Though the claim would not have been unexpected, the community of the realm must have realised that civil war had become a real possibility. The parliament seems to have adjourned to consider the impact of this claim. It reassembled around 28 April and at this point it is likely that John Balliol lodged a counter-claim that, by the accepted rules of inheritance, he and not Bruce was the true heir. He was, after all, a descendant of the elder daughter of David earl of Huntingdon, and Bruce of the younger. However, the widowed Queen Yolande claimed to be expecting a child, a declaration which took the heat out of the debate for the present, and nervously the magnates settled down to await the outcome of the pregnancy.

In the meantime the parliament set about establishing the necessary structures for the government of the kingdom during the interregnum. Firstly, to manage affairs of state, it set up a council of 'keepers of the peace' or 'Guardians'. We might call it a regency council. This council of Guardians was composed of two earls, two bishops and two barons. Analysis of the individuals selected reveals that in its personnel a delicate balance was observed between the two magnate factions that dominated the kingdom. Bishop Robert Wishart of Glasgow and James the hereditary steward of Scotland, were supporters of the Bruces; Bishop William Fraser of St Andrews, Alexander Comyn earl of Buchan and John Comyn of Badenoch were supporters of Balliol. Earl Duncan of Fife may have had equal attachment to both sides. Secondly, the parliament decided that all the nobles should swear an oath of loyalty to whosoever should obtain the kingdom of Scotland *by reason of nearness in blood to King Alexander III*. This committed the magnates to accepting the rightful heir whoever that should turn out to be: Alexander's posthumous child, or, failing that, Margaret, the Maid of Norway, or, failing that, whoever was adjudged to be nearest in blood to the king. It was a formula everyone could sign up to. Thus no decision was taken, but the contending parties were bound to accept an ultimate decision, and civil war was warded off – for the time being.

During the summer of 1286 however, the government began to panic. On 7 August a second embassy was dispatched to Edward with all haste to seek his counsel and protection. Evidently the queen had lost the child, but understandably news of the miscarriage was kept secret as along as possible for fear that the rival magnate camps would resort to arms. It is not surprising that the Bruces, who must have known that their legal claim was the weaker, reacted violently as rumour of the miscarriage spread. Robert the Noble and his son Robert Bruce VI assembled their principal allies in September 1286 at Turnberry Castle – Patrick, earl of March, and his sons; Walter Stewart, earl of Menteith, and his sons; James the Steward and his brother John; and Angus Mór MacDonald, Lord of Islay, and his son Alexander – and bound them, together with two Irish magnates, Richard de Burgh, earl of Ulster, and Thomas de Clare, in a pact of mutual assistance. This arrangement, known as the Turnberry Band, ostensibly involved some commitment to an expedition to the west of Ireland, where both the earl of Ulster and de Clare had interests. Much more significant however was the expression of solidarity among all these magnates present at a critical juncture in the fate of the kingdom of Scotland. There is an implication that all would stand fast against the Comyns. It is even possible that the Bruce faction was preparing to bring in Irish allies to support Robert the Noble in his bid for the throne.

In the winter of 1286–87 the Bruces seized control of three castles in the south-west of Scotland – the royal castles of Dumfries, Wigtown and the Balliol castle of Buittle – securing the Solway Firth for the reception of their Irish allies. This violence was clearly intended to menace or intimidate John Balliol. But the coup failed. No Irish allies arrived, and James, the hereditary steward of Scotland, chose not to stand by his commitments to the Bruces, but instead, acting as Guardian, assisted in regaining the castles and putting down the Bruces' aggression. By May 1287 it was all over. The action had amounted to little more than an aggressive gesture. Besides those involved in the Turnberry Band there were other magnates who might have joined the Bruces but did not: the earls of Fife, March, Atholl, Lennox and Mar, Bishop Wishart of Glasgow, not to mention lords of the second rank, such as Soules, Lindsay and Biggar. Robert the Noble, having resorted to arms prematurely and without the support of his coalition, seems to have withdrawn temporarily from Scotland.

It was now clear that Margaret of Norway would inherit the kingdom. It was desirable for the Guardians of the kingdom firstly to have her reside in Scotland, and secondly to arrange a marriage for her, in order that Scotland's future be settled. Eric of Norway was keen that his daughter inherit the kingdom, and was probably delighted to learn that marriage to Edward of Caernarfon, the son of Edward of England, was also a possibility. He sent ambassadors to England to discuss the prospect. Such a match also seemed an attractive prospect to the Scottish Guardians, who were anxious to involve the powerful English monarch in Scotland to prevent any recurrence of violence. However there were two dangers: the English king might use the opportunity to exercise the feudal overlordship, which he claimed to be his right; and there was also a danger that Scotland's separate laws, customs and institutions might be swallowed up altogether if the kingdoms were united by a such a marriage of heirs. We do not know how Edward I had responded to the Guardians' request for counsel and protection. To judge from his later actions, he probably offered to do all he was asked on condition that his overlordship of Scotland was acknowledged. Rather than assent to such a condition, the Guardians decided to manage without his help. They initiated delicate tripartite negotiations with the Norwegians and English about the marriage of the absent Margaret, the acknowledged Lady of Scotland whom all parties agreed should inherit the kingdom. Eric was reluctant to send his daughter to Scotland while it was unstable. The brief rebellion and its suppression had been a blow to the Bruces and for a period of about two years they lost influence. Unrest continued however. Late in the summer of 1289 Duncan, earl of Fife, was ambushed and slain by his own relatives, the Abernethys, an event which is not satisfactorily explained. The earl of Buchan also died, but, probably to avoid exacerbating the situation, these Guardians were not replaced.

The remaining Guardians developed a plan to have the six-year-old Margaret marry five-year-old Edward of Caernarfon, Edward I's heir, who later became Edward II; by such a royal marriage Scotland might enter into union with England yet safeguard the independence of her customs and institutions. Robert the Noble may have retired to his English lands around this time, but he managed to secure appointment as one of four envoys to treat with the Norwegian ambassadors. In November 1289 the ambassadors agreed that Margaret the Maid should come to Scotland or England within a year, into the custody of her great-uncle, Edward I, who would send her to Scotland as soon as the country was settled. This arrangement is known as the Treaty of Salisbury and, as has been pointed out by Professor Nicholson, it was the first recognition by the Scots that Edward I could intervene in Scottish affairs. The Scots had to promise not to arrange any marriage for the Maid without the advice and consent of both Norwegian and English governments; but eventually they succeeded in negotiating a marriage agreement called the Treaty of Birgham, on 18 July 1290. The settlement heralded a union of the crowns, and it was a diplomatic coup to the extent that it avoided having to acknowledge the overlordship claimed by Edward I. By this, the Maid was to marry young Edward and would be given dower lands in England, but the Scottish kingdom was to remain 'separate, apart and free in itself without subjection to the English kingdom'. Although the thrones of Scotland and England would be united in the person of one monarch, each realm would remain separate, and 'the rights, laws, liberties and customs of the same realm of Scotland to be preserved in every respect and in all time coming throughout the said realm and its borders, completely and without being impaired'. Under this arrangement Edward I could be involved in maintaining peace in Scotland but denied a controlling interest; and when, in time, the marriage produced an heir, the crowns of Scotland and England would be joined in a union in which Scotland would be an equal partner. Among the stipulations of the treaty were provisions guaranteeing that there would be no taxation of the Scots except for Scottish needs; tenants-in-chief of the Scottish crown need do homage only in Scotland; elections of the clergy were to be free from interference; and appointments to the customary offices of the Scottish government would continue. The only qualification to the Scottish achievement is that these provisions were agreed subject to 'the right of our said lord [Edward I]', so all along Edward was safeguarding his claim to be overlord of Scotland.

Against considerable odds, the Guardians had then succeeded in landing a future for Scotland that involved neither civil war nor subjection to the English crown. Without doubt Scots saw Edward I as a benevolent and potentially stabilising influence, whom they were anxious to involve in Scotland to stave off unrest. But already Edward was beginning to encroach upon Scottish rights and capitalise upon the weakness of his northern neighbour. Some time between 1286 and 1290, the earl of Ulster took possession of the Isle of Man, and in 1290 an assembly of islanders made over the land of Man to the king of England, taking no account of the Scottish claim. In this, the earl might have been acting on behalf of the Bruce interest, which already looked to Edward I. The Scots appear to have lodged no formal protest. Edward also appointed the powerful bishop of Durham, Antony Bek, to supervise the government of Scotland on behalf of the infant monarchs-to-be, requiring the Guardians to obey Bek.

In October 1290 the situation of Scotland, and the attitude of Edward I of England, were transformed by a calamitous event. Margaret, the Maid of Norway and Lady of Scotland, died in Orkney on her way to Scotland. The risk of civil war between the principal claimants to Scotland now escalated; patently there was an urgent need for authority of some kind to prevent the situation degenerating. The obvious, and indeed perhaps the only source of such authority, was Edward I, who began to set his own terms for acting as protector of the Scottish realm. No one in Scotland raised any objection to his involvement as adjudicator in the question of who was to succeed to the Scottish throne. Intriguingly, there existed a precedent for appeal to an outside monarch to judge in a case of disputed succession. Frederick Barbarossa, the German Emperor, had sat in judgement in the case of the Danish throne in the eleventh century, but it is thought that Edward was probably unaware of this.

As we saw, Robert Bruce VI and Robert VII were both in service at the court of Edward I from around this time. It would be wrong however to overestimate their influence in that large cosmopolitan establishment. The organisation and etiquette of the royal court are bound to have made a huge impression on the teenager and the imposing figure of Edward – decisive, capable and commanding – undoubtedly provided a model for Robert's later kingship.

Edward was still being drawn into the Scottish arena as opposed to forcing intervention, for the Scottish factions were making approaches to him. The first approach was made by the Comyn–Balliol interest. Bishop Fraser wrote in October, warning Edward that the Bruce faction had already taken up arms, that Robert the Noble had come to Perth, near Scone, with a powerful retinue; Fraser asked Edward to come to the border to prevent bloodshed, and to place the rightful heir on the throne. He implied strongly that Balliol was that rightful heir. The document Edward I received from the Bruce faction is known as the *Appeal of the Seven Earls*. The *Appeal* is a blend of invention, tradition and antiquarian myth, and it represents Bruce propaganda of an unsubtle variety. It sought Edward's help against Bishop Fraser and John Comyn, and it reveals that the committee of the Guardians was now dominated by the Balliol interest. It alleged that the Guardians' officers were ravaging Moray. The kernel of the document however is a hitherto unheard of constitutional theory that the seven earls of Scotland had the right to choose the king. Balliol's supporters advanced no such theories and put their faith in the accepted laws of primogeniture. That said, Balliol was not above slipping a timely bribe to Edward I's right-hand man: as 'heir to the kingdom of Scotland'. He sealed a charter granting Edward I's overseer, Antony Bek, lands held by the Scottish king in England, or, should Edward I refuse to allow that, 500 marks-worth of land in Scotland.

Although both letters to Edward I probably exaggerate the extent of disorder, the danger of civil war was looming. Probably to everyone's relief Edward decided that the dispute over the throne of Scotland should be decided by himself, but he would act only in the capacity of Scotland's overlord. In March 1291 he ordered English monasteries to search their chronicles for information on the historic relationship between the two kingdoms. To some Scots it may have seemed – as it now seems to us – that Edward was taking advantage of the vacancy of the Scottish monarchy to clarify to his own advantage the relationship between the kingdoms. Edward travelled to Norham, on the English bank of the River Tweed, arriving in May 1291, where magnates, notaries and lawyers assembled for the court case to settle who should inherit the kingship of Scotland. It is known to history as the Great Cause. The English army was to muster at Norham on 2 June, and the fleet made ready to blockade Scotland so that Edward's judgement might be enforced should this become necessary.

Edward began by establishing rights of jurisdiction over Scotland. He pointed out that Scottish kings were neither crowned nor anointed and represented this as proof that they were subordinate. He asked 'the high men of the Scots' – probably the Guardians – to acknowledge him as overlord. The Scots refused, on the ground that they had no knowledge of his claim, and that only a king of Scotland could respond. Edward then sought such an acknowledgement from the claimants (or 'competitors') to the throne. This was forthcoming, and neither Robert the Noble nor John Balliol, nor any of the other claimants, made difficulty about acknowledging Edward's suzerainty over Scotland. Furthermore they agreed that Edward might take the realm into his own hands, so long as he then granted it to the successful candidate. Edward accepted, and, not without some caginess on the part of the commanders, the royal castles of Scotland were handed over to his keeping. It is unlikely that Edward then installed English garrisons in Scottish castles generally, though he may have done so in the case of Berwick. Edward then took the homage and fealty of the Guardians, bishops and all the magnates of the realm, and arranged that oaths of fealty from as many nobles as possible be collected on his behalf. In June 1291 the

Guardians accepted that their provisional government derived its authority from Edward as superior overlord, a fateful concession that admitted that Scotland was a sub-kingdom rather than fully independent, and that the next king of Scots would be a vassal of the king of England. Edward then made a short tour of the main towns of his sub-kingdom, taking in Edinburgh, St Andrews and Perth. His taking control of castles and his tour of inspection cannot have been well received by Scots of any class. This victory, won without a sword being drawn, Edward would shortly squander, transforming it into a running sore that would plague the last decade of his life.

Robert Bruce VII, the king to be, was sixteen years of age when Margaret of Norway died and he surely followed these events with breathless interest, perfectly aware that his own fate would be profoundly affected by the success or failure of his grandfather's claim. As we have seen, it is around this time that he was knighted, and began to appear on the political stage in the Bruce dynastic interest.

On Edward's return to Berwick, hearings began there in August 1291, and a court of 104 auditors was set up, 40 chosen by Robert the Noble, 40 by Balliol and 24 by Edward. The Great Cause was to last a year and a half, though this included a nine-month adjournment to allow for research. A total of 14 claimants had now stepped into the ring, most of whom were dismissed at an early stage. One of these was John Comyn II of Badenoch, one of the Guardians and leader of the mighty Comyn faction. The rebuttal of Comyn's own fairly weak claim came neither as a surprise nor as much of a setback since he was married to a sister of John Balliol, the odds-on favourite.

Four serious competitors emerged: Bruce, Balliol, Florent Count of Holland and John Hastings, an English baron. Florent V, Count of Holland, lodged a very strong claim, based on his descent from a daughter of Earl Henry, the son of David I, but he lacked sufficient documentary evidence to substantiate it. In fact Florent had been encouraged to enter a claim by Bruce. Aware that his own claim was weaker than that of Balliol, but also that Florent did not have the necessary documentation to prove his still stronger claim, Bruce cut a deal with the count. We have the text of the agreement, sealed on 14 June 1292. If either Bruce or Florent gained the throne, the successful party would grant one third of the Scottish royal demesne to the other, to be held as a fief for service of a mere five knights; and if Bruce were awarded the throne, he would grant to Florent lands in England equivalent to one third of the Scottish royal demesne. Florent had clearly little independent motivation. Bruce appeared to be offering him a chance to gain great wealth at no risk, and so he had agreed to assist Bruce in his scheme. For his part, the devious Robert was clearly anxious to create obstacles in the way of Balliol success. Another of the lesser competitors, also encouraged by Bruce, was King Eric of Norway. His far-fetched claim, made late in the day, was soon dismissed. However, by encouraging Eric's involvement Robert the Noble managed to gain something for his son, and in November 1292 Robert Bruce VI journeyed to Norway to arrange the marriage of his daughter Isabel to King Eric. The guile of Robert the Noble is to be marvelled at: he had prepared two stalking horses, Florent and Eric, and later, in response to events, he had developed a fallback position – that the kingdom might be partitioned. He was utterly determined to get something out of the Great Cause.

The hearings of the Great Cause ground on. The three remaining claimants were all descendants of daughters of David, Earl of Huntingdon (d. 1219), the grandson of David I of Scotland. John Hastings claimed descent from the youngest daughter, Ada, and argued that Scotland was not a true kingdom, but simply a lordship subject to the kings of England and, as such, the territory should be partitioned among the descendants of female co-heiresses, the three daughters, as any landed estate would be divided when male line failed. At this point Robert the Noble argued vehemently that the kingdom could not be partitioned, though later he was to change that position. The court rejected the Hastings argument on the ground that the unity of the kingdom of Scotland should be preserved.

Only Bruce and Balliol remained. Most authorities concur that John Balliol's case was stronger, and that Balliol enjoyed wider support among the nobility and the clergy than the Bruce. Balliol's case was based on the simple law of primogeniture: the kingdom could not be divided, and therefore had to be awarded to the descendant of David of Huntingdon's eldest daughter Margaret, namely himself, her grandson. Balliol therefore had a better case to the throne than either Robert Bruce, the son of the second daughter Isabel, or John Hastings, the grandson of Ada, the third and youngest daughter. Seniority of line, not nearness of degree, was what mattered, in the Balliol view.

Robert the Noble was not daunted by the simplicity of the Balliol claim. His lawyers too accepted (initially) that the kingdom could not be divided. But they maintained that, according to the established laws and customs of Scotland, a living younger son had a stronger claim to succeed than the son of a deceased elder son, and that Bruce, as the *son* of the second daughter, should succeed instead of John Balliol, the *grand*son of the eldest daughter. On this basis he claimed to be 'nearer in blood'. Furthermore, and as we have seen, Robert the Noble claimed that, at a time before Alexander II had children to succeed him, that king had appointed him as his heir, should he come to grief in war. As far as historical precedent went, there is little evidence to support Bruce's assertions. The most recent work suggests that it was 'a hope entertained by the family which may have been built upon hints' made by King Alexander II around 1238, that Bruce had a possible right to the throne. There is nothing that suggests that Bruce had anything but complete conviction in the justice of his own case.

It was universally accepted however that the Scottish throne descended by male primogeniture, and most rules and precedents favoured the Balliol claim. As they saw the case slipping away from them, Bruce's lawyers in desperation conceded after all that the kingdom might be divided and that the descendants of each of the three daughters of Earl David should obtain his third of the land and income. This late change of plea has contributed to the charge that the Bruces were unpatriotic and self-seeking. Not only were they prepared to acknowledge the overlordship of Edward I, they also were prepared to acquiesce in partition of the kingdom. We must bear in mind however that every competitor had acknowledged Edward's overlordship, and that no medieval magnate would turn down the chance of one third of a kingdom.

With defeat staring him in the face, Robert the Noble may have begun seeking assurances from his allies. In October 1292 William earl of Sutherland attested that he had sworn an oath to Sir Robert Bruce of Annandale to assist him with all advice and power to prosecute his claim to the throne of Scotland. When in November 1292 it became clear that the writing was on the wall for Robert the Noble's claim, this was the occasion of a reshuffle of responsibilities within the Bruce dynasty. Possibly to avoid the personal indignity of rebuff by the court at Norham, the Competitor resigned his claim to his son and to his heirs: 'We inform all of you that we have granted, and totally surrendered, to our well-beloved son Robert Bruce, earl of Carrick, and his heirs, the whole right and claim that we had, or could have had, to sue for the realm of Scotland ... we give and grant of our free will, to our son and his heirs, full and free power to sue for the realm ...'

Days later that son, Robert Bruce VI, the earl of Carrick in right of his wife, resigned the earldom to *his* son, Robert Bruce VII, the future king. In fact such a deed could not be legally binding: an earldom was not in the earl's gift and was something that only a king could bestow. But it shows one generation of the Bruce dynasty passing on the torch to the next. Much thought now will have gone into finding a suitable match for the young earl of Carrick. Every marriage among the nobility represented an alliance and every bride brought dower land into the family. In the year 1296 or thereabouts Robert married Isabel, daughter of the earl of Mar; shortly afterwards a daughter was born to them, whom they named Marjorie, probably in honour of Robert's mother.

Edward I pronounced in favour of John Balliol on 17 November 1292, bringing the Great Cause to a close, and bringing bitter defeat to the Bruces. On St Andrew's Day (30 November) 1292 John Balliol was enthroned on the Stone of Destiny at Scone in the time-honoured fashion as King of Scots, being solemnly led to the throne, not in traditional form by the earl of Fife, who was an infant, but by Sir John de St John as the earl's representative. King John did homage to Edward as his overlord. The Comyn family resumed the control of government that it had enjoyed for half a century, and the spoils of high office and royal patronage went to them and their allies. At King John's first parliament, in February 1293, Alexander MacDougall of Argyll became sheriff of Lorn, the royal agent controlling the south-west coastline, confirmation of a dominance that had existed in the previous reign. By contrast, his rival, Angus Mór MacDonald, a supporter of the Bruces, absented himself from the gathering. At the subsequent Stirling parliament of August 1293, the nineteen-year-old Robert Bruce VII was established in his mother's earldom of Carrick. He was sponsored by James the Steward and the earl of Mar. He cannot have avoided paying a relief and performing homage and fealty to King John Balliol, but his grandfather and his father were conspicuous by their absence on the occasion and neither ever did homage to Balliol.

To the delight of the Bruces however, relations between John and Edward soon began to deteriorate. Naturally, the Bruces would side with the English against King John and his Comyn allies. But the great patriarch of the Bruce family, Robert Bruce the Noble, died aged about seventy-five at Lochmaben on 31 March 1295, just a year before war between England and Scotland broke out. He was buried with his ancestors in Guisborough Priory on 17 April.

The genesis of this war between the kingdoms lay in Edward I's deliberate provocation of the Scots, and also to an extent in his need for military service. Edward had defined the relationship between Scotland and England to his own liking: he had defined the status of the kingdom of Scotland and he had chosen its king. That king enjoyed widespread support and the loyal adherence of the long-established dominant magnate interest, the Comyns. Yet though he had put Balliol in the saddle, Edward now refused to let him ride by himself. Instead he allowed, and even encouraged, individual Scots to appeal over the head of their new king to himself as overlord.

Predictably, one of those who appealed over the head of King John to the superior lord was Alexander MacDonald of the Isles, the son of Angus Mór and an inveterate enemy of the MacDougalls who were now in the ascendant in the west of Scotland. The two families had recently been linked by the marriage of Alexander MacDonald to Juliana MacDougall. King John had arbitrated between Alexander and his wife's family in a bitter dispute over Juliana's dower land at Lismore, had given judgement against him, and was now enforcing that judgement by taking temporary possession of that land. Accordingly, Alexander and his wife, Juliana, took their complaint to Edward I, alleging that King John had occupied a part of Lismore and was refusing to hand it over to them. Not surprisingly, Edward found in favour of MacDonald and called the new King of Scots to account. Another such appellant was Malcolm le fitz Engleys, elsewhere known as MacCulian or MacQuillan, a lord of Kintyre who similarly claimed that King John had denied him justice. These were two of a dozen similar appeals made by Scots to Edward I, most of them politically inspired to embarrass the new King of Scots. There was no tradition of appeals from Scottish courts to courts outside the kingdom (except, rarely, to the papal court). Edward no doubt considered that he was merely exercising his rights, but by entertaining such appeals Edward was insulting the dignity of the Scottish king and needlessly rubbing the noses of Scots in the diminished status of their monarchy. Scots were well aware of Edward's subjugation of Wales in 1282–84, and drew the inevitable comparison that their homeland was also being reduced to a mere appendage of England.

King John, as might be expected, refused to acknowledge the legitimacy of such appeals and ignored both them and the inevitable summons before the English court of King's Bench in May 1293. Eventually however he was pressurised into appearing before the parliament of England in the autumn of that year. Facing the wrathful Edward before a hostile audience must have been a terrifying ordeal. John declared that he had no power to answer the charges or anything touching his kingdom without the advice of his people. Then he began to vacillate, renewing his homage and fealty and promising obedience. Edward merely raised the stakes and increased the provocation by demanding the personal military service of King John in the war which now loomed between England and France, as well as the service of ten earls and sixteen barons. King John prepared to submit. No king of Scotland had performed overseas military service at the behest of the English king for a hundred and thirty years, and the Scottish aristocracy were scandalised, as well as outraged that they had been summonsed as vassals to fight Edward's battles for him.

King John's Comyn-dominated council however, inspired perhaps by a Welsh revolt in 1295, resolved upon a stance of firm resistance to Edward's demands. John's objections were overcome by drastic action on the part of his councillors. At a parliament held in Stirling on 5 July 1295 they took management of relations with the French out of King John's hands. In an unprecedented move, a council of twelve, bent on resistance to Edward's demands, was appointed to rule the country and they sent a deputation to King Philip the Fair of France which negotiated an alliance between the government of King John and King Philip. Scots and French drafted a treaty in Paris in October 1295, providing for the marriage of Philip's daughter Jeanne with John's son Edward Balliol. The treaty thus provided for the French to have a permanent interest in alliance with Scotland, something that no monarch of England could tolerate.

Edward I, well aware that matters were coming to a head, demanded in October 1295 the surrender of Berwick, Roxburgh and Jedburgh castles until the end of his war with France, and he insisted that neither Frenchmen nor Flemmings should be permitted to enter Scotland. He met with robust refusal and gave orders in January 1296 for troops from English counties to assemble at Newcastle on 1 March. The council acting in the name of King John meanwhile summoned the Scottish host to meet at Caddonlee on the Tweed on 11 March. Along with the Bruces, two other Scottish earls supported Edward I: Gilbert de Umfraville earl of Angus, an Englishman, and Patrick earl of March. The Bruce family withdrew temporarily from Scotland. Robert Bruce VI, having succeeded to Annandale on his father's death, was obliged to abandon his family estate. The Lanercost chronicle records that the Scottish magnates 'pronounced forfeiture of his paternal heritage upon Robert de Brus the younger, who had fled to England, because he would not do homage to them. Also they forfeited his son in the earldom of Carrick, wherein he had been infeft, because he adhered to his father.'

John Comyn, who had succeeded his father Alexander in 1289, both as earl of Buchan and as Constable of Scotland, took control of the Bruce patrimony; he had probably been granted it as a forfeiture by the council. Edward I had, however, provided a safe refuge for the Bruces by appointing Robert Bruce VI to the command of Carlisle Castle in October 1295. Almost the first blow in the war between England and Scotland was a direct attack on the Bruces. On 26 March seven Scottish earls – Buchan, Menteith, Strathearn, Lennox, Ross, Atholl and Mar – made a surprise attack on the walled city of Carlisle from across the fords of the Solway Firth. Also present was John Comyn of Badenoch III, whom Robert Bruce VII would later kill. But for the presence of the earl of Mar, it is clear that this was not so much a war between England and Scotland as the Comyn faction attacking its traditional enemies. The Scots burnt the suburbs and tried to burn down one of the gates, and a spy within the city created a fire which panicked the citizens for a short while. The citizens, however, broke down the bridge over the Eden, and from the city walls women dropped stones and poured boiling water on the Scots below. Next day the Scots gave up the attack and retired to Annandale. Young Robert Bruce will have helped defend Carlisle on this occasion, and will have gained first-hand knowledge of the city's defences. The next time Carlisle was besieged he would be leading the attack.

On the eastern route into England – the 'East March' – the English host crossed the Tweed to confront Berwick, the largest town in Scotland. One of the English chronicles, the rhyming chronicle of Peter Langtoft, contains snatches of popular song that capture the bitterly chauvinistic, rabidly xenophobic mood in which this war was fought. He records the taunts and jeers of the Scots at Berwick. 'Let him pike and let him dyke', sang the Scots as Edward methodically built fortifications – a ditch and a palisade – prior to his attack. Then Edward unleashed a devastating attack on the poorly defended town. Bower's *Scotichronicon* describes great slaughter: 'the aforesaid King of England spared no one, whatever the age or sex, and for two days streams of blood flowed from the bodies of the slain, for in his tyrannous rage he ordered 7,500 souls of both sexes to be massacred.' Chronicles, written to entertain and edify as well as to inform, are prone to exaggeration and statistics cited in them are not to be taken seriously. Nevertheless, we gather that the storming of the town was accompanied by great bloodshed. Langtoft records the song of the English foot about the massacre:

> Scattered are the Scots,
> Huddled in their huts,
> Never do they thrive.
> Right if I read,
> They are tumbled into Tweed,
> Who dwelt by the sea.

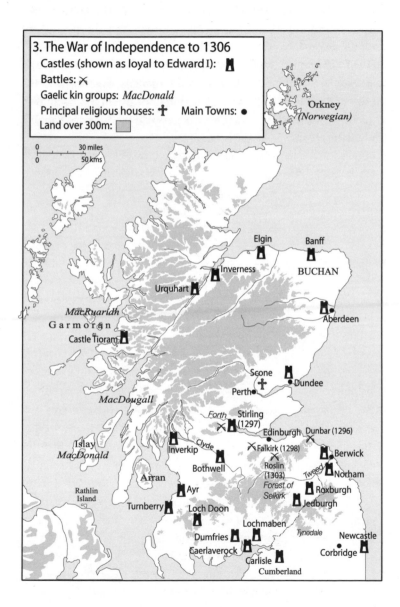

3. The War of Independence to 1306
Castles (shown as loyal to Edward I): ⌘
Battles: ✕
Gaelic kin groups: *MacDonald*
Principal religious houses: ✝ Main Towns: •
Land over 300m: ▨

0   30 miles
0   50 kms

Orkney
(Norwegian)

Elgin   Banff

Inverness   BUCHAN

Urquhart

MacRuaridh
Garmoran

Castle Tioram

Aberdeen

MacDougall

Scone ✝
Perth•   •Dundee

Forth Stirling
✕ (1297)
Edinburgh   Dunbar (1296)
Inverkip *Clyde* ✕ Falkirk (1298)   Berwick

Islay
MacDonald

Bothwell

Roslin
(1303)   Norham
Tweed

Forest of   Roxburgh
Selkirk

Arran

Ayr   Jedburgh

Rathlin
Island

Turnberry

Loch Doon

Lochmaben

Tynedale   Newcastle

Dumfries

Caerlaverock

Carlisle   Corbridge

Cumberland

The Scottish cavalry, led by Ross, Menteith and Atholl, meanwhile raided Northumberland, but when the two main hosts engaged at Dunbar on 2 April there could be no doubt as to which would prevail. Edward I's cavalry, commanded by John, Earl Warenne, and seasoned in recent Welsh and Gascon campaigns, overwhelmed the flower of Scottish chivalry and slaughtered the infantry. The English foot sang rowdily of their victory, and jeered at the Scots for robbing the corpses of nobles on the battlefield:

> The foot folk
> Put the Scots in the poke,
>   And bared their buttocks.
> By the way
> Never heard I say
>   Of readier boys
> To rob
> The robes of the rich
>   That fell in the field.
> They took of each man;
> May the rough ragged fiend
>   Tear them in hell!

After this shattering defeat there was very little resistance except in the west. There Highlanders, under Alexander MacDougall, lord of Lorn, had to be quelled by an expedition from Ireland. Otherwise, Scotland was too shocked to resist. That summer Edward spent in making a stately progress through the towns and castles of the east coast, taking control of Edinburgh after a week's siege, then Stirling, Perth, Aberdeen, Banff, and even reaching Elgin late in July. Edward insisted upon an abject surrender from King John, and obtained it. Ceremonially King John was stripped of regality, and became known as 'Toom Tabard'. The nickname –'the empty surcoat' – conveyed that John had become a nullity. The kingdom was handed over to

Edward I as overlord, and John, the unmade king, was sent south as a prisoner to the Tower of London. The earls of Atholl, Ross and Menteith were also sent into captivity, along with John Comyn the younger of Badenoch. Lesser prisoners were sent to other castles in England. Almost one hundred Scots of the *gentil* classes were made prisoner; many to be released on payment of a ransom or sureties, others of higher rank imprisoned partly to impress upon them the force of Edward's lordship, partly to guarantee good behaviour from their tenants or kinsmen, and partly as trophies to impress and gratify the English.

The treasury, jewels, plate and regalia of the kings of Scotland were loaded onto baggage trains for England, but trophies of another sort were also captured. These were the sacred relics of the kingdom: the Black Rood of St Margaret, a jewelled relic case containing a piece of the cross of Christ; and the Stone of Destiny, on which Scottish kings had been enthroned time out of mind. In English towns and cities the mobs were jubilantly reciting anti-Scottish lampoons and scurrilous jeering songs, recorded in the chronicle of Peter Langtoft:

> The sorcery
> Of Albany
> Cannot prevail.
> [St] Andrew is dead,
> Or he sleeps at the minster.
>
> Their king's seat of Scone
> Is driven over downs
> Carried to London.

Edward was interested in acquiring the magical properties of these objects for himself and his dynasty. In the past he had acquired the most sacred of Welsh relics, a fragment of the true cross called Y

Groes Naid or the Cross of Neath and the crown of Arthur, and had paraded them through the streets before adding them to the shrine of St Edward the Confessor, the saint whom Edward regarded as his spiritual mentor. He had brought the Cross of Neath with him on his triumphal journey through Scotland in 1296, and he obliged Bishop Wishart to swear fealty to him on that very relic. To Wishart, Scotland's leading churchman and patriot, the message was clear: Edward had appropriated to himself all the power of Scotland, temporal and spiritual, as he had already appropriated that of Wales.

It was just as important to send out an unmistakable signal to the Scots that there would be no subsequent Scottish king unless Edward consented. He decided to rule Scotland as 'superior lord', without intermediary, and through mere officials. With the war won and Scotland's humiliation complete, Edward was delighted to pass over responsibility for Scotland to a lieutenant. Warenne was appointed, and as he tossed Warenne the great seal of Scotland Edward cheerfully remarked, 'When you get rid of a turd, you do a good job.' At the August 1296 parliament in Berwick an ordinance for the government of Scotland was drawn up, detailing how Edward would henceforth rule the kingdom.

What then of the Bruces? Bower records, and we have no reason to doubt it, that Robert Bruce VI chose an opportune moment, approached Edward I and delicately reminded him that, now the Balliol claim to the throne had been overthrown, as runner-up in the Great Cause he was in line for employment as vassal-king of Scotland. This demeaning request elicited the richly deserved and crushingly scornful response, 'Do you think I have nothing better to do than win kingdoms for you?'

3

Resistance and survival in occupied Scotland (1296–1306)

Edward's conquest of Scotland in 1296 had been a pushover and, as Scots were well aware, he had just finished prosecuting the last of three bitter wars to subdue Wales. The kingship of Britain was beckoning, as Peter Langtoft, canon of Bridlington, acknowledged:

> Now are the islanders all joined together,
> And Albany reunited to the regalities
> Of which King Edward is proclaimed lord.
> Cornwall and Wales are in his power
> And Ireland the great at his will.
> There is neither king nor prince of all the countries
> Except King Edward, who has thus united them.

A man grounded in hard political realities, Edward himself can hardly have been under the illusion that his subjection of Scotland was complete, but for now he had to switch his attention to France, a far more powerful enemy.

Scots also knew that the humiliation of their homeland was going down rather well in England. An intensely conservative people, they had just witnessed astounding change in the accepted order of things. Most will have been profoundly shocked at the degradation of Scottish kingship, the humiliating defeat of their lairds in battle and the sacrilegious removal of the sacred relics of the kingdom. They regarded the terms of the Treaty of Birgham as the standard for an acceptable union with England, but Edward I had ignored those terms, trampled all over Scottish sensibilities and made every effort to destroy Scotland's separate identity.

Had the English presence been limited to the imposition of a few disciplined castle garrisons, it is possible that the Scots might have tolerated it for a time. Had the change of regime had little practical effect on the great mass of the people, it might have lasted. In fact the new order presented three serious threats to the well-being of the people: security of landed property was jeopardised; financial exactions impoverished every social class; and the horrendous prospect of enforced military service overseas loomed. To these elements, which are the principal causes of the uprising of 1297, the widespread sense of outrage at English triumphalism and humiliation of the Scots must surely be added.

Any threat to security of landed tenure was sure to provoke a violent reaction from the propertied noble classes, and an atmosphere of uncertainty prevailed early in the autumn and early winter. Edward had imprisoned many of the Scottish leaders, and they remained in prison well into 1297. It remained to be seen whether they would be restored to their lands. Already, in the summer of 1296, Edward's officials had traversed the country, extracting an oath of fealty to Edward from every substantial freeholder in the land and taking evidence of it. These written and sealed testimonials, over 1,500 of them, were recorded on a document known as the Ragman Roll. The very approach to collection of these fealties, methodical and legalistic as it was, will have generated fear of dispossession. For why should Edward want these proofs of sworn loyalty if it were not to extract military or other services? The Bruces, now back in possession of Annandale, acquired a new neighbour, as the former Balliol lordship of Galloway was awarded to the Englishman Henry Percy. Robert Bruce VI, lord of Annandale, and his son Robert Bruce VII, earl of

Carrick and future king, were sworn and appear on the roll along with all the others. But not everyone of note was represented on the Ragman Roll. Malcolm and William Wallace, the former a vassal of the Steward, are not recorded as having sworn. Lower down the social scale, they will have been more easily omitted, and the absence of their names is not proof of principled opposition.

Financial exactions certainly increased as a result of the change of regime. Edward had installed Hugh Cressingham as treasurer of Scotland, and his task was to raise money for Edward's war with King Philip the Fair of France. Cressingham's exactions were such that by May 1297 he was able to send the huge sum of £5,188 to the English exchequer. It was customary for a king to obtain parliamentary sanction for the collection of taxes, but this sum was raised by gathering in the king's debts, and the profits of justice, fines, wardships and marriages. In England a general 'prise' or seizure of wool was conducted as part of royal policy. This also applied in Scotland and must have been hugely unpopular with great religious houses that produced the wool, and the merchants of the east-coast ports who exported it. It was probably Edward's long-term intention to pay for this wool, just as, technically, the casual seizures of goods and transport by the king's ministers – also known as 'prises' – were all supposed to be paid for in the long run. But these financial expedients thoroughly alienated the merchants of the towns and country people living in proximity to castle garrisons. Cressingham, a fat and unpleasant man, was loathed by the Scots.

It was, however, the prospect of having to serve overseas that appears to have caused most alarm. The widespread belief was that Edward intended to 'seize all the middle people of Scotland to send them overseas in his war, to their great damage and destruction'. Early in June 1297 Edward began to release the captured Scottish nobles from prison in return for promises to serve in his planned campaign against France in Flanders. Those released included many of the governing Comyn–Balliol faction: the two John Comyns of

Badenoch – the elder and the younger – John Comyn earl of Buchan, Alexander de Balliol and Alexander earl of Menteith. Accordingly, the magnates who governed large swathes of the country returned to their estates, and leadership was restored to a defeated people. Edward expected them to begin enlisting their tenantry in preparation for service overseas.

In the west, Gaelic clans realigned themselves in accordance with the new order. Under the Comyn-dominated governments of Alexander III and King John, MacDougall had been in the ascendant and MacDonald excluded from royal patronage. But on the defeat of the Scots this situation was reversed: the MacDonalds had sided with the English – and the Bruces – against their traditional enemies, and reaped the benefits of having backed the winner. Alexander MacDonald of Islay and his younger brother Angus Óg became Edward's chief agents in the region, leaving the MacDougalls excluded from patronage, but far from powerless. On release from imprisonment at Berwick in May 1297, Alexander MacDougall of Argyll and his son John went on the rampage, attacking MacDonald, Campbell and MacSween territories. This son, John of Argyll, known as John Bachach ('the Lame'), was later to emerge as one of Robert Bruce's most inveterate foes. To counter this threat, Edward's government appointed Alexander MacDonald of Islay as baillie of Kintyre, formerly an office held by James the Steward, and baillie in the sheriffdoms of Lorn, Ross and the Isles, privileged positions formerly held by Alexander MacDougall. Thus in the summer of 1297 the MacDonalds were struggling, on Edward of England's behalf, to restrain this widespread MacDougall rebellion.

The violence in the west had probably never ceased since 1296 and can largely be explained by traditional animosities, but clear centres of revolt specifically against Edwardian government crystallised in the south-west, in the Forest of Selkirk and in the north of Scotland. While the lord of Annandale himself, Robert Bruce VI, remained aloof, still clinging perhaps to the remote possibility that Edward I would install him as sub-king, the revolt in the south-west was nourished by the traditional allies of the Bruces, the former cronies of Robert the Noble, James the Steward and Bishop Wishart of Glasgow. Both are accused by English chronicles of stirring up this revolt, which began in May 1297 in parts of Galloway. Further north, in Lanark, William Wallace – who was one of the Steward's affinity – attacked and killed William Hesilrig, the English sheriff, and the rising became widespread. In the far north meanwhile Andrew Moray led entirely separate attacks on the English garrison at Castle Urquhart that same month. Finally, in Aberdeenshire, remarkably, the English sheriff defected to the side of the rebels. These originally unconnected revolts, mobilised, naturally, by aristocratic leaders, enjoyed widespread support from all classes.

The myth that Wallace was a commoner who led a popular uprising has scant foundation in history. Wallace himself was the son of a knight, and he was soon joined by Sir William Douglas (known as 'the Hardy'), the Steward's brother-in-law and another ally of the Bruces. Together they mounted a daring raid on the court of the English justiciar William Ormsby while it was in session at Scone. Though Ormsby escaped, the rebels captured valuables and horses. After this they made for the cover of Selkirk Forest, 'the cradle of insurrection' which provided virtually impenetrable shelter for malcontents. These outlaws attracted a large following, which they began to fashion into an army.

James the Steward abandoned his covert support for the rebels for open participation and joined Wallace and Douglas in July, leading into rebellion a further group of disaffected Scottish nobles, including not only Robert Wishart, Bishop of Glasgow and former Guardian, but also MacDuff, the son of the ninth earl of Fife, Alexander Lindsay and the young Robert Bruce VII, the earl of Carrick. The future king was now twenty-two and in joining the rebels he seems to have been acting independently or perhaps even in the face of his father's disapproval. The lord of Annandale was careful to have nothing to do with rebellion, and seems to have abandoned his patrimony once more for the safety of Carlisle. Young Bruce's involvement in rebellion was not in the family interest. What possessed him to risk life, limb and inheritance by joining the rebels is unknown; it looks as though he had fallen under the influence of his grandfather's friends Bishop Wishart of Glasgow and the Steward, and, if we may trust Bruce's reported words, they had inspired him to patriotic resistance.

When first suspected of sympathy with the rebellion, the young earl was obliged by the bishop and citizens of Carlisle to swear an oath of loyalty to the king on the sacred host and on a relic called the sword of St Thomas in Carlisle Castle. As Penman stresses, St Thomas was a saint especially revered by the Bruces. Swearing a falsehood on this relic may have cost him dear psychologically and damaged his reputation and honour. Having done so, Robert left the city, and, to allay suspicion further, he feigned an attack on the lands of Sir William Douglas and burnt a part of them. He carried off Douglas's wife and children, but took them, not to the king's custody in Carlisle, but to safety in Annandale. It may be at this point that he first met the young James Douglas, heir to Sir William, who was to become his faithful lieutenant and close friend. In Annandale, Robert called together the knights of his ancestral patrimony and addressed them. These words are put into his mouth by the hostile chronicler Walter of Guisborough:

My dearest friends, you know and it is true that recently at Carlisle I swore an oath as you know and have heard, but it is null and void since it was extorted by force. I did this thing from fear for the body, but not of my own free will. For this I am contrite and deeply penitent. I hope nevertheless that the benefit of absolution will follow shortly. No man holds his own flesh and blood in hatred and I am no exception. I must join my own people and the nation from which I was born. I ask that you please come with me and you will be my councillors and close comrades.

Readers should note that the chronicle stops short of making Robert say that he was born *in* Scotland. Young Bruce was then believed to have acted out of patriotism, and he may well have done so. The lord of Annandale, Robert Bruce VI, however, was having nothing to do with the revolt, and because of this the men of Annandale refused to follow his heir. They told young Bruce that they would give him a response on the morrow, but most slipped away under cover of night to avoid refusing him.

The chronicler adds the not improbable observation that 'even at that time it was noised abroad that Carrick aspired to the kingship'. However that might be, the sources show that Bruce was in the forefront of fomenting rebellion. A letter to King Edward from Cressingham of 23 July reports the opinion that 'if you had the earl of Carrick, the Steward of Scotland and his brother ... you would think your business done'. Little was achieved in any case by the Steward, Wishart and Bruce: by June they found themselves hemmed in by superior forces led by English magnates Henry Percy and Robert Clifford, who were both to become hardened veterans of the Scottish wars. Yet the Scots did not surrender but instead quibbled over surrender terms, and in this way they pinned down Percy and Clifford's army for almost a month. They bought time, while William Wallace in the Forest of Selkirk and Andrew Moray in the far north spread rebellion. By 24 July Percy and Clifford had captured Sir Alexander Lindsay and Sir William Douglas, who was kept in irons in Berwick Castle 'still very savage and abusive', having failed to produce hostages for his release. Soon afterwards Sir William was sent to the Tower of London, where he died, leaving his son James to avenge him.

Wishart, the Steward and Bruce were expected to surrender at Irvine on 8 August, and Cressingham had high hopes that their expected surrender in the south-west would mean the end of the rebellion. On 4 August he wrote to the king, 'Sire, across the Scottish Sea [the Firth of Forth] your peace is still disturbed, so it is said, as a result of the deeds of the earls who are there. But at all events, we hope that if the business with the bishop of Glasgow and the others on the feast of St Laurence [8 August] goes well, we will have the people on the far side of the Scottish Sea at our mercy, by God's grace.' Percy and Clifford came away from the capitulation at Irvine with the impression that they had pacified the whole of southern Scotland, and that rebellion south of the Forth was over. They even convinced Cressingham, who had raised a large infantry force in Northumberland and was preparing to enter Scotland, that there was no need for a further expedition. Bishop Wishart was in prison by July. Imprisonment of a clergyman was contrary to canon law, and Wishart's case would bring papal disapproval on King Edward. The Steward was released, doubtless on sureties and delivery of hostages. One of the terms suggested for Bruce's release had been the handover of his baby daughter Marjorie as a hostage, but it is not at all certain that this was agreed. Indeed there is no record of Bruce surrendering; he may have escaped somehow. If he did surrender at Irvine, it can only have been briefly and without commitment because it is quite clear in the aftermath of the Battle of Falkirk that his standing was high with the patriots.

Elsewhere rebellions continued to spread and began to coalesce. Wallace, operating out of the vast Forest of Selkirk, was amassing and training large numbers of foot soldiers and gathered sufficient strength to besiege Dundee castle. In the north-east Andrew Moray had taken the castles of Inverness, Banff and Elgin. By a remarkable miscalculation on Edward's part, the Comyns – John earl of Buchan and his brother Alexander and John of Badenoch III – instead of being sent to Flanders, were dispatched to keep in check the northern revolt. Edward must have believed that by the taking of sureties and hostages they had been reduced to complete dependence on him. At first they were ineffectual in Edward's service; then Buchan openly changed sides and joined the rebels. Only the fact that he was serving in Flanders kept John Comyn of Badenoch the elder loyal to Edward. The return of the Comyns was especially significant. North of the Mounth they had tremendous prestige, and throughout Scotland they will have been looked to for leadership. If this presented a problem for those elements of the revolt associated with the Bruce faction, there is no reflection of it in the sources. Letters to Edward from Hugh Cressingham reveal the disintegration of the occupation administration: '[24 July 1297] Sire, let it not displease you, by far the greater part of your counties of the realm of Scotland are still unprovided for with keepers, as well by death, sieges or imprisonment; and some have given up their bailiwicks, and others neither will nor dare return; and in some counties the Scots have established and placed bailiffs and ministers, so that no county is in proper order excepting Berwick and Roxburgh and this only lately.'

The reference to the Scots appointing baillies and officials of their own reveals the degree of organisation behind the revolt, and such organisation can only have come from the aristocratic governing element. With much of the pre-1296 local government restored to the country, the rebellion acquired further legitimacy and vigour. The earls of Buchan, Strathearn, and Carrick too, if, as we suspect, Bruce was still with the rebels, will have contributed levies of men from their estates, and there may have been other elements of compulsory military service at work. With the authority of at least two earls behind them, Wallace and Moray began to issue writs in the name of King John, and they continued to have Dundee under siege.

Edward's lieutenant in Scotland, John earl of Warrene, never actually resided in Scotland: he found that the climate was not conducive to his health. But, though the king himself was absent in Gascony, Cressingham's letters eventually had effect in Westminster, and in September Warenne at last felt obliged to bestir himself. He marched with a substantial force from Berwick to Stirling. On the slopes north of the River Forth Andrew Moray and Wallace's forces had combined and lay in wait for Warenne's army to cross Stirling Bridge. Twice on the morning of 11 September 1297 the English army crossed the bridge, but each time it was summoned back to await Warenne's command. He had slept in. On the third occasion, the Scots waited until half of the force had crossed the bridge, then they charged down the slopes at the English, cutting their army in two. The half of the English army which was on the bridge or waiting to cross could only watch as the other half was butchered. Warenne was on the south side, with those waiting to cross, but the hated treasurer found himself on the far bank, cut off and vulnerable.

> Hugh de Cressingham, not accustomed to the saddle,
> From his steed in its course fell under foot.
> His body was cut to pieces by the ribalds of Scotland,
> And his skin taken off in small thongs
> As an insult to the king, whose clerk he was ...

The battle of Stirling Bridge was a landmark victory that restored Scottish confidence and pride, erasing the memory of the debacle at Dunbar. Stirling Castle at once capitulated. There was only one significant loss on the Scottish side: Andrew Moray appears to have been mortally wounded in the battle. There is a report that he was killed, but letters were written in his name at some time after the battle, indicating that he did not die straightaway. He lingered at least until 7 November, the date of a document in which Wallace and Moray are described as 'Leaders of the Army of Scotland'. An immediate consequence of this outstanding victory was that Wallace's prestige soared, and on Moray's death he became sole Guardian. The Scottish Church rallied behind Wallace, and in Rome it was able to achieve the consecration of the patriot William Lamberton as bishop of St Andrews. This extraordinarily able ecclesiastic then brought the plight of the Scots to the notice of the French and papal courts.

After the battle Wallace resumed prosecution of the siege of Dundee and, having captured also the town (though not the castle) of Berwick, he announced to merchants of Lübeck and Hamburgh that liberated Scotland was open for business. His principal achievement, however, was his protracted invasion of the East and West Marches of England.

A contemporary chronicler, Walter of Guisborough, describes the panic in Northumberland after the battle of Stirling Bridge, where there was no doubt what was in store: 'The Northumbrians were petrified with fear and they evacuated from the countryside their wives and children and all their household goods, sending them with their animals to Newcastle and various other places. At that time the praise of God ceased in all the monasteries and churches of the whole province from Newcastle to Carlisle. All the monks, canons regular and the rest of the priests and ministers of the Lord, together with almost the whole of the people fled from the face of the Scot.' Another chronicle, the *Chronicle of Lanercost*, summarises the Wallace invasion of northern England: 'After this ... the Scots gathered together and invaded, devastating the whole country, causing burnings, depredations and murders, and they came almost up to the town of Newcastle; but turned away from it and invaded the county of Carlisle; there they did as in Northumberland, destroying everything; and afterwards they returned to Northumberland, to devastate more fully anything they had overlooked previously; and on the feast of St Cecilia, virgin and martyr [22 November 1297], they returned to Scotland.'

This is a broadly accurate summary for it corresponds with information gleaned from financial accounts of manors destroyed. After sporadic raids led by others, Wallace led an army apparently composed of infantry spearmen south from Berwick towards Newcastle, but then shied away from that formidably large – though as yet unwalled – town and moved westwards into Tynedale, burning Bywell and Corbridge. At Newminster and Hexham he extracted a ransom for sparing the monasteries. Hexham was still recovering from the Scots' last visitation in 1296. Then Wallace advanced upon Carlisle. That city began to prepare for assault, and Robert Bruce VI was replaced as garrison commander by John Halton, Bishop of Carlisle, probably because he was a Scot; nowhere is it alleged that he was disloyal, or that members of his family were fighting alongside Wallace. Carlisle was already menaced by Gallovidians, and ten Gallovidian hostages were delivered to the city in an effort to gain it further protection. Wallace and the 'Army of Scotland' arrived outside the city at Martinmas (11 November), and a clerk was sent into the city to demand its surrender to 'William the Conqueror'. Wallace was impressed by the defences, however. The citizens had prepared engines to resist a siege, whereas he himself had no siege train. He did not attack, but left a force to keep the city garrison in check while he devastated Cumberland as far as Inglewood Forest and beyond. Then around 18 November Wallace and the Gallovidians together marched eastwards, re-entering Tynedale. Again he visited Hexham Priory. Scottish troops – Gallovidians, perhaps – stole even the sacred vessels from the altar. The hostile chronicler Walter of Guisborough says that Wallace apologised to the canons for the behaviour of a 'rough and uncivilised people who had no shame'. Wallace was embarrassed because when he had passed by the priory a week or two earlier, he had issued a letter of protection to the canons, no doubt in return for a hefty ransom. Now, on this return journey to Newcastle, he could not persuade the men of Galloway who were accompanying him to respect that immunity.

After two days Wallace left the priory and marched on in the snow towards Newcastle. The town had not yet been fully encircled by defences and the citizens prepared for the worst. They organised watches, the castle was garrisoned and three war-engines rehabilitated. It was now about 23 November. Wallace, however, failed to attack: 'The courageous men who were in charge of Newcastle braced themselves and went out of the city a little way, despite the fact that they were very few against many. Seeing this, the Scots veered away from the city, divided among themselves the spoils, and handing over to the Gallovidians their share, they departed to their own regions.'

The English reports of the invasion reveal that Wallace was unable to capitalise fully on the signal victory of Stirling. He seems to have presided over, rather than led, a five-week rampage through northern England, a large infantry force, boldly challenging Carlisle and Newcastle, but ill-equipped to assault either. Wallace was embarrassed by the behaviour of his men at Hexham, suggesting that he could not control the men of Galloway. Perhaps Wallace had intended an assault on Newcastle, but his men were unwilling to risk losing their spoils. We may indeed wonder how far the raid was an expression of Wallace's strategic ambitions and how far it was motivated by popular feelings of vengeance and euphoria in the wake of the victory at Stirling.

Wallace's fascination with major strategic points – Berwick, Newcastle and Carlisle – is reminiscent of earlier invasions of England by David I and William the Lion. Yet Wallace appears to have been indecisive, attracted by the great strategic prizes of Newcastle and Carlisle but aware that his army was poorly equipped to capture either. It is true that he captured the towns of Berwick and Dundee, but the only castles he took – apart from Stirling, which had surrendered after the battle – were the comparatively unimportant ones of Dirleton and Jedburgh. A decade later Robert Bruce had learned from Wallace's experience in northern England: his first raids on the same territories threw all strategy to the wind, making the organised collection of ransoms and booty their priority. His were cavalry raids, which avoided battle, rather than invasions by massed bodies of slow-moving infantry. Memories of the Wallace invasion however will no doubt have contributed to the decisions by the northern English counties to pay the extortionate ransoms demanded by Robert Bruce when he became king, rather than risk repetition of the horrors of 1297. Only when he had reduced the surrounding countryside to his obedience did Bruce apply pressure on the strategic towns of Berwick and Carlisle.

In the absence of her king, England was reeling from the shock of defeat and invasion. As a knee-jerk reaction to defeat at Stirling Bridge, writs of array were issued for the assembly of an improbably large 33,400-strong infantry, mostly from the English shires and the remainder from Wales. Horrified by the impudence of the Wallace invasion, all the resources of the English governmental machine were brought to bear and actually produced a force of 18,500 men, an army of unmanageable proportions, which gathered at Berwick in early 1298. On its approach Wallace evacuated the town, aware that he was unable to hold it. This vast force was impossible to feed, and to the enormous relief of Edward's Scottish administration, instructions arrived from the English king in February that nothing was to be attempted until his return. The levies were disbanded. A winter invasion of Scotland was impossible for any army, and such a vast army would simply have starved. Some retaliation had already taken place, for around Christmas Warenne and Robert Clifford had raided Annandale and destroyed ten villages.

The English still held the major castles of Scotland: Berwick, Edinburgh and Roxburgh, but Wallace increased the pressure on them all, keeping their garrisons busy. Wallace was well aware that he would soon have to face Edward in battle, and he probably spent the spring and summer of 1298 training levies. He was knighted by one of the earls who supported him, to make acceptable to the aristocrats his election as sole Guardian of Scotland and in recognition of his achievement at Stirling Bridge.

That summer, the Scots scored a significant diplomatic victory. Bishop-elect Lamberton had been able to evade the English blockade and make the voyage to Rome for consecration there on 1 June 1298. Then he travelled to Paris, to join a small group of Scottish émigrés at the French court. They were able to persuade both King Philip and Pope Boniface VIII to write to Edward demanding the release of King John Balliol and a cessation of Edward's attacks on the Scots. It was a significant step in the escalation of diplomatic pressure against England, but it would be a year before the English king would be forced to make any concession, and for now nothing would stop his invasion of Scotland. With a united English aristocracy at his back, Edward mustered a force of 25,000 foot – 11,000 of whom were Welsh – and 3,000 cavalry. The logistical preparations for such a force were, however, inadequate. Edinburgh and Carlisle were the only locations to which some grain was sent in advance, and ships intended to provision the army were delayed by contrary winds. The Welsh foot-soldiers turned out to be unreliable, but Edward may have been forced to use them because so many of the English had already served their forty days outside the kingdom of England at their own expense in the previous winter. As this force advanced into Scotland it became clear that Wallace had very thoroughly removed from their path all possible means of sustenance, 'a scorched earth' tactic that threatened to weaken the English severely before battle was joined. This too would be later emulated by Bruce. In an effort to cheer up his starving troops, Edward's Welsh foot-soldiers were given wine, and violence broke out between the Welsh and the English knights. The Welsh withdrew from the army, and threatened to take no further part in the war. As the English passed through the town of Linlithgow they saw the massed spears of the Scottish army on a mountain in the distance.

Wallace had clearly realised the sense in postponing battle as long as possible, to make the most of dissension in the enemy ranks and draw them deep into hostile territory. However the earls upon whom Wallace depended may not have countenanced anything but conventional warfare, and Wallace's own position would have been profoundly weakened had he allowed the English to reoccupy Scotland. Open battle was therefore inevitable, although the folly of taking on a superior force had already been demonstrated at Dunbar in 1296. A little beyond the town of Falkirk the Scottish force prepared to give battle, and on the feast of St Mary Magdalene, 22 July, they faced the mighty English host.

Unlike Edward's army, which was largely paid and for which accounts survive, nothing exists to reveal the size of Wallace's force. However, David Caldwell has argued that he might have had a larger

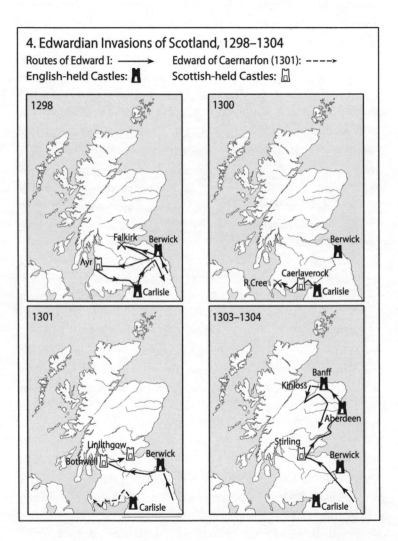

4. Edwardian Invasions of Scotland, 1298–1304

Routes of Edward I: ———→   Edward of Caernarfon (1301): - - - -→
English-held Castles: 🏰   Scottish-held Castles: 🏰

1298
Falkirk   Berwick
Ayr
Carlisle

1300
Berwick
Caerlaverock
R.Cree
Carlisle

1301
Linlithgow   Berwick
Bothwell
Carlisle

1303–1304
Banff
Kinloss
Aberdeen
Stirling   Berwick
Carlisle

force of foot spearmen than is usually allowed: perhaps as many as 20,000. The challenge before Wallace was to withstand the might of Edward's armoured cavalry with an army substantially composed of foot soldiers. He drew up his army of spearmen in three densely packed 'schiltroms' or blocks radiating iron spearheads. A small marsh and loch between the armies provided some natural shelter for the Scottish centre from the charge of the English heavy cavalry. So that they would not give way before the impact of the charge, Wallace had each schiltrom 'anchored' to its chosen position by means of ropes tied to wooden stakes driven into the ground, which formed makeshift circular palisades. These then were the rings he referred to in his famous remark to the foot soldiers before the battle, 'I have brought you into the ring, now see if you can dance.' In the gaps between the schiltroms he placed such archers as he had, and in the rear he kept the small numbers of cavalry that Scottish nobles – James the Steward, the earls of Buchan, Strathearn, Lennox, possibly Atholl and Menteith too – had committed. Should the worst come to the worst, Callendar Wood lay to the rear of Scots, which might provide cover for fleeing infantry.

It was perhaps the best possible arrangement that could be devised for such an unequal battle, but it was not good enough. The aristocratic Scottish horsemen fled the field early without making any contact with the English. Those with most to lose, they had weighed up the odds and made the rational, if ignoble, last-minute decision to avoid personal commitment, leaving their tenants to face the enemy. English cavalry rode down the Scottish archers positioned between the schiltroms, then turned their attention to the now isolated formations of spearmen, who had to withstand the impact of repeated charges. Periodically each schiltrom was subjected to the hail of crossbow bolts and arrows from the Welsh bowmen and eventually – as they ran out of manufactured missiles – of stones. The schiltroms were stationary targets for missiles and cavalry charges, and eventually, despite the palisades of ropes and stakes, they could not hold together. Battle turned to slaughter. In fleeing to the woods behind them, great numbers of Scottish spearmen were killed; others drowned in the loch; still others were ridden down by the pursuing English cavalry. The English lost 110 horses and 2,000 infantry were killed. That figure takes account only of the paid element of the English force. There is no estimating Scottish losses, but they must have been far in excess of those sustained by the victors.

Neither of the two Robert Bruces was at the battle of Falkirk, which is why neither appears on the heraldic Falkirk roll of arms. In Fordun, there survives an account that blames a Robert Bruce for the loss of the battle, but this is a lie intended to blacken the name which has escaped expurgation by Bruce's hagiographers. In fact Robert Bruce VI was then serving Edward I on the western march, and had been dispatched to raise troops from his lordship of Annandale. The younger Robert continued to enjoy high standing with the patriots after the battle and was subsequently elected joint-Guardian, so he certainly had not come to the peace of Edward, but nor was he at the battle as he was not among those who forfeited lands for fighting against the king. He was most likely on his estates at Turnberry. He may have been sulking, unwilling to fight battles for King John Balliol and unable to stomach fighting alongside the Comyns. He probably met his father at this juncture, who will have tried to persuade him to come into the peace of Edward I, but evidently young Robert decided to persevere in his resistance to the king of England. Perhaps the patriot leadership were already dangling before him the prospect of Guardianship to keep him on board.

After the battle the victorious English advanced into Fife. They occupied St Andrews, but one report says that Edward, out of respect for the local saint, ordered that the town should not be sacked. Perth, however, was destroyed. Edward then turned westwards through the Forest of Selkirk and marched towards the earldom of Carrick. One of the English chronicles carries a report that the Scots were regrouping in Galloway, and it seems that Edward was anxious to confront them. It is very likely that the Comyns and the earl of Carrick – who emerged as the leaders of resistance in the aftermath of the battle – had retreated to family estates in the south-west. Bruce indeed may have previously arranged that the Bruces' Irish allies should contribute forces to the west of Scotland. For in what may have been an echo of the Turnberry Band, Antrim magnate Thomas Bisset arrived with his followers on the island of Arran in order, according to Walter of Guisborough, 'to assist the Scots, as was commonly said'. Once he learned of the outcome of the battle, however, Bisset changed his stance and claimed that he had come to help the English and actually received a grant of the isle of Arran from Edward. The Guisborough chronicle records that 'hearing of the approach of the king, Robert Bruce the son fled from his face and he burnt that castle [Ayr] which he held'. It is the first concrete report of Bruce's activities since the surrender at Irvine. It is also significant that the young earl is associated with the burning of castles to deny them to the enemy. This tactic he subsequently developed into a hallmark of his style of warfare.

At Ayr Edward waited for a fortnight for ships carrying provisions to appear while his army starved a second time, and then he retreated, first to Dumfries, thence to Lochmaben. In Annandale the Bruces' retainers held the ancestral castle at Lochmaben but, probably in the aftermath of Stirling, they had at last declared for the patriots. Now, they had no choice but to surrender, and Edward spared their lives. He destroyed the stone castle of Robert the Noble of Lochmaben, and re-using the stone, built afresh on a site nearby. Adjacent to this new castle, he built a wooden palisade covered in mud to render it fireproof. Such structures were known as peels, and they enlarged the accommodation and hence the protective capacity of castles. They could be speedily erected, and at no great expense; in time peels were attached to many castles in English-held Scotland including Dumfries, Linlithgow and – significantly – at Selkirk, always a focal point of resistance. Edward then made arrangements for the garrisoning and

Robert Bruce

provisioning of castles throughout Scotland, and reorganised the occupation. Garrisons at Berwick, Edinburgh, Stirling (abandoned by the Scots after the battle), Roxburgh and Jedburgh were all carefully provisioned, and captaincies were established over wide areas: Eskdale, Edinburgh, Nithsdale, with Patrick, earl of March, appointed as Guardian of Scotland South of the Forth. Lack of provisions however meant Edward could no longer stay in Scotland, and he led the bulk of his army across the Solway, reaching Carlisle in September.

For the Scots, the saving grace of the year 1298 was that Edward was unable properly to follow up his victory. The remains of the Army of Scotland and many of the nobles – Buchan and Lamberton the most prominent – regrouped in the shelter of Selkirk Forest. There, in the weeks following the rout, the internal politics of the patriots were played out to a remarkable conclusion. It was decided that after such a defeat Wallace could no longer remain as sole Guardian. Wallace may have been moving towards the conclusion that the Scots could never achieve victory by their own efforts, for a year later he left for Paris to lobby the French king for support. In his stead Robert Bruce earl of Carrick and John Comyn of Badenoch the younger were elected joint Guardians of Scotland. This was the John Comyn who Robert Bruce was to murder in 1306. The heirs of both hostile noble factions had evidently decided to bury differences for the time being and co-operate to resist the occupation. How this was achieved or what the heads of the two families thought we do not know; Bruce may have co-operated because he was given a position of honour and influence equal to that of the Comyns, but he will not have compromised on his family's claim to the throne.

The patriot government of northern Scotland was resilient enough to withstand defeat at Falkirk, and it still functioned in the name of King John. It was probably based upon the Comyn lordships of the north-east, still largely unscathed by warfare. In the north the court of the justiciar of Scotia – which office was filled by John Comyn, earl of Buchan – still held pleas, and sheriffs still collected revenues for the government of the guardians, and not just for north of the Forth. During the joint guardianship of Bruce and Comyn, their official documents commenced in the following words: 'Robert Bruce, earl of Carrick, and John Comyn the son, Guardians of the kingdom of Scotland in the name of the famous prince the illustrious King John, together with the bishops, abbots, priors, earls, barons and other magnates and the whole community of the realm ...' Bruce of course would much have preferred there to be no mention of King John, but he was prepared to acquiesce as long as John remained at a safe distance.

Edward fully intended to return to Scotland in the following season, 1299, and before the summer of 1298 was out he had issued writs for the next season's campaign and laid plans for the supply of his garrisons. His hand had been immeasurably strengthened by the Anglo–French peace of 1298, negotiated through the arbitration of Boniface VIII. This was a cynical agreement by which England and France reined in their mutual antagonism in order that each might concentrate on suppressing its smaller northern neighbours. Thus the English abandoned their erstwhile allies, the Flemings, to the tender mercies of Philip IV. The French did rather better by their allies, the Scots. Before distancing themselves from the Scottish alliance they wrung a highly significant concession from the English, namely the release of King John from English into papal custody. A number of political difficulties however rendered it impossible for Edward to contemplate campaigning in Scotland in the summer of 1299. One was his impending marriage to Margaret, the sister of Philip the Fair, a major state occasion which, given the political importance of the marriage, called for the utmost delicacy in planning and protocol. Another was the truculent attitude of the English baronage. Edward seized as forfeit all the lands of many Scottish nobles who had fought against him. These he granted out to English magnates, in order to give them a stake in the conquest of Scotland: the earl of Lincoln, for example, was awarded the office and lands of James the Steward; Robert Clifford was given the Maxwell castle of Caerlaverock; and, later, Henry Percy was granted the lands of Ingram Balliol. It was the first major redistribution of forfeited estates. The grantees, however, were left to gain possession and extract revenue from Scottish estates, and the king's apparent generosity cut little ice with his magnates. The Falkirk campaign had been possible because king and magnates had acted from shared outrage at the Wallace invasion, but these circumstances were not to be repeated. Already the earls of Norfolk and Hereford had fallen out with Edward over his grant of Arran to Bisset which had been made without their advice. They were now demanding that the king abide by concessions he had made, and which he was now unwilling to stand by.

An exchange of prisoners was achieved in April 1299, and it is interesting to note that the Scots had captured some middle-ranking English lords: William fitz Warren, Marmaduke de Thweng and William de Ros. Resistance against the occupation mainly took the form of slow exertion of pressure on English garrison castles by encirclement, cutting off supplies and ambush. But it was also a war of mounted raids, known as *chevauchées*, designed to impoverish and terrorise populations adhering to the enemy, another tactic subsequently developed by Robert Bruce.

Patriot nobles mustered at Peebles for a raid from the cover of Selkirk Forest. A council was held there on 19 August 1299. The report of a spy who witnessed the council provides a remarkable insight into the tensions prevalent within the patriot camp:

> At the council Sir David Graham demanded the lands and goods of Sir William Wallace because he was leaving the kingdom [for Paris] without the leave or the approval of the Guardians. And Sir Malcolm, Sir William's brother, answered that neither his lands nor his goods should be given away, for they were protected by the peace in which Wallace had left the kingdom, since he was leaving to work for the good of the kingdom. At this, the two knights gave the lie to each other and drew their daggers.

The next sentence reveals that Bruce and Comyn factions were quite literally at each others' throats:

> And since Sir David was of Sir John Comyn's following and Sir Malcolm Wallace of the earl of Carrick's following, it was reported to the earl of Buchan and John Comyn that a fight had broken out without their knowing it; and John Comyn leaped at the earl of Carrick and seized him by the throat, and the earl of Buchan turned on the bishop of St. Andrew's, declaring that treason and lese-majesté [an offence against the dignity of a sovereign power] were being plotted. Eventually the Steward and others came between them and quietened them.

The meeting ended with Bishop Lamberton being admitted as a third Guardian in an effort to maintain some semblance of unity.

Edward's allies and garrisons in Scotland paid the price for his failure to campaign in 1299. That summer the patriot commander Herbert Morham was able to cut lines of supply to the ninety-strong English garrison at Stirling, and they began to starve. Bruce continually tried through the autumn to force the English garrison out of Lochmaben. He had no success. But in November the long siege of Stirling ended in the surrender of the English garrison. For the Scots this was a major strategic prize that promised to enlarge significantly the area under the sway of the patriots.

In the west too, Edward's agents the MacDonalds sustained a serious defeat as the MacDougall revolt continued unabated. The Annals of Ulster record that in that year 'Alexander MacDonald, the person who was the best for hospitality and excellence that was in Ireland and in Scotland, was killed, together with a countless number of his own people, who were slaughtered around him, by Alexander MacDougall.' It used to be thought that the Alexander who died in 1299 was Alexander Óg, son of Angus Mór. In the Barbour narrative which commences in 1306, Angus Óg is portrayed as the unrivalled chieftain at Islay, and Barbour builds him up as a staunch ally of Robert throughout his career. However, the MacDonalds, like all the Gaelic lordships, were prone to faction, internal dissension and instability. It is now thought that Barbour, writing in the 1370s, exaggerates the role of Angus Óg to suit the personalities at the court of his patron and that, in reality, Angus was a lesser player at least until 1318. The Alexander MacDonald who died in 1299 is likely to have been the brother, not the son, of Angus Mór. The MacDonald lordship passed to Alexander Óg in 1299 and he probably survived right up until 1318, though he may not have been dominant for the whole of this period. Another MacDonald chief, Donald of Islay, appears in 1308 and takes a prominent role until he too died in 1318. Angus Óg MacDonald only emerges as a something of a troublemaker around 1310, in the service of Edward II. In the *Gaidhealtachd*, the tensions, violence and slaughter took place not just between the lordships, they often occurred within them.

Horrified at the surrender of the key fortress of Stirling above all, Edward made a rash attempt to mount a winter campaign, summoning 16,000 men to appear at Berwick in the middle of December, but for this he did not have the support of his earls. Only 2,500 men turned up, and these stayed only a few days before deserting. Despite this, there was no doubt that the English would field a formidable army in the summer of 1300.

By May 1300, however, Robert Bruce had ceased any co-operation with Comyn, and at a patriot parliament held at Rutherglen in that month he no longer appears as a Guardian. Clearly great personal animosity had resurfaced between himself and John Comyn of Badenoch III. Bruce's decision to leave – or his removal from – the Guardianship seems to have been related to Edward I's agreement in July 1299 to surrender King John Balliol into papal custody in France. One of the factors that made this possible was an oath King John had taken on 1 April 1298 never to set foot in Scotland or have anything to do with Scots. Balliol and Comyn elements among the

Scots were delighted at the release of their king and at once began working towards a restoration of King John to Scotland. This Bruce could not stomach, and he ceased his involvement in the patriotic resistance. His place in the Guardian triumvirate was taken by Ingram de Umfraville, a magnate firmly aligned with the Comyns.

The purpose of the Rutherglen parliament had been to concert resistance to the expected English invasion of 1300. Edward had decided this time to enter Scotland by the Western March, presumably to try to break the hold of the patriots on the south-west, where lay the Bruce territories of Annandale and Carrick, the Balliol lordship of Galloway, the Steward's lands and the bishopric of Glasgow. Tenants of these lords had all been strongly supportive of the patriot cause. The English army was to proceed along the Solway coast accompanied by a provisioning fleet. The main action of the campaign was the siege of Caerlaverock Castle, lately recaptured by the Scots and a threat to the English garrisons at Lochmaben and Dumfries, and to the security of the Cumberland littoral. The siege, which commenced in July, involved battering rams and trebuchets, and was an awe-inspiring demonstration of the power of Edward's siege train. As they advanced westwards, the English met with resistance on the banks of the River Cree, where there was a brief engagement between the English and the main Scottish cavalry force, led by the Comyns. The Scottish cavalry soon took flight, as they had done at Falkirk, but Edward was unable to pursue the Scots further. He stayed in south-west Scotland, supervising the garrisons and organising the occupation until, in October, he could stay no longer. He met Scottish envoys at Dumfries, and in a recorded exchange with their envoys we see that what rankled with Edward, what above all he could not tolerate, was the Scots' perceived breach of faith with him: 'Every one of you has done homage to me as chief lord of Scotland. Now you set aside your allegiance and make a fool of me as though I were a weakling!' Nevertheless he granted the Scots a truce until the following summer. Of Bruce there is no mention,

Robert Bruce

and it seems he took no part in the 1300 campaign. In Professor Duncan's opinion he was sulking. Excluded from the Guardianship, he took nothing to do with the patriotic resistance, for the prospect of fighting for King John was anathema to the Bruces.

The Scottish diplomatic effort at the papal and French courts, headed by Bishop Lamberton, had borne further success in June 1299 when Boniface VIII sealed the papal letter to Edward I known as 'Scimus Fili', a text clearly inspired by the strong Scottish lobby at the curia. However it was received by Edward I only in the autumn of 1300. This papal broadside was an outright denunciation of the Edwardian occupation. It claimed that 'from ancient times the realm of Scotland belonged rightfully, and is known still to belong, to the Roman church'. It reminded Edward of his undertaking in the Treaty of Birgham that 'the realm should remain for ever entirely free and subject or submitted to nobody'. It accused Edward of taking advantage 'at a time when the realm of Scotland lacked the protection of a ruler', and concludes that 'no-one who considers [these things] can doubt that the realm of Scotland belongs to the Roman church, and that it was not, and is not lawful for you to dominate it by force and to subjugate it to your rule.' No wonder that Edward could not bear to listen to this as it was read to him by an archbishop, but exploded with wrath. 'By God's blood! For Zion's sake I will not be silent and for Jerusalem's sake I will not be at rest, but with all my strength I will defend my right that is known to all the world!' Boniface urged Edward to present his case to rule Scotland before the papal court. The Scots had effectively captured the weapon of papal favour. Since the papal letter advanced no arguments specifically in favour of King John's rights, the Bruce faction may have had the upper hand in lobbying at the papal court.

Two responses were prepared by the English. One was a letter from Edward I, dispatched in May 1301, rehearsing the historical evidences supporting the English claim, accusing the Scots of terrible atrocities and explaining that Edward could not accept papal mediation in this matter. Another was a letter, ostensibly from the barons of England – though no doubt written by royal clerks – protesting their king's claims in equally strong terms. In Rome meanwhile the Scottish delegation, ably led by Master Baldred Bisset, argued powerfully that the Anglo–Scottish dispute should be submitted to the papal court. Any homage done by Scottish kings was only for lands they held in England. In a much-admired *processus*, carefully designed to appeal to papal interests, Bisset advanced five proofs – from papal privilege, common law, prescription, past history and documentary evidence – to demonstrate that Scotland owed Edward I no allegiance. However, the focus of the Scottish diplomatic effort was switching to France, whither King John had now been transferred, out of papal custody and into that of the French king. Philip the Fair saw in Balliol a very useful pawn in his attempts to undermine Edward I. The prospect of a Balliol restoration was growing, and from exile King John was now free to influence events in Scotland.

By the campaigning season of 1301 there had been further changes in the Guardianship. Bishop Lamberton and his colleagues Comyn and Umfraville resigned and were replaced by Sir John Soules acting as sole Guardian; one chronicler reports that Soules had been elevated to the guardianship on the prompting of King John. Changes in the wording and seals of documents emanating from the patriot government also suggest a more prominent role for the exiled king: where previously the names of the Guardians had appeared at the head of such deeds, they were now replaced by the name of King John, with Soules, the Guardian, appearing only as a witness.

The English invasion of 1301 materialised as a two-pronged attack, much more complex and formidable than that of the previous year. Edward himself led an army from Berwick up the River Tweed to Selkirk and Peebles, and then into the valley of the Clyde to besiege Bothwell Castle in August; his son Edward of Caernarvon, Prince of

Wales, led a force along the Solway coast all the way to Loch Ryan. With the help of a force from Ireland, the prince's vanguard was able to capture Turnberry in September. As earl of Carrick, Robert Bruce VII could not afford to stand aloof from resistance to this invasion, for Turnberry was the principal castle of his earldom. Presumably it was Bruce's garrison that held out against the prince of Wales until September 1301, and it was the militia of his earldom that menaced the English garrison thereafter. Yet Bruce was involved in resistance only in so far as invasion threatened his own lands, and he left it to the Comyn earl of Buchan to lead the patriot efforts against king and prince, and to Soules and Umfraville to attack the English occupying Lochmaben on 7 and 8 September.

Having increasingly distanced himself from the patriots, Robert Bruce decided early in 1302 to return to allegiance to Edward I. The prospect of a Balliol restoration presided over by the Comyns was something he could not tolerate since it would remove completely all possibility that he would succeed to the throne. Moreover, in the peace concluded between the English and French at Asnières in January, provision was made for lands of Scots who had not submitted to be handed over to French administrators. Such an arrangement would deprive Robert of the revenues of his earldom for an indefinite period, and quite possibly place him at the mercy of the Comyns who could expect to receive favourable treatment from the French.

However, probably the main reason why Robert changed sides at this point was that he had managed to negotiate generous terms from Edward. The text of the agreement has survived. Robert and his men were guaranteed life and limb, lands and tenements and freedom from imprisonment. Edward would compensate him should the terms of a treaty or a papal ordinance affect the tenure of the Bruce estates, so that Robert would not suffer from French administration of his estates. Robert was granted the wardship and marriage of a son of the earl of Mar. The child, Donald of Mar, was Robert's nephew. Mention is made of Robert's 'claim' in a further clause. This might just refer to his claim to lands or titles, but it seems to have a wider meaning, and it could encompass his claim to the throne of Scotland. There was of course no question of Edward permitting an independent monarchy of Scotland; the kingship of Scotland envisaged at this time can only have been as a vassal or sub–king to Edward I. If we interpret this document correctly, it seems that Edward not only allowed Robert to persist in his claim to the throne, but intimated that under certain conditions he might even facilitate it:

> Because [either 'the king' or 'Robert'] fears that the kingdom of Scotland may be removed from out of the king's hands (which God forbid), and handed over to Sir John Balliol or to his son, or that claim may be brought into disrepute, or reversed and contradicted in a fresh judgement, the king grants to Robert that he may pursue his claim and that the king will hear him fairly and hold him to justice in the king's court. If by any chance it should happen that the claim must be adjudicated elsewhere than in the king's court [for example, in the papal court], then in this case the king promises Robert assistance and counsel as before, as well as he is able to give it.

Why should Edward have given Robert Bruce a chance to air his claim to the Scottish throne? It seems that even Edward I, whose armies were marching into Scotland virtually on an annual basis, was now prepared to concede the *possibility* of a Balliol restoration. It might suit his diplomacy towards France and the papacy to tolerate it. The above passage seems also to admit of the possibility of a re-run of the Great Cause in the papal court. Edward may have permitted Robert to persist in his claim to the Scottish throne since, in the event of a Balliol restoration, he could use Robert to destabilise the Scottish monarchy. Edward would work hard to ensure that there would be no Balliol restoration in Scotland, but, if it came to it, he had in Robert Bruce a willing and pliant rival for the sub-kingship.

Robert had gained security for his lands and titles, without, apparently, compromising his claim to the throne. His father, Robert Bruce VI, was probably delighted at his change of sides. It brought additional benefits to the family: Edward Bruce appears in the service of the Prince of Wales in April 1304, and Alexander Bruce, the clergyman, received the living of Kirkinner near Wigtown for his maintenance. Robert was able to travel into England to attend parliament, as he did in October 1302, probably following an instruction to make a public gesture of obedience and loyalty. On this journey he may well have visited his father or family properties in England. We know he stayed in England over the winter and visited Cambridge in the spring of 1303 to give a feast there, as was traditional, on the occasion of Alexander Bruce's becoming Master of Arts. Another benefit that came Robert's way as a result of his return to Edward's allegiance was a second marriage. The fate of Robert's first wife, Isabel of Mar, is uncertain; most probably she had died. This second marriage was to Elisabeth de Burgh, daughter of Richard de Burgh, earl of Ulster. It was a most desirable match, and Edward might have dangled the possibility of it before Robert to persuade him to defect. The earl of Ulster was the most powerful magnate in Ireland, and a traditional ally of the Bruces, as the Turnberry Band of 1286 testifies. The earl's sister Egidia – also known as Gelis – had married James the Steward, so Bruce's marriage strengthened the long-standing alliance of these three families. Altogether we have no reason to believe that Robert's change of sides was an anguished decision, or that defection cost him anything in terms of esteem among his peers in Scotland. No one at the time levelled the charge of treachery at him so far as we know. Contemporaries probably acknowledged that Robert was merely pursuing family interest and his claim to the throne of Scotland by other means, and acting in a predictable and understandable way.

Professor Barrow draws attention to an interesting letter written by Bruce in March 1302, just after he had changed sides. It is a promise to the Abbey of Melrose that, though in the past he had often drafted the abbey's tenants of Maybole into the army of the earldom of Carrick, conscience now troubled him and henceforth he would never compel the tenants to military service unless there was a summons of the common army of the realm. While Bruce's piety and his particular devotion to Melrose Abbey is unquestioned, the timing of the promise suggests that the earl of Carrick was not overly concerned to provide troops for his new master.

The truce between Edward I and the patriots ensured that there was no campaign in 1302, yet a dramatic turn of events in Scotland was effected by a battle in faraway Flanders. At Courtrai on 11 July the haughty aristocrats of the French heavy cavalry suffered a comprehensive humiliation at the hands of the Flemish foot-soldiers, weavers and townsfolk who opposed Philip the Fair's efforts to control them. It was a landmark battle: the first significant occasion in the Middle Ages when infantry defeated cavalry. In the long term of course this development boded well for the Scots, and in that sense Courtrai prefigured the victory of the Scottish foot at Bannockburn. But in 1302 it spelt disaster for the Scottish cause. In the words of Barrow, it 'did more to make Scotland an English province than any other single event of these years'. For the result of the French king's defeat was that he was forced to abandon all support for the Scottish patriots and for restoration of the Balliol monarchy. In the autumn of 1302 the Guardian, John Soules, led a delegation of Scottish aristocrats to Paris to try to persuade the French king to continue his support, but it was to no avail.

While Soules in France struggled to ward off disaster, John Comyn of Badenoch took over the role of acting Guardian at home and enjoyed considerable success. Together with Simon Fraser, Comyn scored a remarkable victory on 24 February 1303, sallying out from the shelter of Selkirk Forest to ambush Edward's lieutenant in Scotland, Sir John Segrave, and the clerk of the royal wardrobe, Ralph Manton, at Roslin near Edinburgh. Manton, a central figure in the bureaucracy of occupied Scotland, was killed, and many knights, including Segrave, were taken prisoner. The peel of Selkirk, designed to project the English occupation into the very depths of the forest, was captured by the Scots.

Though it represented a considerable achievement, this victory was set in context by the inevitable summer invasion. The Edwardian invasion of 1303 was larger, more penetrating and, consequently for the Scots, more demoralising than any that had gone before, and there was no mistaking the English king's sense of purpose. On 20 May 1303 Edward concluded a further peace with Philip of France and, thus secured on his southern flank, he concentrated his undivided ferocity upon the Scots. All the resources of England and her satellite territories were marshalled as never before and devoted to crushing Scottish resistance. In July a large Irish contingent led by the earl of Ulster landed in the west to reduce the castles of Bute and Inverkip. Robert Bruce, earl of Carrick, was also active in Edward's service. He was ordered to call up 1,000 foot from his sheriffdom of Ayr, and, in co-operation with two Galloway chiefs, Gibbon MacCann and Dungal MacDowall, a further 1,000 from Carrick and Galloway. Bruce himself seems to have remained on the Western March with John Botetourt during the campaign. Three prefabricated pontoon bridges, designed to project the English army across the Firth of Forth, were floated up the North Sea coast. Sir William Oliphant, commanding the Scottish garrison at Stirling, held grimly on while the great host passed by, but in August the English attacked and overcame the Scottish garrison at Brechin. Edward continued his march along the east coast, through Aberdeen, to Banff and as far as Kinloss Abbey. There he halted in mid September, and during October he returned by a more inland route, by way of Kildrummy, Brechin and Scone. Early in November Edward settled into winter quarters in Dunfermline Abbey, where he was joined by his queen.

During February 1304 Edward dispatched an expedition deep into Selkirk Forest to locate Fraser and Wallace. In this Bruce was ordered to participate, and he joined John Segrave, Robert Clifford and William Latimer. They routed the patriots, but both Fraser and Wallace escaped. No clue survives as to how Bruce might have felt at participating in this action. To pursue the former leader of Scottish resistance, his comrade-in-arms, perhaps his former commander, must have been deeply uncomfortable for him – to say the least. Stories that Bruce captured Wallace but released him unbeknown to Clifford must be dismissed as a later fabrication by Robert's hagiographers. It had been four years since, during the row in the patriot camp in Peebles, the Wallaces had last shown themselves supporters of the Bruce faction, and this episode illustrates how the Edwardian conquest of Scotland had changed the face of politics beyond all recognition.

Wallace was now an isolated figure. Most other Scottish commanders, including the Guardian, John Comyn, decided that resistance could no longer be maintained. That same February the great majority of Scottish patriots sued for peace. This was partly an acknowledgement that they had been overwhelmed by the military might of England, partly exasperation at the failure of King John to throw in his lot with his beleagured subjects. The patriots no longer enjoyed the support of the King of France or of the pope, and now they resigned themselves to a general surrender while there was still a little room for negotiation with Edward I. Comyn sought that Edward would rule Scotland according to the laws and customs in the time of Alexander III; that any departure from them should be sanctioned by the assent of the good people of Scotland; that nothing should be enacted to the prejudice of the Scots; and that no hostages be taken. Edward, on the other hand, was unwilling to accept all the Scottish leaders into his peace until Wallace had been captured. A series of compromise agreements were reached, whereby certain of the patriot leaders were to be exiled for varying periods of time, depending upon the extent of their involvement with the resistance. Scottish nobles whose estates had been granted to Englishmen were to be given the opportunity to buy them back. Edward could have insisted upon much tougher terms. Simon Fraser also surrendered, though it is clear that Edward detested him. As it was, he was saving the fullness of his vengeance for the Scottish garrison of Stirling, and for William Wallace.

In the spring of 1304, Edward besieged or 'invested' Stirling Castle and unleashed upon it all the refinements of medieval siege technology, including primitive explosives. Engines of war – battering rams and catapults – were collected from Brechin, Aberdeen and Berwick. Robert Bruce contributed siege machines of his own. Lead was stripped from the roofs of nearby churches to provide counterweighs for catapults, and cotton thread, sulphur and saltpetre – the ingredients of Greek fire – were assembled, presumably to make bombs. The siege of Stirling was a showcase for contemporary warfare; in fact Edward ensured that the whole prospect – ingenious contraptions at work, fires, explosions, heraldic banners and shields, feats of arms – could be viewed at a safe distance by the ladies of the English court from a specially constructed oriel window. Within the castle, the heroic garrison, led by Sir William Oliphant, sheltered from the explosions in caves deep within the bedrock, but emerged to rain crossbow bolts and stones on the attackers. Oliphant may have felt deserted by his king, who had not arrived to lead the resistance; he claimed to hold the castle, not of the Guardian, Sir John Soules, nor yet of King John, but, in reference to the Scottish royal standard, 'of the Lion'. Thus Oliphant considered that he held the castle in trust for the monarchy or kingdom of Scotland. Gazing across at the enemy ranks, however, the defenders discerned the heraldic devices of their erstwhile comrades John Comyn, Alexander Lindsay, David Graham and Simon Fraser and became aware that these hitherto staunch patriots had already made terms with Edward. Robert Bruce earl of Carrick was also present among the besiegers. On 20 July Oliphant decided he could hold out no longer and offered surrender. Edward showed no magnanimity whatsoever and refused to give the defenders peace until he had tried out his new and terrible siege engine, the Warwolf. At last, on 24 July, he allowed them to surrender, and Oliphant's brave men emerged, barefoot and faces besmirched with ashes, symbolising abject contrition, to throw themselves on his mercy. The king made it plain that they were lucky to be granted life and limb, and he hanged only the man responsible for betraying the castle to the Scots four years earlier.

Victorious, Edward returned to England that summer with Scotland all but subdued. Only William Wallace remained at large. On the day after the siege of Stirling had ended, Edward had dispatched Comyn, Lindsay, Graham and Fraser to capture Wallace by 13 January 1305, if they wanted easier surrender terms. In August 1305 the greatest patriot of the age was captured as he lay with his mistress – according to Peter Langtoft's chronicle – by John Stewart of Menteith's men. Wallace was taken to London where a show trial rehearsed the accusations against him: he had spared none who used the English tongue, he had slaughtered children, widows and nuns, and he had rebelled against his feudal lord. No account was taken of the facts that Wallace had never sworn fealty to Edward, and did not acknowledge Edward as his lord. No opportunity was given for him to answer the charges. By the standards of the age this was all to be expected: Wallace was not of high birth and he had waged war without particular regard to chivalry. As Edward's biographer points out, 'there was no reason why Edward should have treated him with compassion or respect'. But the barbarism of the execution is inexcusable by any standards. Wallace was dragged by horses for four miles from Westminster to Smithfield, hanged, cut down while still alive, disembowelled and beheaded. His head was placed on London Bridge, and the body quartered, with parts dispatched to Newcastle, Berwick, Stirling and Perth. Wallace had been unloved by the Comyn faction, and though he hailed from within the Bruce camp we must assume that Robert Bruce had made every effort to hunt him down in 1304. It is hard to see how he can have escaped from participating in that shameful pursuit. Nevertheless, from what we can now tell, others in Scotland bore the opprobrium. King Edward's treatment of a former Guardian must have generated considerable popular outrage in Scotland. It is likely that the Bruce coup of 1306 owes something of its popular support to revulsion at Wallace's brutal execution.

In September 1305 Edward addressed the problem of the future government of England's latest satellite territory. Ten Scots met with twenty of the king's counsellors to draft the Ordinance for the Government of Scotland. In the text, Scotland is referred to not as a realm or kingdom, but merely as a 'land'; its status is thus relegated to that of Ireland. A royal lieutenant – John of Brittany – was appointed to serve as Guardian, with a council of twenty-two Scottish aristocrats. Other offices included a chancellor, a chamberlain, and four pairs of justices, each pair consisting of an Englishman and a Scotsman. The sheriffs and castellans appointed were mostly Scots, but the more important castles and the sheriffdoms of the south-east were given to Englishmen. The council of twenty-two was to embark upon a comprehensive review of Scottish law. In this document none of the attention to detail manifest in his settlements of other lands is shown, and one gains the impression that, at the age of sixty-four, Edward I was enormously relieved to have finally settled the Scottish question. Bruce, who had recently entertained hopes of being vassal king, was to have but a minor role in the settlement. He was among those nominated to sit on the Guardian's council and, as he held the young heir to the earldom of Mar in wardship, he was to install a constable in Kildrummy Castle, the principal seat of that earldom.

In 1305 Edward I appeared to have completed his exhausting undertaking of reducing Scotland to obedience. Indeed he had hammered the Scots into submission, but it is also true that he had been obliged to reach accommodation with the powerful aristocratic Comyn faction, and, having finally secured their co-operation, he could now govern through their resources of lordship, patronage and castles. Edward could have done so much earlier, had he been in a position to devote to Scotland his undivided attention. The costs, even in terms of hard cash, were staggering. His biographer estimates that the campaign of 1300 cost £40,000–50,000, and that of 1303–04 may have cost £80,000. For Edward's earlier conquest of Wales there had been a higher proportion of his income available; he had conquered Scotland at a time when there were many other calls on his resources. True, there were distant highlands and islands where Edward's writ did not yet run, but, as he had control of all the centres of authority he could be confident that his peace had been widely imposed. True again, he was unloved, had no purchase on the hearts and minds of the Scots and must have been resented by virtually all, yet he was now in a position to divide and rule, to administer vast resources of patronage and coercion. As was the case for any medieval monarch, he had little need of consent from the population at large so long as magnates could be relied upon to co-operate, however begrudgingly. Given a competent heir to cement his achievements, continued co-operation from Scottish magnates and the absence of any alternative to his rule, Edward's conquest might have lasted indefinitely. In 1305 Scotland's fate had been sealed; the Edwardian super-kingdom had arrived.

4

'Playing at kings and queens' (1306)

Murder, revolution and enthronement

Robert Bruce's actions in the spring of 1306 ensured that Edward I died angry, bitterly disappointed that a coveted prize, the conquest of Scotland, had slipped exasperatingly from his grasp. They re-opened the Anglo-Scottish wars, began the demise of the powerful Comyn affinity and introduced the Bruce–Stewart dynasty to the Scottish throne. By any standards the dark deed of that February evening and the subsequent revival of the Scottish monarchy was a defining episode in Scottish history and in the history of these islands. Robert Bruce VI had taken no action that we know of since 1296 to promote the family's claim to the throne, or shown any significant interest in Scottish affairs. Had his son lived a similar trouble-free life in the service of Edward I, Scottish identity and the very concept of Scotland might today have been totally different: a quaint medieval survival, a distant half-forgotten memory, or possibly lost altogether.

The reconstruction of the events of 10 February 1306 with which this book opens is based upon the narrative of the chronicler Walter of Guisborough who, though hostile to Bruce, is not as hostile as others and is the best near-contemporary source for these events. As we will see, despite bitter hostility between Bruce and Comyn, a deal or agreement for mutual assistance seems to have existed. Bruce appears to have sought a meeting on neutral, consecrated ground. John Comyn had ridden from Dalwinston accompanied by his uncle, Sir Robert Comyn. Bruce was accompanied by three knights and perhaps others besides. The principals greeted one another with a kiss though, the Guisborough chronicle points out, it was not the 'kiss of peace'. Walter of Guisborough describes what happened:

> They were speaking together with words which seemed peaceful; suddenly, in a reversal and with different words, [Bruce] began to accuse him of betrayal, in that [Comyn] had accused him to the king of England, and had worsened his position to his harm. When [Comyn] spoke peaceably and excused himself, [Bruce] did not wish to hear his speech but, as he had conspired, he struck him with foot and sword and went away out. But [Bruce's] men followed [Comyn] and cast him down on the paving before the altar, leaving him for dead ... Robert Comyn, his uncle, ran to bring him help, but Christopher Seton, who had married Robert's sister, met him, struck his head with a sword and he died ... [John] Comyn still lived, for the friars had carried him down to the altar vestry to treat him and for him to confess his sins. When he confessed and was repentant, by the tyrant's [that is, Bruce's] order he was dragged out of the vestry and killed on the steps of the high altar.

So it seems discussion had turned to argument, and argument to jealous rage. The question is whether murder was intended in a sacrosanct church, of all places. Surely Bruce would not have handed such a propaganda weapon to his enemies. John Comyn did not die outright before Bruce left the church; and Bruce subsequently ordered him to be dragged out of the vestry and finished off by the altar. The two-stage nature of the murder suggests that the assault had not been premeditated but that, once commenced upon, it had to be completed. Later writers relate that Roger Kirkpatrick of Closeburn and James Lindsay finished off the dying Comyn on Bruce's behalf, but there is no evidence for that. The subsequent letter of excommunication specifies that Bruce's companions were Alexander Lindsay and Christopher and John Seton. Bruce had surely intended to assume the leadership of a united Scotland, not plunge the country into years of bitter civil war by murdering the leader of a rival patriot affinity, but it seems that he had blundered across his Rubicon, and will have realised immediately afterwards that the die was cast. Perhaps he proclaimed his intention to seize the throne there and then; at any rate his men hurried off to seize Dumfries Castle. Bruce's *coup d'état* had not got off to the smoothest of starts. However, as we shall see, there is an alternative reading of those events.

There has been an endless speculation as to what drove Robert Bruce VII to take such drastic action. However, by 1306, it is clear that three preconditions for action on his claim to the throne had been met, three factors that had made it impossible for him to act on it had been removed. The first of these was the sudden impossibility of a restoration of the exiled King John Balliol, caused by defeat on the field of Courtrai of King Philip the Fair's power, upon which that whole idea had depended. The king of France would not now be able to impose that upon Edward I, and it left the Bruce claim to the Scottish throne a plausible option for a revival of the Scottish monarchy. The second was the death of Robert Bruce VI on 21 April 1304. The elder Bruce had resided on his properties in the south-east of England, but on the collapse of Scottish resistance to Edward I early in 1304, he decided to repair to his principal Scottish lordship once more. However, he died on that return journey to Annandale and was buried at Holm Cultram Abbey in Cumberland. This meant that Robert Bruce VII acquired a considerable increase in prestige and resources as he became lord of Annandale, head of the family and the Bruce claimant to the throne of Scotland. Accordingly, he did homage to Edward I and came into his inheritance on 14 June. Henceforth, there would be no recurrence of the episode in 1297, when the Annandale knights had refused to follow the young heir into rebellion. The third factor permitting of a Bruce bid for the throne was the looming prospect of Edward I's death. At 65, Edward was very old by medieval standards and every courtier fawning upon the domineering old man anticipated that a Pandora's box of possibilities would spring open on his demise. Cultivating the heir to the throne, covert alliances and plotting are all the order of the day when a king's death is not far off. In the heady mix of succession politics there were many unknowns. For example, in 1305, on his capture, the patriot leader Sir William Wallace was found to be carrying documents implicating certain of the Scottish magnates in a conspiracy; tantalisingly, we know nothing of their contents.

In Scotland, a number of factors were making for a violent reaction against the sullen *pax Edwardiana* that was imposed on Scotland. Surely outrage seethed among the Scottish nobility at Edward's trampling on every Scottish sensibility, at the foreign occupation, disinheritances, looting of precious relics, arbitrary seizures and exactions of oaths and hostages. This outrage must have been exacerbated by the provocative execution of William Wallace, whom Edward I had humiliated, tortured and killed in 1305. Wallace was a former Guardian of the realm and a military leader who had commanded huge popular respect in Scotland. Bruce must have shared this widespread indignation and probably hoped to harness it to his own ends. Furthermore, as the old king neared his end, a climate of expectation must have been brewing, a sense of imminent catastrophe dimly reflected in the rumours and forebodings inspired by the prophecies of Merlin and Thomas of Erceldoune referred to in Barbour's *The Bruce* and in the letter of 15 May 1307 discussed in the following chapter.

In these circumstances it was easy for Edward's Scottish administration to make dreadful errors. One such was the appointment on 26 October 1305 of Bishop William Lamberton as one of the four Guardians to hold office until John of Brittany, nominated as Lord Lieutenant in the Ordinance of 1305, could take up his duties. The bishop had a long history of supporting the patriot cause when political circumstances had allowed, and the appointment rates as a significant mistake. Indeed, it was almost as huge an error as Edward's underestimation of Robert Bruce himself.

We may be certain that Robert Bruce had never abandoned his designs on the throne and was preparing for Edward's death as the moment when he would act. It appears from letters written in the wake of the murder that Bruce had been provisioning castles in the south-east of Scotland, Ayr and Dunaverty. In the winter of 1305–06, he was biding his time, strengthening his position and probably awaiting the old king's death.

However, the question remains of what impelled Robert Bruce to risk everything – estates, family honour, life and limb – by murdering Comyn and leaving Edward I's fealty. Was he inspired by patriotism to act against his own interests, or pushed by declining fortunes? There are conflicting assessments of Bruce's position at court. Barrow takes the view that Bruce, as earl of Carrick and lord of Annandale, married to a daughter of the most powerful magnate in Ireland, holding Ayr and Kildrummy castles, and with three royal forests in his keeping, had everything to lose. 'Potentially, he had never been richer or more favoured.' He implies that belief in his right to the throne motivated Bruce to act contrary to his own material interests. Prestwich however contends that Bruce had grounds for discontent with royal service which drove him to act as he did. Like all Edward I's magnates, he faced great difficulty in recovering expenses from the king. He was owed money on account of expenditure incurred as sheriff of Ayrshire and Lanarkshire, and there was trouble over certain rights he claimed in Annandale. Prestwich's judgement is that Bruce's expectations of loyal service had not been realised, he was goaded into rebellion and 'with more careful handling by Edward, it is very likely that Bruce would have remained a valuable ally of the English'. Certainly, Bruce endured the changeable fortunes of the courtier. In March 1305 he was prominent at the Westminster Parliament. He sought and received the lands of Sir Ingram de Umfraville in Carrick; he was consulted as to how Scotland should be represented at the subsequent parliament; and the following April he was among those charged with supervising election of those representatives and with the defence of Scotland. Yet when that subsequent parliament met in September 1305 Bruce was not present. He was relegated by the Ordinance to a minor role in the government of Scotland; and the lands in Carrick were restored to Umfraville. Furthermore, Edward I attempted to collect from Bruce debts allegedly owed by his father. Probably, like his father, Robert still harboured fond expectation of eventually being asked to take on the role of vassal-king of Scotland, and was disappointed at Edward's continued refusal to employ him in this capacity.

It may be that in February 1306 Bruce feared a sudden and catastrophic fall from grace, and was driven to desperate measures to escape awful consequences. Had he been planning a revolt, as we suspect, he may have dreaded revelation of his preparations. Pacts agreed with other magnates, made a couple of years earlier, may have been simple efforts to secure support or neutralise opponents at court; or they may have been preparations for revolt, or capable of interpretation as such. One such pact Bruce made on 11 June 1304 with William Lamberton, bishop of St Andrews, while watching Edward I's showpiece reduction of Stirling Castle, the last patriot stronghold in Scotland. We have the text. By this pact, each promised to aid the other in the event of future perils, 'to be of one another's council in all their business and affairs at all times and against whichever individuals'. It is an innocent enough agreement of a fairly standard nature and not remarkable of itself, except that it lacks the normal clause 'exempting fealty to our lord the king'. That may be just a scribal error, but it leaves open the possibility that these confederates were prepared to assist one another in activities which Edward would consider treasonable. Lamberton was probably not the only Scottish magnate with whom Bruce allied himself. Judging by his swift and enthusiastic reaction to the dramatic events of spring 1306, it is most likely that Bishop Wishart of Glasgow was also party to whatever Bruce may have been hatching. It also seems likely that some similar arrangement had been entered into with John Comyn III of Badenoch, who had also been at the siege of Stirling. Although there was long-standing animosity between them, an accord may have been brokered by the Scottish bishops keen to see revival of the monarchy. Versions of a deal between the two men are recorded in both pro- and anti-Bruce chronicle traditions, relating either that Comyn broke the agreement by revealing Bruce's intentions to Edward I, or that Bruce was incensed by a report that Comyn had done so. The Barbour narrative poem *The Bruce*, which commences with this episode, includes the latter version. Either way, almost every early source alleges that Bruce and Comyn had made a deal, and that in 1306 Bruce was plotting something to which Comyn would not assent.

The figure of John Comyn III of Badenoch is central to the story. He is known to history as the 'Red Comyn', although that name properly pertains to each successive head of that branch of the Comyn family. He headed the aristocratic faction that had been in the ascendant in Scotland for the thirty years prior to 1296. During that time, the Comyns had used royal power and office to establish and extend a network of patronage especially in the north of the country. John Comyn II had been a Guardian, and John Comyn III had been sole Guardian from the autumn of 1302 until the general submission of the patriots to Edward I in February 1304. John III's wife was Joan de Valence, sister of Aymer de Valence who was a rising star in the court of Edward I, a magnate already with considerable military experience in Scotland and soon to become earl of Pembroke. John was also the victor of Roslin, a patriotic victory of such moment that the Scottish ambassadors in Paris wrote to him: 'It would gladden your hearts if you knew how much your honour has increased in every part of the world as a result of your recent battle with the English.' He had thus considerable military prestige among the patriots as well as all the kudos that lineage, extensive lands and patronage could bestow. Equally with Robert Bruce, John Comyn was leadership material; and they hated one another. It was jealousy of the Comyns that led Bruce to sulk on his Carrick estates while other patriots faced Edward I in battle at Falkirk in 1298. To get Bruce back on board, the patriots had had to offer Bruce a share in the Guardianship. As we have seen, that compromise ended with Comyn seizing Bruce by the throat in the camp at Peebles in August 1299. There is no doubt: Comyn was a great man in his own right, a worthy rival to Bruce and there was bad blood between them.

However, the real question is whether John Comyn III was actively pursuing a claim to the throne in his own right. If not, then Robert Bruce had no real necessity to kill him and Comyn's murder in the Greyfriars' church at Dumfries is likely to have been unintended, unplanned, perhaps the result of an uncontrollable rage. If yes, Comyn's murder begins to take on the character of a political assassination. For years, historians have taken the former view, which goes a little way towards reducing the guilt of Robert Bruce. At Norham in July 1291, Comyn's father, John Comyn II, had presented a claim to the throne at Edward I's tribunal but it had not been vigorously pursued as John Balliol was effectively a Comyn puppet. That claim, of descent from King Donald III (1093–97), was made without prejudice to the claim of John Balliol, and had been dismissed early in the proceedings. Nevertheless, John Comyn III would have considered his claim to the throne by way of his mother, Eleanor Balliol, superior to any Bruce claim because he came of the senior line of descent. However, in addition to these ancestral claims, John Comyn III was also a nephew of the exiled King John Balliol; he was, in fact, John's closest adult male relative. And as John was unlikely to be reinstated, John Comyn, as the leading member of the senior royal line was an obvious candidate for the throne.

It is to be expected that, during the reign of Robert I, any material suggestive of Comyn regality would be assiduously expunged from the historical record. Yet Dr Alexander Grant has identified contemporary material that denigrates the Bruce claim to the throne and implicitly supports a claim by John Comyn. The verses occur in the *Liber Extravagens*, the supplementary book in Bower's chronicle, and while they do not openly support a Comyn kingship, they are dismissive of Bruce and Balliol claims alike and express longing for a candidate to assume the throne of Scotland. Grant uncovers similar Comyn-for-king sentiment in the *Scalachronica*, the chronicle written by Sir Thomas Gray. Therefore John Comyn may well have been actively pursuing the Scottish throne and the implications are as follows: John Comyn III's candidacy was a direct threat to Bruce's claim to the throne, and for Bruce to become king, Comyn had either to be neutralised somehow, or eliminated. This is a long way, of course, from being proof that the Bruce affinity murdered Comyn for his royal title; but it certainly increases the likelihood that Comyn's murder was premeditated. Given the existence of their mutually exclusive claims to the throne and the antagonism and mistrust between the two men, Comyn's care to meet Bruce only on hallowed ground as a guarantee of safety seems to have been inadequate.

When the heads of both families met in the Greyfriars Church at Dumfries on 10 February 1306, there will have been considerable tension. Comyn and Bruce were rivals for the throne, even though at this stage it was probably only the vassal kingship that was in contention. As we have seen, there had always been deep suspicion and animosity between the Bruce and Comyn factions, and these same men had actually come to blows at the council meeting in Peebles in 1299. But besides tension, they will have shared a feeling that, one way or another, things were coming to a head.

After the murder, Robert Bruce rode back to Lochmaben to raise the tenantry of Annandale, this time with much greater authority than he had done in 1297. A letter survives, written by an unknown author in the English garrison at Berwick in March 1306, which gives detailed information on Bruce's movements in the weeks after the death of John Comyn. The author explains that he himself is engaged in reinforcing the peel at Berwick, and that he is none too sure of the support of local people and soldiers. He then lists the fortifications held by Robert, and the provisions available to them:

> Sir, the news in these parts is that the earl of Carrick holds the king's castles of Dumfries and Ayr, and the castle of Dalswinton which belonged to John Comyn, and the castle of Tibbers which belongs to Richard Siward, and he holds this Richard, and William Balliol, in prison as he did before; and of the stores which were in the castle of Ayr, there are in the town in the hands of merchants, a good hundred casks of wine and other stores in great plenty. He has had his castle of Dunaverty in Kintyre provisioned for a long period.

This acquisition of castles and accumulating of stores tells us that Bruce had been preparing for some time, building up his strength and consolidating his position. Robert Boyd, a prominent member of Bruce's retinue, had taken Rothesay by trickery, and was besieging Inverkip. The writer describes Robert's efforts to raise an army:

> The earl of Carrick has made war in Galloway to cause the people to rebel with him, but they have answered in accord that they will never rebel against the king for any man living … Sir, the earl of Carrick has been at Glasgow and Rutherglen and in those districts, and has received the fealty of the people where he has come, and has charged them to be ready to go with him with rations for nine days when they receive a day and night's notice … The evil bishop remains at Glasgow as his chief advisor, and the earl comes often, and they take … their counsel together, and they are mustering all the support that they can find from every quarter …

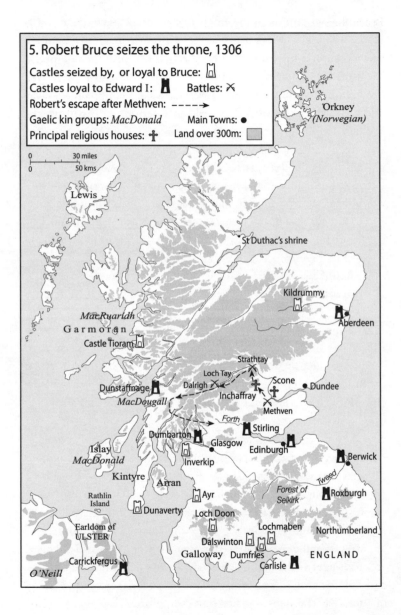

5. Robert Bruce seizes the throne, 1306

Castles seized by, or loyal to Bruce:
Castles loyal to Edward I: Battles: ✕
Robert's escape after Methven: - - - - →
Gaelic kin groups: *MacDonald*   Main Towns: ●
Principal religious houses: ✝   Land over 300m:

0   30 miles
0   50 kms

Orkney
(Norwegian)

Lewis

St Duthac's shrine

MacRuaridh
G a r m o r a n
Castle Tioram

Kildrummy

Aberdeen

Strathtay

Dunstaffnage   Loch Tay
Dalrigh ✕   Scone   Dundee
MacDougall   Inchaffray
Methven ✕

Forth   Stirling

Dumbarton   Glasgow   Edinburgh
Berwick
Inverkip

Islay
MacDonald   Kintyre   Arran   Ayr   Forest of   Roxburgh
Selkirk

Rathlin   Dunaverty   Loch Doon
Island

Earldom of   Lochmaben   Northumberland
ULSTER   Dalswinton
Galloway   Dumfries   ENGLAND

Carrickfergus   Carlisle

O'Neill   *Tweed*

Bruce then was in open rebellion. It is no wonder that the people of the 'otherwise-minded' province of Galloway, ever hopeful of further autonomy from Scotland, refused Bruce their support. Nevertheless he had taken care to ensure that his castles were well provisioned. The distribution of the castles seized (along the Solway and Carrick shoreline) suggests an expectation of help from the Western Isles or Ireland; Bruce was falling back on the same plan that his grandfather had entertained both at the Turnberry Band and in his rebellion of 1286–87. While Edward and Neil Bruce stayed with Robert in 1306, there is no mention in narratives of the other brothers, Thomas and Alexander Bruce, who may already have been dispatched to the Western Isles to muster galloglass. The Berwick correspondent also reports that Bruce intended to garrison and hold his own castles against the king's forces, but that he would destroy other castles. From other sources we learn that the rebellion was spreading in the Bruce heartland of the south-west. Christopher Seton and his brothers held for him Tibbers and Loch Doon castles. The young Thomas Randolph – later to become Robert's most trusted lieutenant and earl of Moray – adhered to Bruce, in spite of his father's loyalty to the Balliols.

Bruce then left Lochmaben to consult with 'the evil bishop', Robert Wishart, at Glasgow. On the way there, at Arickstane, Barbour says that he met for the first time the young James Douglas, son and heir of Sir William Douglas the Hardy who had died in the Tower of London in 1298. They probably met earlier, in 1297, as we have seen. Douglas threw in his lot with Bruce in the hope of recovering his patrimony, which Edward I had granted to Robert Clifford. Other early adherents of the Bruce cause were earls Alan of Menteith and Malcolm of Lennox.

Bruce spent some time in conference with Bishop Wishart who absolved him of the sin of killing of Comyn and administered an oath that, as king, Bruce would abide by the direction of the clergy of Scotland. The oath was probably a traditional one, expected of any candidate for kingship, but the Scottish clergy was from this time onwards supportive of the Bruce monarchy. According to the *Scalachronica* of Thomas Gray, the bishop gave him 'robes and the attire with which Bruce had himself vested and attired on the day' and 'a banner of the royal arms which he had long hidden in his treasury'. The banner was clearly that of Alexander III. Bruce was no longer interested in the vassal kingship of Scotland, but now aspired to nothing less than the revival of the independent monarchy. This is all borne out by subsequent charges against the bishop sent by Edward I to the pope. The bishop will also have advised on a suitable date for enthronement. If the revival of the kingship were to be credible, all traditional forms would have to be observed as far as possible. Enthronement in the penitential season of Lent would not do. Easter, with its connotations of resurrection and rebirth, would have been ideal, but nine days before Easter, on 25 March, came the feast of the Annunciation, which was not reckoned as Lent. Since time was of the essence, they settled for the earlier date. They dined, and then the bishop bade him 'go to secure his heritage by all the means that he could'. Leaving Glasgow, Bruce advanced against John Stewart of Menteith, the sheriff and constable of Dumbarton. John refused to surrender the castle of Dumbarton to Bruce's supporters, Alexander Lindsay and Walter Logan.

Bruce did not assault Dumbarton, but took his growing entourage across the River Forth, as the Berwick correspondent explained: 'On the day that this letter was written John of Menteith informed me that the earl of Carrick had crossed the sea with 60 men-at-arms. And sir, if the people on the other side are trustworthy, which I do not misdoubt, he will have but a short stay with them.' The sea referred to is clearly the Firth of Forth, known as 'the Scottish Sea'. The letter continues:

> Sir, however you are given to understand of the earl of Carrick, he is nevertheless attempting to seize the realm of Scotland and to be king ...

The king's council ordered him to deliver up the king's officers,
and the king's castles in his hands, and the towns which belonged to
John Comyn, and should belong to the king on the death of John
(on whom God have mercy), but to this, Sir, he has made no answer.

Sir, the chamberlain commanded him to do the same thing …
and he replied that he would take castles, towns and people as fast as
he could, until the king had notified his will concerning his demand,
and, if he would not grant it to him, he would defend himself with
the longest stick that he had.

Edward's council of Scotland and chamberlain had therefore
called on Bruce to desist and surrender, but Bruce had aggressively
demanded something of the king and expected a response. His
demand might have been for a comprehensive royal pardon or for
Edward to bestow upon him the vassal kingship, but since neither
was likely to be forthcoming, he was proceeding regardless with his
seizure of the kingship. Apart from anything else, it was only as king,
with a king's power to raise armies, that Bruce could withstand the
vengeance of the Comyns. The outraged Comyns and their allies –
Sir John Mowbray, Ingram de Umfraville, the earls of Buchan and
Atholl, Alexander Abernethy and others – were mustering their
forces at Liddesdale and preparing to take vengeance on Bruce.
Atholl was feigning, however, and subsequently joined Bruce.

Revival of the kingship was not proceeding quite as Bruce had
planned, and he was improvising frantically. No doubt he had
envisaged leading a united Scottish reaction to English occupation,
but there was no disguising that the 'community of the realm' was
divided, and that the greater part supported the more legitimate Balliol
claim and preferred the Edwardian settlement to the usurpation
of a murderer. However, Bruce's support among the higher clergy
probably reflects the Scottish Church's historic insistence upon
independence from the archiepiscopal authority of York. Bishop
Wishart, who had recently been granted timber for the steeple of

Glasgow Cathedral, used it instead to make siege engines to attack Kirkintilloch Castle. Everywhere but in Galloway Edward's intrusion upon the rights and liberties of the kingdom, the humiliation of the Scottish king and the execution of William Wallace had been deeply resented. Bruce was borne to the throne upon that groundswell of emotion. As he advanced from Dumbarton on Scone his retinue will have been daily increased by fresh adherents of every class, delighted at the revival of the kingship, but whose commitment remained to be tested. In those heady spring days as Lent neared its end, it may have seemed that, along with monarchy, the very nation was being reborn. News spread, and expectant crowds gathered for a cherished spectacle they had despaired of ever again witnessing. All was not optimism, of course. In April, May and June lands and titles of the chief rebels were declared forfeit and parcelled out to followers of Edward. Annandale was granted to Humphery de Bohun, the earl of Hereford; Robert's earldom of Carrick to Henry Percy; the earldom of Lennox to John Stewart of Menteith and that of Menteith to John Hastings.

The feast of the Annunciation fell upon a Friday. Walter of Guisborough, the most reliable of the chroniclers, records that four bishops and five earls were present at the ceremony. We know of three bishops at most. Robert Wishart and David Murray, bishop of Moray, were there on the Friday, and, when he had heard the news of Comyn's murder, Bishop William Lamberton, as chief of edward's council of Scotland, delayed and obfuscated the council's reaction to the Bruce coup, then fled from Berwick across the Firth of Forth, arriving at Scone to celebrate mass for the new king on the Sunday following, Palm Sunday. He may even have been present earlier, at the enthronement, since he was later accused of showing Bruce 'honour on the day of coronation'. The identity of the fourth bishop we do not know, but the abbots of both Scone and Inchaffray were both in attendance. We know of four earls present, besides Bruce himself: the young Donald, heir of Mar, who was Robert's ward, Malcolm of

Lennox, Alan of Menteith and John of Atholl, a recent adherent. It was a creditable turnout of the great and good, sufficient to be convincing. Crucially, however, the earl of Fife was absent, the heir being sixteen-year-old Duncan, soon to become the fourth earl, who was currently in the wardship of Edward I and therefore unavailable. The earl of Fife's traditional role of leading the king-elect to the throne was central to proceedings. But for the enthronement of John Balliol in 1292, when the earl was a child, a substitute had had to be found, and on this occasion too a substitute became available. This was Isabella of Fife, the young heir's aunt, who was also countess of Buchan, being married to John Comyn earl of Buchan. Atholl had escorted her to Scone from her house, emptying the stables of Buchan's horses as he did so, to thwart pursuit. Isabella is reported in English chronicles as Robert's mistress. However this may be, she must have had strong motivation for such flagrant defiance of her husband.

On the appointed day, Lady Day, all the essential ceremonies were observed. The new king was acclaimed by clergy, nobles and people in the abbey church, and then led out to the churchyard where the time-honoured ceremony took place under the gaze of a crowd of onlookers. The clergy girded Robert with a sword, administered the oath and placed a robe on his shoulders. Much of the regalia were missing, having been looted by Edward I. The rose-sceptre and the Stone of Destiny now lay at St Edward's shrine in Westminster Abbey. Professor Duncan observes of this ceremony, 'The place, Scone, and the inaugurator, a representative of the earl of Fife, were important, but the Stone was quietly forgotten.' The high point of proceedings was when Isabella of Fife led Robert Bruce to whatever throne or ornamental chair was provided. To underline the significance of the moment, she then placed a coronet on his head, though this was not recognised as part of the ancient rite. A Highland poet or *seanachaidh* read aloud the new king's genealogy reaching back to Kenneth MacAlpin, and beyond to Fergus son of Erc, the mythical ancestral ruler of Dal Riata, the ancient Irish kingdom and homeland of the Scots. The day ended with a feast and the taking of fealties.

On the Sunday following, high mass was said by Bishop Lamberton, and this was followed by the taking of homages and fealties. Among those who adhered to the new king, adding significantly to his legitimacy, was Alexander Scrymgeour, the King of Scots' hereditary royal standard-bearer, who had served all the Guardians in turn. Furthermore, Scrymgeour bore the very banner of Alexander III. The significance of regalia and ceremony was allegedly wasted upon Robert's wife, Elisabeth de Burgh, who reportedly berated her husband for 'playing at kings and queens'. Whatever her views were, from this point in the narrative onwards it behoves us to refer to Robert Bruce as Robert I of Scotland.

Enthronement was necessary pageantry. It was vital that Robert Bruce should undergo the sacramental change from mere mortal to Robert I, King of Scots and representative of divine order in the world. But it did not alter the harsh facts that the new king had perhaps only a quarter of Scotland under his sway, and that powerful enemies were bearing down on him. Preparations for a campaign had been set in train by the English government on 1 March. In England too a pageant was held, in May 1306. Following the knighting of Edward of Caernarfon, the prince of Wales, all the 267 newly made knights were invited to a 'feast of the Swans', where they each pledged an oath of chivalric symbolism, 'to the Swan', to avenge the death of John Comyn; then they set off to join the campaign. In the streets, meanwhile, popular satirists jeered at Bruce's makeshift ceremony. They scoffed at 'King Hobbe' or 'Mad King Robin' and they gleefully predicted that the new king's reign would not last for long: 'I think you may be King of Summer,/King of Winter you will not be.'

For the new King of Scots the period after the enthronement was one of frantic activity to strengthen his power-base by capturing castles, making friends and issuing promises – 'friends and friendship purchasing' as Barbour puts it. He travelled north, where David

Murray, Bishop of Moray, was rousing the people to a patriotic crusade. Edward I subsequently complained to the pope that 'The flock of the Bishop of Moray, who assembled to the help of the said Robert, and still hold themselves with him, have done this owing to the incitement, preaching and exhorting of the said bishop, because he told them that they who rebelled with Sir Robert to help him against the king of England and took the part of the said Sir Robert, were not less deserving of merit than if they should fight in the Holy Land against pagans and Saracens.' Robert captured and destroyed Forfar Castle on his way north. He visited Banff, and extorted cash from the merchant communities of Aberdeen, Dundee and Perth by taking hostages. At Aberdeen, Bruce spent a week or so, establishing his queen and his daughter Marjorie in the care of a band of faithful knights: his brother Neil, Alexander Lindsay and Robert Boyd. At Perth, the bailiffs were thrown in prison and threatened with death until they paid £54, which Robert then took as rents that were due to him as king. He may have attacked and damaged the fortifications of all three towns, for Edward I had them all repaired the following year. When Malise, earl of Strathearn, refused to provide military support for the new king, Robert, accompanied by Atholl, advanced against him. He marched to Fowlis, one of Strathearn's castles, and held two meetings with Strathearn to demand his support; gave him a few days to think it over; then in exasperation had him seized and held on the Isle of Inchmahome, where at last the earl submitted. Strathearn had good reason to be cagey: not only was he not a natural ally, being married to a Comyn, but Edward I held hostage his only remaining son.

Domestic reaction against the Bruce coup was initially swift, but then months were wasted waiting for the English to arrive in strength. The letter from the Berwick correspondent shows that, though taken utterly by surprise, the opposition were nevertheless in a strong position. All the main castles of Lothian and the east were provisioned, the peel of Selkirk was in safe hands, and already a hundred Northumberland foot were on their way to Berwick. As early as 22 February – a mere twelve days after the murder of John Comyn – Tibbers castle had been recaptured; on 3 March Dumfries fell to forces hostile to Bruce. These actions were probably taken by garrisons already in Scotland; it was summer before the English entered Scotland in strength. On 5 April Edward appointed Aymer de Valence, the brother-in-law of the murdered Comyn, as his lieutenant in Scotland. Henry Percy and Robert Clifford, leading a force of 100 cavalry, closed in on the Bruce heartland of south-west Scotland. Robert, having taken more castles than he could garrison, left the castle at Ayr slighted and abandoned. At last, in June, Aymer de Valence advanced from Berwick towards Perth and Dundee with 300 cavalry and a large force of infantry; Barbour tells us he was accompanied by the Scottish magnates Philip Mowbray and Ingram de Umfraville. At Cupar in Fife, Valence arrested the elderly and defiant Bishop Wishart; at Scotlandwell near Kinross, Lamberton also surrendered, though he first dispatched his ward Andrew, son and heir of James the Steward, into Robert's care. Valence then occupied Perth.

Buoyed up by the apparently widespread support at his enthronement, Robert knew that if he could confront and defeat Valence there was every chance that vindication of his right on the battlefield would cause support for his kingship to snowball further. Strathearn had proven unreliable in providing levies, but Robert had nevertheless managed to gather a considerable army and besieged Strathearn in his manor house at Kenmore in Perthshire. Robert laid waste his estates and had him arrested for a time. Strathearn played for time and only just managed to avoid commiting himself until Robert was at last distracted by the advance of Aymer de Valence on Perth. With Robert were the earls of Lennox and Atholl, his brother Edward Bruce, Thomas Randolph, Hugh Hay, Sir David Barclay and Sir Simon Fraser, once again in revolt. It was scarcely a sign of confidence, however, that many of Robert's knights wore white shirts over their surcoats, masking their heraldic devices so that, in the event of defeat, they would not be identified and suffer loss of lands or a traitor's death.

On 26 June Robert challenged Valence to come out of the town and fight in the open, but Valence declined, responding that he preferred to wait until the morrow. Robert's men broke up to make camp at Methven and forage for firewood but, just then, in the twilight, Valence attacked with devastating effect. A cavalry charge put to flight the infantry and surprised Robert's knights. The chronicles report that Robert was almost captured. Barbour describes how Philip Mowbray seized the reins of Robert's horse and cried, 'Help! Help! I have the new-made king!' Christopher Seton, however, attacked Mowbray, causing the bridle to slip from his hand. Barbour puts as brave a face as he can on the defeat, but Robert's forces were clearly routed, and they were pursued from the field by knights of Valence's company. Malcolm, earl of Lennox, slipped away quietly to his estates. Thomas Randolph was one of those captured, and he was fortunate to have his life spared. But sixteen prisoners were tried and executed at Newcastle in August, and a further eleven were taken to York. Simon Fraser, whom Edward I hated deeply, was also captured and, like Wallace, taken to London where he suffered a gruesome execution for the gratification of the mob.

Pursuit was hot, for there were great rewards in ransoms and royal favour to be had for those who captured significant personages. Robert and the remnants of his cavalry fled westwards along Strathearn, into the territory of St Fillan, whose relics were reverently maintained by the Abbey of Inchaffray, a recipient of the king's generosity in later years. During his flight Robert perhaps considered himself protected by the saint or may have been sheltered by the abbot. He was still accompanied by Edward Bruce, the Northumberland knight Walter Burradon, Gilbert Hay, Neil Campbell and a few others, and with them he crossed over the mountains into Strathtay. There, however, the pursuers, led by the Gascon knight Giles d'Argentan, caught up with them. The Bruce party suffered a further defeat, but they must have acquitted themselves well, since they caused horses to be lost by the pursuers. Great was the delight of English songsters at Robert's discomforture: 'Now King Hobbe to the moors has gone/To come to town he has no desire.'

Certainly there was nothing left to Robert now but further flight into the wilderness. It is impossible to imagine that he could avoid despair on taking to the heather after Methven and Strathtay. He had gambled and lost heavily. Whether he cursed his ambition for bringing ruin on his family and friends, he surely regretted deeply whatever had transpired in the church at Dumfries, for it had set in motion a chain of events that could now – it seemed – only end in death and disgrace. Working from the benefit of hindsight, commentators have tended to exaggerate such faint glimmers of hope as remained to him. Recovery from this desperate position was by no means inevitable, however; it was, rather, miraculous.

5

'Through the Mountains and from Isle to Isle' (1306–07)

Defeat and exile

In the dark moment that followed his defeats at Methven and Strathtay, Robert Bruce must have drawn upon wells of self-belief, fortitude and confidence that few possess. For about a fortnight he and his men kept to the high glens and hillsides. Fortunately it was summer, and one pictures the erstwhile grandees sheltering in the 'sheilings', or temporary dwellings of herdsmen in the high pastures, binding wounds and struggling to find grazing sufficient for the horses. The Scottish chronicles describe the outlaw life of Robert's band of loyal followers in the Mounth. For this episode, the nadir of the hero-king's career, Fordun sets the desolation of his hopes and the ruin of his fortunes against the indifferent sea and sky:

> the aforesaid king was cut off from his men and underwent endless woes, and was tossed in dangers untold, being attended at times by three followers, at times by two; and more often he was left utterly alone without help. Now passing a whole fortnight without food of any kind to live upon but raw herbs and water; now walking barefoot, when his shoes became old and worn out; now left alone in the islands; now alone fleeing before his enemies; now slighted by his servants, he abode in utter loneliness.

The solitude described here is, however, a literary device demonstrating despair. In Barbour's *The Bruce* the king does not want for company, but lives nonetheless a miserable existence:

> They spent many days as outlaws
> Suffering hardship in the Mounth
> Eating flesh and drinking water …
> Thus in the hills lived he
> Till the most part of his menie [retinue]
> Was tattered and torn. They had no shoes
> Save those they could make of hide.

The new king's tribulations were only just beginning. The MacDougalls were advancing on him from the west. In the *Gaidhealtachd*, news of the murder of John Comyn and the inauguration of a Bruce king had had profound repercussions. Until this time Alexander MacDougall had been in continual revolt against the authority of Edward I's chief lieutenant in the area, Alexander Óg MacDonald. In accordance with the general surrender of 1304, the MacDougalls had entered the peace of Edward I. But such was the strength of the bond between the Comyns, Balliols and MacDougalls, and such the fear of a Bruce kingship, that the news of Comyn's death and Bruce's enthronement swept the MacDougalls into the camp of Edward I to avenge the murder and terminate the Bruce coup. The MacDonalds, by the same token, suddenly found their firm allies, the Bruces, to be anathema to Edward's government, and their inveterate foes, the MacDougalls, on Edward's side. Thus a complete about-turn in the politics of the region had occurred: the former rebel MacDougalls now siding with Edward I, and Edward's erstwhile agents in the region, the MacDonalds, siding with the Bruces against him.

At this juncture there comes to prominence John of Argyll, or John Bachach –'the Lame' – MacDougall, who was to remain a thorn in Robert's side for many years. Known to Barbour as 'John of Lorn', this was the son of Alexander MacDougall of Argyll and a daughter of John Comyn of Badenoch I and therefore he was a full cousin of that John Comyn whom Bruce had murdered. Though his father was still active, John took over the leadership of the powerful MacDougall affinity. Such was the bitterness which John harboured against the Bruces that Barbour was moved to write:

> This John of Lorn hated the king
> For the sake of his uncle Sir John Comyn.
> Were he able to slay or capture him,
> He would not value his life at a straw,
> Provided that he could take vengeance on him.

Accordingly John sought out the remnants of Robert's forces where they skulked in the mountains following their defeats. In July, near the head of Strathtay at Dalry, he found them. In Barbour's account Robert's party was attacked but saw off a thousand axe-wielding Argyllsmen, who nevertheless slew and injured many of his horses. Barbour makes a rare admission that Robert withdrew from the battlefield, and he also discloses that James Douglas and Gilbert Hay were wounded. Probably Barbour has turned defeat into victory; John of Argyll seems to have been victorious yet unable to destroy the Bruce force entirely. Here, in later life, Robert I established a priory of Strathfillan, at Glendochart, as though in gratitude for a great mercy at this place.

Now thrice defeated, Robert dispatched John, earl of Atholl, with all the party's horses, to join the queen at Kildrummy Castle. This relieved him of the difficulty of finding grazing for the warhorses. Atholl had instructions to take the ladies of the Bruce party from Kildrummy to a seaport in order that they might escape to Norwegian territory in the Orkney Islands, or to Norway itself. In Norway, Isabella, Robert's sister, lived as widowed queen, and there his dependants would find asylum.

However, Neil Bruce remained at Kildrummy after the ladies had departed, and there he prepared to resist a siege, a decision that suggests tremendous but misplaced faith in his eldest brother. According to the Barbour narrative the royal ladies were accompanied by the young James Douglas. *The Bruce* includes vignettes of Douglas finding food for the ladies, bringing them now venison, now eels, now salmon and trout caught by hand. But Aymer de Valence, enormously strengthened by the arrival in Scotland of a large expedition under Edward of Caernarfon, was closing in on the Bruces. By 3 August he was at Aberdeen. Soon afterwards the English besieged Kildrummy. The castle fell to them in September, betrayed by one of the garrison, who set fire to the stocks of grain. Neil Bruce was delivered into the hands of the prince of Wales as a prisoner. Atholl, Queen Elisabeth and Robert's daughter Marjorie were captured at St Duthus or Duthac's sanctuary near Tain by William, earl of Ross. In early September Donald, the heir to Mar, was taken either at Kildrummy or at Tain. Violation of sanctuary was a serious taboo, and, although Ross later defected to the Bruces, King Robert subsequently bound the earls of Ross to pay £20 annually for six chaplains at St Duthac's sanctuary at Tain to say masses for the souls of earlier kings and for that of John, earl of Atholl.

Aged, and embittered at the sudden renewal of resistance in Scotland, Edward I exacted a terrible vengeance on Robert's adherents. On account of his rank Atholl was taken to London for a show trial and then, for that same reason, hanged from a gallows thirty feet higher than anyone else, cut down, beheaded and burned. The English knight Christopher Seton, Robert's brother-in-law and his castellan at Loch Doon, suffered hanging in Dumfries. Seton's wife, Christina Bruce, later founded a chapel for him at Dumfries, and Robert provided an income to pay for masses for his soul. Christopher's two brothers were also executed. Mention has already been made of the sixteen prominent supporters of Bruce hanged at Newcastle in August. When they surrendered on or around 10 September the garrison of Kildrummy Castle was also hanged;

and in October Neil Bruce was tried before Edward of Caernarfon, drawn by horses through the streets of Berwick, then hanged and beheaded, along with Sir Alan Durward and several others.

Edward I's treatment of the female prisoners was more discriminating, which may suggest that some of the Scottish ladies showed a spirited defiance of the English king, while others did not. The punishment meted out to Mary Bruce and Isabella of Fife, the countess of Buchan, was most inhumane, even by the harsh standards of the time. To make an example of them they were confined, each in a separate cage open to public gaze, one at Roxburgh, the other at Berwick. The cage of the countess was constructed in the shape of a crown, recalling her role in Robert's enthronement, and is described as 'a little wooden chamber in a tower of the castle of Berwick with latticed sides, so that all might look in from curiosity'. Each cage was to be equipped with a privy, and the ladies were to be attended by Englishwomen. At first the twelve-year-old Marjorie, Robert's daughter, was sentenced to be similarly imprisoned, but Edward relented and she and Christina were entrusted to the custody of Henry Percy. The countess was not released from her cage until June 1310, when she was sent to a convent in Berwick; we do not know how long Mary Bruce had to endure this degrading punishment. This spiteful treatment of the ladies of the Bruce court is indicative of the depth of Edward's rage at those who ruined his settlement of Scotland. Robert's de Burgh queen, who may perhaps have disapproved of his coup and then sought leniency from Edward on this account, received the lightest punishment. She was detained at the royal manor of Burstwick in Yorkshire, and given two elderly companions whose demeanour was to be 'not at all gay' – sometimes taken to mean that they were not allowed to smile.

Yet Edward I was a complex character, and even in the midst of all this cruelty and bloodletting he found reasons for clemency towards some. Three knights, Alexander Seton, Robert Boyd and Alexander Lindsay, were apparently released. Young Thomas Randolph, who had also been captured, was released and he reverted to the peace of the English king. The boy Donald, heir of Mar, was retained and brought up at the court of Edward of Caernarfon, to whom he became so attached that he refused to leave in 1315 when prisoners were exchanged.

Mercifully ignorant of the bloodletting and humiliation that was to befall his followers, Robert and his ragged company, which Barbour puts realistically at 200, proceeded on foot across the Mounth late that August. Options were closing all around him. The enmity of the MacDougalls seems to have deterred him from approaching the western coast. Over eighty miles of hostile territory lay between the fugitives and the Forest of Selkirk, the established locale for outlaws and dissidents. Bruce family territories of the south-west were now subdued and enemy garrisons were installed in them. Remaining options cannot have seemed attractive. Some of his supporters, such as David, Bishop of Moray, had made it to safety in Orkney. There was always Ireland, where local kings could defy the will of the English king with impunity, though Robert had perhaps already appealed to his father-in-law, the earl of Ulster, and been spurned. Only in the highlands and islands of western Scotland could he expect shelter, but he had to keep on the move. Barbour suggests plausibly that Robert's immediate goal was Kintyre; from there he would be able to flee to any of these further destinations.

The Barbour narrative is vague at this point. He describes how Neil Campbell departed to collect ships, while the king set off for Loch Lomond, reached it on the third day, spent a day and a night getting his men across the loch in the only boat available, and thence into Lennox. Duncan, however, has reconstructed a more probable itinerary. Robert must have led his men by foot through Breadalbane and then south to the coast at Loch Fyne – at which point Neil Campbell left the main band to gather boats – and thence to Glenkinglass, Arrochar and Tarbet, where Loch Lomond was crossed in an easterly direction, and so on to Lennox. Barbour's account of the day and night spent crossing Loch Lomond, and hunting venison in the earl of Lennox's forests in Gartmore fits more easily into this sequence. Hearing the king's hunting horn, Malcolm, earl of Lennox rode to meet Robert and greeted him joyfully, for he had believed that Robert had died on the field at Methven. Lennox provided a feast for the hungry fugitives. After this Neil Campbell rejoined the main party, Duncan suggests, in the vicinity of Kilcreggan on Loch Long. Campbell had provided ships with sails and oars and they all set off down the Clyde estuary for Bute en route to the open sea. Malcolm, however, delayed and was last to set out. His ship was hotly pursued by enemy vessels, perhaps from Dumbarton, where John of Menteith, to whom Edward I had recently awarded Malcolm's title and earldom, was in command. Barbour relates how, to slow down the enemy, Malcolm cast overboard various pieces of harness and gear, which the enemy took time to take on board, and in this way the earl escaped to rejoin the fugitive king.

From Bute, Robert and his men sailed to Kintyre, where they were warmly received, probably not by Angus Óg MacDonald of Islay as Barbour has it, but by Malcolm MacQuillan, the lord of Kintyre and owner of Dunaverty. It is evident from the Berwick correspondent that in February MacQuillan had placed Dunaverty at Robert's disposal for the coup. Perched on a rocky headland at the tip of the Kintyre peninsula, Dunaverty must have ideally suited Robert's needs. Barbour claims that it was Robert's intention to winter in Dunaverty, yet at this point in the narrative Robert feared treachery:

> Nonetheless in many ways
> He dreaded treason
> And therefore, as I heard men say
> He trusted completely in no-one
> Until he knew him truly.

This is hardly surprising, since Robert had potentially such a price on his head. Penman puts Robert's fear down to dynastic infighting among the leading MacDonald chiefs. Barbour states that Robert stayed in Dunaverty only three days on account of his fear, but the real cause of his abrupt departure appears to have been the arrival in Kintyre of a substantial force to attack the fugitive king in his lair. Early in September the English lord John Botetourt, accompanied by John of Menteith, arrived to besiege Dunaverty. Clearly they understood that Robert was within the walls, and they transported two siege engines from Carlisle to smash their way in. At the end of September the castle fell, but to their dismay the besiegers' quarry had already fled.

Around 20 September the Bruce party embarked again. Barbour describes an unhurried departure from Dunaverty in several ships borne by a strong but favourable wind, bearing Robert and his followers to Rathlin Island off the coast of Antrim. He was accompanied by his brother Edward, Malcolm of Lennox and Neil Campbell, who were with him in Kintyre; Malcolm MacQuillan, lord of Dunaverty, was probably also of the party. MacQuillan was a useful man. His relatives had served with the earl of Ulster and had lands on the Antrim coast. Though not a Gaelic kin group, the MacQuillans were nevertheless in the business of supplying galloglass mercenaries. Barbour's description of the crossing, which owes much to Virgil, is memorable:

> They raised sail and set forth,
> Soon passing by the Mull
> And entered soon into the race
> Where the current was so strong
> That strong waves, which were breakers,
> Rose like hills here and there.
>
> The ships glided over the waves,
> For they had a wind blowing fair.
> Nonetheless, anyone who had been there
> Would have seen a great shifting

> Of ships. For sometimes some would be
> Atop the waves, as if on a hill-top
> And some would slide from top to bottom,
> As if bound for hell,
> Then rise up suddenly on the wave,
> And other ships nearby sank into the trough.

This voyage of Robert Bruce to Rathlin, like that of Bonnie Prince Charlie 'over the sea to Skye', is often invested with a special, almost mystic, significance. In both instances the fate of the Scottish nation personified in royalty is entrusted to the waves: nature intervening to save the embodiment of Scotland from the clutches of the enemy. However, Robert himself would have seen the voyage as no significant departure. The whole western coast from the Hebrides to Ulster and further west was a cultural unity, linked by seasonal travel along shipping lanes and easily traversed. Rathlin he may have considered a Scottish island, rather than part of Ireland.

Far from fleeing his homeland, Robert was taking to a highway that for generations had borne MacDonald, MacDougall, MacRuaridh and MacSween galloglass, not just between Erin and Alba, but to all the far-flung islands of the *Gaidhealtachd*. Undoubtedly Robert was now intent upon recruiting such mercenaries from three principal sources. The first source was MacDonald, based at Dunyvaig on Islay; the second the 'Lady of Garmoran', Christina MacRuaridh, or as she is known 'Christina of the Isles', doubly related to the Bruces through the family of Mar. Her late husband, Duncan of Mar, had been both Robert's brother-in-law by reason of his first marriage to Isabel of Mar, and also his brother-in-law by reason of his sister's marriage to Garnait, earl of Mar. The third possible source of military support from the *Gaidhealtachd* was Domnall O'Neill of Tyrone, who headed a loose federation of allies in the north of Ireland. To persuade these Gaelic magnates that it was in their interest to support him, to weld together their scant resources by skilful diplomacy and thus create armies will have taken a supreme effort. Unfortunately we know very little about how this remarkable achievement was accomplished, and these autumn and winter months of 1306–07 are crucial missing pieces from the jigsaw of Robert's life.

It is hard to believe that Rathlin was Robert's intended destination; either the Irish mainland or Islay would have been more attractive. Barbour, who specifies Rathlin, records that the people of the island fled with their cattle to a 'right stalwart castle' and that Robert negotiated with them. No such castle existed on Rathlin, and Barbour might be describing action on any of larger Western Isles. The men of the island did homage and fealty, and while Robert stayed they undertook to send him every day provisions for 300 men. The size of Robert's requirement increases the probability that the 'Rathlin' scene belongs to an arrival on a much larger island, more able to sustain the Bruce court, or that it may have been repeated on various landings on others of the Western Isles.

During the autumn and winter, Robert and his envoys journeyed to and fro among the Western Isles, calling in debts, twisting arms and promising the world in return for military service and ship service. Against all the odds, a letter of King Robert which seems to belong to this period has survived. It is addressed 'to all the kings of Ireland, to the prelates and clergy and the inhabitants of Ireland', and is a letter of credence, borne by Robert's envoys to Irish Gaelic kings. It appeals to the supposed common racial origin of the Irish and Scots:

> Whereas we and you, and our people and your people, free since ancient times, share the same national ancestry and are urged to come together more eagerly and joyfully in friendship by a common language and by common custom, we have sent over to you our beloved kinsmen, the bearers of this letter to negotiate with you in our name about permanently strengthening and maintaining inviolate the special friendship between us and you, so that with

God's will our nation may recover her ancient liberty. Whatever our
envoys or one of them may on our behalf conclude with you in this
matter, we shall ratify and uphold in the future.

Our nation may recover its ancient liberty? To modern ears it sounds as
though Robert conceived of a single Gaelic nation, and that he offered
an alliance of Gaelic peoples against the dominance of England. Such
sentiments are not uncommon in Gaelic poetry of the period, but
only rarely were they expressed politically. It is best not to take this
sort of language at face value. The letter demonstrates only that the
Bruces knew how to introduce themselves to a Gaelic audience; it
does not mean that they were prepared to lead the Gaelic world into
conflict with the Anglo-Norman. The flowery appeal to common
language and custom would cut ice only if accompanied by the threat
of force, or by silver, and lots of it. The Bruces consistently pedalled
this 'pan-Celtic' verbiage in their dealings with Ireland – and Wales
– when it suited them, and the Irish and Welsh understood it for the
posturing it was. Probably the king's brothers Thomas and Alexander
were the plenipotentiary envoys empowered by this document. The
'letter to the Irish' survives as an exemplar in a formulary or a copy-
book compiled for Scottish royal clerks. In such exemplars, the capital
letters 'A' and 'B' are generally used to mark the places where the clerk
should insert the names of the royal envoys, but at the end of this
missive the capitals used are 'T' and 'A'. Professor Duffy pointed out
that the copyist must have neglected to change the initials used in the
original, initials that can only refer to Thomas and Alexander Bruce,
whom Robert was evidently sending as the bearers of this letter to
all the kings, prelates, clergy and inhabitants of Ireland. Indeed,
conspicuously absent from events in Scotland, they may have been
whipping up support in the *Gaidhealtachd* since February 1306. Later
in 1306 they are described as 'leading a piratical existence', which may
suggest that they moved among the Western Isles gathering a force of
ships. If Thomas and Alexander received assistance from Irish kings,

it is likely to have come from the O'Neills of Tyrone and their allies. As we saw earlier, there may have been ties of kinship and fosterage linking the Bruces to the O'Neills.

During the winter of 1306–07 Robert pieced together his coalition. Traditional loyalties to the Bruces were no doubt cited and played upon to maximum effect. Christina MacRuaridh duly acknowledged Robert as king, and placed at his disposal the lordship of Garmoran, a sprawling collection of lands and islands that stretched from the Outer Hebrides to the shores of Loch Linnhe. She was also rumoured to be Robert's lover during these months. Then, at Martinmas, Robert sent 'many Irishmen and Scots' across to his earldom of Carrick to collect the rents then due, and this would have given him cash with which to bribe those West Highland chiefs and Irish kings who could not be otherwise be persuaded to support him.

As Robert and his brothers laboured to raise an army of galloglass, the king of England was not unaware of their activities. Hugh Bisset, the lord of Rathlin and a vassal of the earl of Ulster, commanded a squadron in the North Channel. In January he was ordered to equip his ships and join John of Menteith among the isles off the coast of Scotland, cutting off Robert Bruce's retreat. Edward I added that he 'held this business greatly at heart'. Four lords were paid for expenses in inquiring as to the whereabouts of 'enemies, rebels and felons of Scotland, who had come to Ireland and been received, with religious persons and others, within the liberty of Ulster, and in seizing those enemies and their harbourers and conveying them to the castle of Dublin.' This reference to 'religious persons' could include Alexander Bruce. Simon Montacute, a Somerset baron who had designs on the Isle of Man, was put in command against rebels 'lurking in Scotland and the isles between Scotland and Ireland'. The earl of Ulster, like his daughter, Robert's queen, clearly wanted nothing to do with Robert's ambitions and made no difficulties for royal agents involved in the pursuit. The sheriff of Cumberland was ordered to commandeer vessels and sent them to Ayr, which became a naval base for Montacute, Bisset and another commander, William le Jettour, all of whom were engaged in the hunt for Bruce. By February they had at their disposal 15 vessels and 200 sailors, and they patrolled the waters around Arran and Bute. Also at Ayr was the victor of Methven, Aymer de Valence, with significant land forces. Evidently the Bruces were expected to attempt a landing on the Scottish mainland. Edward's correspondence betrays deep anxiety for news about the whereabouts of the Bruces and the progress of the hunt. Occasionally he received reports from spies. Montacute was one of those paid for information about Scots received in Ulster. Robert's agents had been busy seeking military support from the earl's restless Gaelic vassals, and Edward's spies were monitoring their activities. On 6 February 1307 Edward considered that Aymer de Valence had been too cautious, and he instructed his treasurer, Walter Langton, to write to Valence and the others at Ayr, telling them that the king understood from elsewhere that they had made such a hash of the pursuit that they dared not tell him. Five days later he wrote directly to Valence in the same terms. Edward had heard nothing of the sort, but, lying in his sickbed in Lanercost Priory, he was consumed by anxiety for news, anxiety which probably hastened his demise.

The Bruces could not wait for Edward's death, however, for the good weather would allow Montacute's squadrons to penetrate even to the outer isles. They prepared to land on the Scottish mainland in two stages. Towards the end of January 1307, Robert arrived in Kintyre, and remained thereabouts for a month or so, evading Montacute's patrols. At around the same time James Douglas and Robert Boyd – neither of whom had accompanied the king on his voyages – mounted an attack on Brodick castle on the Isle of Arran from the mainland. They failed to capture it, but managed to link up with Robert nevertheless. Then on 9 February 1307 a second force, of eighteen galleys, led by Thomas and Alexander Bruce, made a landing in Galloway. This force included Sir Reginald Crawford, a former sheriff of Ayr; Malcolm MacQuillan; and 'a certain Irish kinglet', and the landing was interpreted as a revenge attack on the people of Galloway for their failure to support Robert's kingship. The Galloway chieftan Dungal MacDowall attacked it upon landing, and only two galleys escaped. The following payment, made in the wardrobe of the prince of Wales on 19 February, explains the fate of the leaders: 'To Dungal MacDowall, captain of the army of Galloway, coming to the court of the Prince at Wetheral and leading in his company Sir Thomas Bruce and Alexander his brother and Sir Reginald Crawford, traitors of the king, having captured them in battle, together with the heads of certain other traitors of Ireland and Kintyre, cut off by the said Dungal and his army … 1 mark.' From this it appears that Malcolm MacQuillan – who was the traitor of Kintyre – and the Irish chieftain had been killed in battle by the Gallovidians. Alexander ought to have been spared on account of his status as dean of Glasgow; nevertheless all three prisoners were taken to Carlisle for execution. Thomas was drawn at the tails of horses through the streets, hanged and beheaded on 17 February; the other two were hanged and beheaded. For his good service MacDowall received a further £40 and was knighted at Easter, but he earned the lasting enmity of the remaining Bruce brothers.

According to Barbour, Robert, lurking on Arran or elsewhere in the Clyde estuary, sent a spy by the name of Cuthbert to Carrick, who found that, through fear of the English, the men of the earldom could no longer be relied upon. Cuthbert decided therefore against setting alight a beacon, the signal for Robert to cross; nevertheless a fire was lit which Robert and his men mistook for the signal, and they crossed into Carrick around 10 February. The earldom had been subdued the previous summer, and it was occupied by enemy troops, both in castle garrisons and billeted in villages. It comes across quite strongly from Barbour that, far from welcoming home their exiled earl, the people of Carrick displayed little residual loyalty to the Bruces and an abiding fear of the English:

Both high and low the land was then
Occupied by Englishmen
Who scorned above all else
Robert Bruce the doughty king.
Carrick was then given entirely
To Sir Henry the lord Percy
Who in Turnberry castle then
Was with almost three hundred men
And he so dominated all the land
So that everyone was obedient to him.
This Cuthbert saw their wickedness
And saw the folk wholeheartedly
Become so wholly English, both rich and poor
That to none dared he disclose himself.

A little further on in the narrative Barbour returns to this theme:

When the king and his folk were
Arrived, as I told you earlier
He stayed a while in Carrick
To see who would be friend and who foe.
But he found little support
And, although the people sided with him in part,
Englishmen so harshly
Governed them with threats and power
That they did not dare show him any friendship.

Robert's own earldom was utterly hostile to him. The common people, whatever their true sympathies, had no confidence that he would triumph in the long run, and therefore no guarantee of protection from the vengeance of the English.

Edward I, at Carlisle, was as well informed about Robert's landing as he had been about that of Thomas and Alexander. Fifteen knights

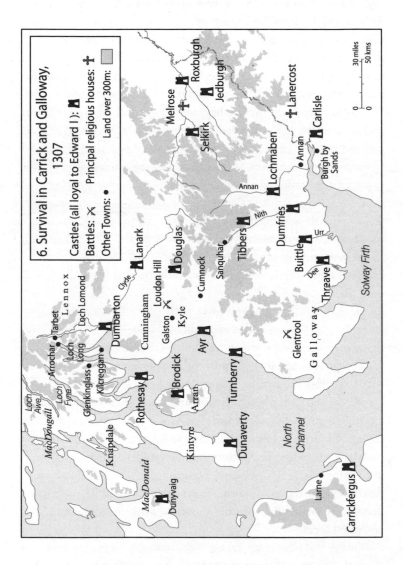

6. Survival in Carrick and Galloway, 1307

Castles (all loyal to Edward I): ⚔
Principal religious houses: ✝
Battles: ✕
Other Towns: •
Land over 300m:

and some forty other cavalry were immediately dispatched against Robert, led by John Botetourt, and four hundred and sixty foot soldiers were sent to reinforce Aymer de Valence. Henry Percy, to whom Robert's earldom of Carrick had been granted, also mobilised to capture him. Robert seems to have not only successfully evaded these forces, but after a time to have inflicted humiliation on Percy. His band surprised Percy's baggage train, and captured horses and silver plate. Percy scuttled into the safety of Turnberry Castle, and did not stir until a force of Northumberland infantry arrived to enable his evacuation. The English and their allies searched for Robert for the remainder of the spring.

Unable to rely on his former tenants and confronted with an enemy superior numerically and with every other conceivable advantage, Robert remained in the hills and moors. Moorland, marshland and hill country, impenetrable to heavy cavalry, became his 'favourable territory', where he was safe, and the enemy ill at ease. He relied on ambush and surprise to make the best use of his small force. Choosing his ground carefully, he would suddenly emerge to win a minor skirmish and then retreat once more into the wilderness. He preferred small engagements, thus minimising his losses and capitalising upon the snowball effect of a series of small victories. He never engaged the enemy unless sure of victory. He terrorised unsympathetic villages and local communities, forcing them to pay large fines, to provide supplies or military service. Thus he created a local 'climate of insecurity', where lords could not guarantee protection to their vassals, and where the writ of the king of the England could not run. Immensely negative and destructive in the short term, these tactics eventually permitted Robert to broaden the basis of his own lordship, to create, in effect, 'liberated areas'.

This is all instantly recognisable to the modern mind as guerrilla warfare, 'the war of the flea', where all strategy is tossed to the wind in favour of tactical advantage. Faced with a stark choice between ignominious survival and a traitor's death and the end of his dynasty, Robert stooped to modes of combat that were plainly beneath his royal and lordly dignity. Having had three brothers executed and his wife, child and sisters captured and many loyal friends lost to this brutalising war with Edward I, he was perhaps driven to the conclusion that victory could not be won through chivalric feats of arms; but that victory, however squalid, must be won at all costs. Guerrilla warfare did not come easily to haughty feudal lords to whom honour and chivalry were everything, who considered themselves born to lead the cavalry charge with heraldic banners flying proudly, and whose very breeding revolted at 'churlish' modes of combat. In medieval Christendom the conduct of knights was often barbaric – especially when fighting non-Christians or social inferiors – yet it was uncommon for knights fighting their peers to adopt systematically tactics of ambush, surprise and terrorism to offset numerical disadvantage. Later Robert received a dressing down for his 'unchivalrous' methods from his nephew, Thomas Randolph, who, after he had rejoined the king, criticised him thus:

> You rebuke me,
> But rather you should be rebuked.
> For since you made war on the king of England,
> You should strive to prove your right by open fighting,
> And not by cowardice or cunning.

For that insolence Randoph was held in confinement, but the criticisms he reportedly voiced may have been widely shared.

Following his raid on Percy's baggage train, Robert's next successful action was indeed the stuff of guerrilla warfare: a ruthless massacre. Barbour describes how, in a village near Turnberry, Bruce and his men descended upon English troops billeted therein, and dispatched many of them in their sleep. Even Barbour seems a little shame-faced about the episode, and he puts these unconvincing words of justification into Robert's mouth:

> And even if we killed them all when sleeping,
> No man could reproach us for it
> For a warrior should not bother
> Whether he can overcome his enemy by might or guile,
> So long as good faith is always maintained.

At night the screams of the surprised troopers were heard by Percy's garrison inside Turnberry Castle, but none dared venture out. Only when the Northumberland infantry arrived did Percy leave the safety of the castle. When he regained Turnberry, Robert did not however take possession of it, which would have offered the enemy a target, but slighted the castle to ensure that it could afford the enemy no further protection. For the present he preferred to remain on the run. Destruction of castles became another central plank in Robert's strategy. He systematically destroyed fortifications to rob lords of the security that these afforded. In doing so, he forced them to choose sides.

After this Robert's guerrilla band received some adherence from the local gentry. Barbour describes how a lady of that country, 'who was closely related to him' – though nameless in the poem – was 'greatly cheered at his arrival'. She contributed forty men to his force, and gave Robert the grim news of the fates that had befallen the ladies of his household, his brother Neil, the earl of Atholl and Christopher Seton. It is speculated that this lady was Robert's mistress. She is often identified as the mother of Christina of Carrick, whom Robert decreed many years later should be paid an annual allowance of forty shillings.

> Many times she comforted the king,
> Both with silver and with food
> Such as she could get in the land.

In the middle of March, John Botetourt was searching for Robert in Nithsdale, with a large force of cavalry. Evidently he found him, for compensation was paid to Botetourt for horses lost on 12 March. Perhaps as a result of Botetourt's losses the English government ordered levies of northern English footsoldiers to assemble at Carlisle on 15 April 'to pursue Robert Bruce and his accomplices who are lurking in the moors and marshes of Scotland'. On 17–18 April a force of 10 knights and 23 esquires were sent to Glen Trool until 30 April, and this was reinforced by 300 archers of Tynedale, sent to Carrick and Glen Trool from 10 April to 3 May. This then was probably the occasion of the battle of Glen Trool, recounted in Barbour as Robert's first significant victory, against a force of Scots and English led by Sir Aymer de Valence sent into Glen Trool to try to ambush the king while he and his men – Barbour says they numbered 700 – were at rest.

Barbour stresses that Robert at this time was vulnerable to betrayal. He recounts that Sir Ingram Umfraville had offered £40-worth of land in return for Robert's murder, and includes two versions of an episode where three men set out to kill him. A one-eyed Carrick man, of sturdy build, and his two sons lay in wait for Robert one morning as he rose to answer a call of nature. Robert was accompanied only by a page carrying a crossbow, but he was accustomed to wear his sword at all times. With these weapons Robert dispatched all three would-be assassins. In a similar episode, the king and his unnamed foster-brother spent the night in an abandoned farmstead in the company of three traitors. Although the king triumphed – as always – his foster-brother was killed, and 'the king went forth, sad and angry, grieving tenderly over his man'.

In one of the most famous of these episodes from Barbour, men from Galloway attacked Robert's camp one evening, and used a bloodhound to follow the king's trail. Robert's entourage was pursued into rugged terrain, where the king became separated from his followers and, at a narrow ford, single-handedly held off the 200-strong enemy. Later in the text it is John of Lorn, or as we know him, John of Argyll, who hunts the king with hound and horn, 'as if he were a wolf, a thief, or a thief's accomplice'. These episodes, some representing different versions of the same tale, others several episodes rolled together, and others no doubt borrowings from classical or Celtic myth, all represent facets of an important development: that myths of Robert's strength, courage and worthiness grew as events unfolded. It can also be inferred from the Barbour text that changes were gradually occurring. The size of Bruce's force was increasing. There is mention of a royal banner which signified Robert's presence and kingship: it is perhaps the banner of Alexander III. Whole districts began to declare for Robert: 'he made the land of Kyle obedient to himself', and 'the greater part of Cunningham held to his lordship'.

Barbour does not neglect the activities of his other hero, James Douglas. All the returned exiles were anxious to recover possession of their own lands and rents, and Douglas and his men set out to recover his patrimony. In the first of many tales of ingenious tricks played by the Scots to dupe castle garrisons, Barbour describes how Douglas disguised his men as a convoy of peasants leading pack animals laden with grain to the Whitsun fair at Lanark. This episode may then be dated to May 1307. The convoy wound its way close by Castle Douglas in Lanarkshire, tempting the garrison to sally out and capture the grain. As the garrison approached, Douglas's men threw the sacks, filled only with grass, off the saddles and, mounting the horses, attacked the sortie and raced towards the undefended castle. Douglas gained access and paid the remaining soldiers to clear off; then he knocked down the wall of the castle and destroyed its houses so that it was useless to the enemy. That was only a temporary success however. Robert Clifford, to whom the castle had been granted, was subsequently given £100 and twenty-one masons to make good the damage, and the castle was repaired and garrisoned that summer.

Around 10 May there took place the encounter between the Bruce band and Aymer de Valence at Loudon Hill. Walter Langton, bishop of Lichfield, the royal treasurer, was touring the garrisons of the south-west, making payments to ensure their loyalty. For security, he was accompanied by Valence. Robert was clearly interested in capturing the chests of silver coin that travelled with the treasurer, and he prepared to ambush him first at Galston, then at Loudon, where a good firm road ran through marsh on both sides. Robert prepared the ground by digging three ditches to fortify his position on the road, and his men, used to running, hiding and guerrilla fighting for a year now, prepared with apprehension to face the approaching cavalry:

> Their bascinetts were all burnished bright
> Gleaming in the sun's light;
> Their spears, their pennons and their shields
> Lit up all the fields with light
> Their best bright-embroidered banners,
> Horse of many hues
> Coats of armour of diverse colours
> And hauberks which were as white as flour
> Made them glitter, as though they were like to
> Angels from the kingdom of heaven.

Valence's impressively armoured cavalry was routed by Robert's force of entrenched spearmen, who, Barbour suggests, numbered about six hundred, and Valence was forced to flee to Bothwell. Robert did not get his hands on the treasure, however, nor did his men get the chance to plunder the enemy, as Valence's force seems to have retired largely intact. But a letter from the English court shows that the defeat put Valence once more in bad odour at court: 'The king had been much enraged because the Guardian of Scotland [Valence] and the other folk had retreated before King Hobbe without doing any exploit.' This letter also reveals that prior to the battle, Douglas – whom we are used to considering as Robert's faithful friend – had been thinking about defecting to the English. That revelation, more than any other, demonstrates just how precarious Robert's position was in the spring of 1307.

Even so, while Robert himself was contained in the south-west of Scotland, there is evidence that in distant parts the Bruces' frantic diplomacy in the *Gaidhealtachd* over the previous winter was beginning to take effect. Written in Forfar, a hundred miles from Glen Trool and across the Scottish Sea, a letter of 15 May suggests that events in the south-west were being closely watched and exaggerated to suggest the imminence of Bruce's ultimate triumph: 'I hear that Bruce never had the good will of his own followers or of the people generally so much with him as now. It appears that God is with him, for he has destroyed King Edward's power both among English and Scots.' Robert of course had done nothing of the sort as yet. But the Forfar correspondent identifies the propagandists who had so demolished the morale of the Scottish opposition:

> The people believe that Bruce will carry all before him, exhorted by false preachers from Bruce's army men who have previously been charged before the justices for advocating war and have been released on bail, but now are behaving worse than ever. I fully believe, as I have heard from Reginald Cheyne, Duncan of Frendraught and Gilbert of Glencarnie who keep the peace beyond the Mounth and on this side, that if Bruce can get away in this direction or towards the parts of Ross he will find the people all ready at his will more entirely than ever, unless King Edward can send more troops, for there are many people living loyally in his peace so long as the English are in power.
>
> May it please God to prolong King Edward's life, for men say openly that when he is gone the victory will go to Bruce. For these preachers have told the people that they have found a prophecy

of Merlin, that after the death of 'le Roy Coveytous' the people of
Scotland and the Welsh shall band together and have full lordship
and live in peace together to the end of the world.

This hugely significant letter raises a number of points. Firstly, it
illustrates the power of millenarian preaching in the medieval
world, and use of prophecy to magnify rumour and create real
opportunity from remote possibility. This is not the first time in the
life of Bruce that we have encountered political prophecy, the 'media
spin' of its day. Robert, or his allies among the clergy, had dispatched
such preachers far and near, fomenting a sense of foreboding and
imminent change. Secondly, the letter serves to remind us that the
Scottish clergy – not just its lower orders, but at least four bishops
– were largely supportive of the Bruce claim to the throne; we
have already encountered Bishop David Murray preaching holy
war on Robert's behalf. Thirdly, it points up the serious gap in
our knowledge: the unknown agreements forged during Robert's
sojourn in the Western Isles. That northern districts should be in
such expectation of Robert's ultimate victory, while he himself was
merely living the life of a successful bandit in the south-west, takes
some accounting for. Support for the Bruce cause in Ross can only
have been the result of MacRuaridh influence, coupled with the
distance and terrain that preserved the north-west from English
reprisal. One is tempted to suggest explanations for which there is no
evidence: was there perhaps a growth in the population, and hence
in the military significance, of the north-west? Professor Barrow
found that Bruce consistently recruited his armies from north of
the Forth, and there is evidence that northern Scots accompanied
Robert on his later raids into England.

The contrast between the expectations expressed in the Forfar
letter and Bruce's precarious though improving position in the
south-west is remarkable. Following his creditable display in the
open field at Loudon Hill, Robert considered it prudent to retreat

to the mountains once more. Barbour portrays him hunting and relaxing in the safety of a deep glen, behaving with rather more nonchalance than his position would warrant. He relates that the English, 'riding by night, keeping to cover by day' arrived secretly within a mile of Robert's location, and that they sent a beggar-woman to spy on him. The beggar, however, aroused Robert's suspicions; he had her seized, and she confessed that Valence and his men were already closing in on him through the woods. Quickly Robert donned armour and prepared to fend off the attack, and the English fled in such disarray, Barbour recounts, that their leaders fell out with one another. As spring turned to summer, Robert's strength increased. In mid-June Glen Trool was again the focus of English activity and a raid against Robert was mounted. Duncan shows that 23 horses were lost in a pursuit of Robert Bruce between Glen Trool and 'Glen Heur', which location Barrow identifies as the glen of the Palnure Burn, some eight miles south of Glen Trool. Such English losses suggest that Robert was in fact on the offensive and doing the pursuing.

A fortnight later there came the news that the Forfar correspondent had dreaded. On 3 July Edward of England had ridden out of Carlisle, aware that only his presence would restore the situation in south-west Scotland. Heading for Dumfries, he spent the night of 6 July at Burgh by Sands, but he was found dead by his servants the following morning. His officials, well aware of the effect that news of his death would have in Scotland, at first attempted to suppress it. There was no let up in the search for Robert Bruce. That month John of Argyll was at Ayr with a force of 800 men – a figure which we can tell from administrative sources that Barbour gives correctly – and he was accompanied by Robert's nephew, Thomas Randolph, still loyal to Edward I. In the Barbour narrative John set out with a tracker dog to find Robert, then in the vicinity of Cumnock. Although Robert's band split up, the tracker dog always stayed in hot pursuit of the king's group. John sent an advance party of five men, fleet of foot, to head off Robert. The hero-king dispatched four of these enemies, and his foster-brother the fifth.

On the news of his father's death, Edward of Caernarfon travelled from London to take charge of the campaign, and he was in Scotland on 31 July. He advanced to Dumfries, where he divided his army into three columns and set out in pursuit of the rebel earl of Carrick. He moved through Tibbers and Sanquhar before reaching Cumnock, where he stayed ten days. During this time Robert did not dare to put his head above the parapet and avoided action. But Edward retired to Carlisle on 1 September. His campaign was perfunctory, for he was required to return to England for the obsequies of his great father, to hold a parliament and to attend to arrangements for his own marriage and coronation. Requiring Aymer de Valence for other services, he relieved him of the Scottish command and appointed instead the less able John of Brittany.

When Edward II departed, Robert celebrated with a vengeful attack on the hated Gallovidians – the first of many. In this way the remaining Bruce brothers, Robert and Edward, exacted revenge from those who six months previously had captured Thomas and Alexander and handed them over for execution. By 25 September Gallovidian refugees were pouring across the border, seeking safety and grazing for their herds of cattle in Inglewood Forest. Dungal MacDowall and Dungal MacCann wrote to the king of England appealing for help, complaining that the Bruces were forcing the men of those parts to perform military service. The Bruces pursued the refugees mercilessly, carrying war into England for the first time. On the English West March keepers of the peace had to be appointed 'for the preservation of those parts from incursions of the king's enemies and to punish rebels', and the Cumberland knight Thomas de Multon was ordered to assist the keepers 'owing to the thieving incursions of Robert Bruce'. The Bruces exacted tribute from the men of Galloway in the form of a fine to leave them in peace. This was to become another hallmark of Robert I's warfare.

Towards the end of September Robert steeled himself for a tremendous gamble and moved decisively northwards. It was a bold step, but necessary, for his position was still far from secure in the south-west, the area where Bruce dynastic influence might have been expected to predominate. Clearly, Robert too had heard those rumours of growing support for his cause in the north which the Forfar correspondent had reported. To seek allies and to broaden the basis of his kingship he had to move northwards. His great adversary Edward I having gone to his reward, Robert was anxious to capitalise upon any faltering in the English war effort. His most dangerous foes however were Scottish, and Robert now turned northwards to face his bitterest enemies: the magnate faction that had governed Scotland for fifty years, the Comyns, and the implacable MacDougall lords of Argyll.

6

Recovering the kingdom (1307–11)

With the death of 'le roy coveytous' in July 1307, and with Robert's decision the following September to move beyond the heartland of Bruce dynastic influence, the war and Robert's life entered a new phase. Gone were the days of struggling frantically for survival in the wake of the catastrophies of Methven and the Galloway landing. Robert and his allies were seizing the initiative and carrying war to the enemy. The period witnessed the devastation of three centres of resistance to his power: Buchan, Galloway and Argyll; a fourth centre, Lothian, Robert was not yet strong enough to reduce. In the Barbour text two principal themes emerge. The first is how the Bruce faction managed to overcome the overwhelming material advantages of their enemies by cunning and guile. This is illustrated by the capture and destruction of many castles garrisoned by their enemies. The second theme is the increasing recognition in Scotland of Robert as king. Barbour portrays the period in terms of an inexorable *Risorgimento*, as the Scottish people come to their senses and recognise the hero-king, but we know different. Civil wars are always more savage and bitter than foreign wars, and even in the Barbour narrative the scale of bloodletting is apparent as Robert Bruce recovers his kingdom with ruthless perseverance.

This escalation of the struggle was made possible by the long-anticipated demise of Edward I and the accession to the English throne of his son. Edward of Caernarfon, Edward II as he now was, was neither the colossus of statesmanship nor the genius of imperial expansionism that his father had been. A contemporary described his character in these terms:

> This Edward was fair of body and great of strength, and unsteadfast in manners, if men shall believe what is commonly told. For he forsook the company of lords and sought out the company of harlots, singers, jesters, carters, delvers, ditchers, rowers, shipmen and bootmen, and other craftsmen; he also gave himself up to much drinking. He would lightly share confidences and hit men who were about him for the merest offence, and he did more by the advice of other men than by his own. He was generous and solemn in feast making, loquacious and inconstant, irritated by his enemies and cruel to his own. He loved strongly one of his favourites and did him great reverence, worshipped him and made him extremely rich. From this came hatred to the lover, evil speech and backbiting to the loved, slander to the people and harm and damage to the realm.

Thomas of Castleford is more pithy: 'this Edward was wise in word, and fool in deed.' Edward II was considered by the English nobility of the day to be an undignified character. He was homosexual, and the favourite referred to above was a Gascon knight called Piers Gaveston whom, to the disgust of the magnates, Edward elevated to the earldom of Cornwall. Like his father, Edward II was anxious to maintain and increase the power of the English monarchy, and that included holding onto Scotland by every conceivable means, but he lacked his father's single-mindedness, his powerful influence over the English feudal nobility and his overbearing personality. Soon Edward II developed a deep-seated hatred of the most powerful of all the English nobles, Thomas of Lancaster. Altogether, the second Edward was an opponent of lesser stature than Edward I had been, and Robert was fortunate that Edward I's successor was incompetent and under-mighty. One English annalist records a possible saying of Robert: that 'he feared the bones of the dead king more than he did the live one, and that it was a greater feat of war to wrest six inches of territory from Edward I than to gain a whole kingdom from his son'.

The character of the English king directly affected the nature of the war Robert was engaged in. Edward II had left Scotland on 1 September 1307 without confronting Robert and his guerrilla band, and he did not return until 1310, allowing Robert three years in which to establish a secure power base. In retrospect we can see the magnitude of this error; 1307–10 were the 'locust years' of English occupation, when what was dearly won by the strenuous efforts of the previous reign was recklessly frittered away. Military and financial support for garrisons and Scottish communities that accepted Edward II's kingship were sorely neglected; a catastrophic error which Robert did not fail to punish. To Edward's supporters in Scotland, dependent upon a distant and distracted government, the offer of *suffraunce de guerre* or purchased truce always seemed attractive. Naïvely they trusted that time was on their side, that the English king would sooner or later come to help them; whereas Robert offered truces only to neutralise the strong while picking off the frightened and vulnerable. In time it became clear that the faraway English king promised much and delivered little, while Robert presented an immediate and pressing threat to increasingly isolated lords and communities.

Barbour tells us that Robert set out northwards in September 1307 with his brother Edward, Gilbert Hay, Sir Robert Boyd and others. His small army marched swiftly, but grew significantly along the way. There are no details of the ninety-mile journey to the north-west; his force marched down the Clyde, north along Loch Lomond and over the mountains to the head of Loch Linnhe. Moving with great speed, he will have been very careful to avoid any encounter with John of Argyll. Malcolm, earl of Lennox, appears to have rejoined the king, and Robert received naval support on the western flank from

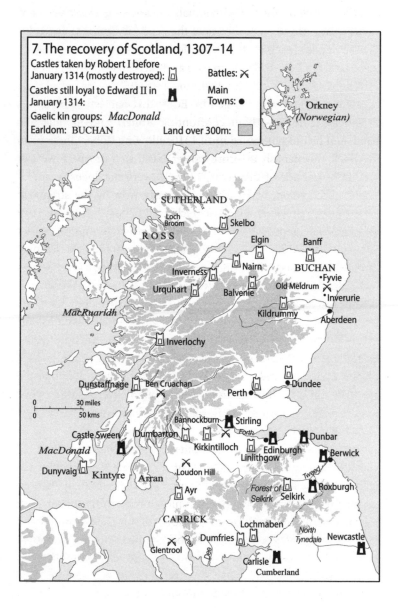

7. The recovery of Scotland, 1307–14

Castles taken by Robert I before January 1314 (mostly destroyed):

Castles still loyal to Edward II in January 1314:

Gaelic kin groups: *MacDonald*

Earldom: BUCHAN

Battles: ✕

Main Towns: ●

Land over 300m:

Orkney *(Norwegian)*

SUTHERLAND

Loch Broom

Skelbo

ROSS

Elgin

Banff

Inverness

Nairn

BUCHAN

Urquhart

Balvenie

Old Meldrum
•Fyvie
•Inverurie

MacRuaridh

Kildrummy

Aberdeen

Inverlochy

Dunstaffnage

Ben Cruachan

Perth

Dundee

0   30 miles
0   50 kms

Bannockburn

Stirling

Castle Sween

Dumbarton

Forth

MacDonald

Kirkintilloch

Edinburgh

Dunbar

Linlithgow

Berwick

Dunyvaig

Kintyre

Arran

Loudon Hill

Ayr

Forest of Selkirk

Selkirk

Tweed

Roxburgh

CARRICK

Lochmaben

North Tyndale

Newcastle

Glentrool

Dumfries

Dee

Carlisle

Cumberland

MacRuaridh and MacDonald galleys. In the rear, James Douglas remained in Selkirk Forest, the haven that had sheltered Wallace and Simon Fraser before him, and Douglas's following became sufficiently threatening to necessitate the garrisoning of Carlisle Castle from 16 April 1308 to Michaelmas following (29 September).

Robert moved quickly to besiege the Comyn stronghold of Inverlochy Castle, arriving on 25 November 1307. Inverlochy was the key to the Great Glen, the obvious corridor to the north. The Comyns were surprised; evidently they had not provisioned the castle adequately and it was handed over to Robert 'by the deceit and treason of the men of the castle'. Robert probably slighted Inverlochy, as he destroyed all the castles that fell into his hands at this stage. He then moved rapidly north-east along the glen, destroying Castle Urquhart on Loch Ness along the way. Probably the galleys were hauled or carried overland between the lochs of the Great Glen, allowing Robert to move rapidly and amphibiously. To the north and west lay the hostile territories of Caithness, Sutherland and Ross. In a letter to Edward II William, earl of Ross, offered explanations as to why he was forced to come to terms with Bruce:

> we heard of the coming of Sir Robert Bruce towards the parts of Ross with a great power, so that we had no power against him, but nevertheless we caused our men to be called out and we were stationed for a fortnight with three thousand men at our own expense, on the borders of our earldom and in two other earldoms, Sutherland and Caithness and [Bruce] would have destroyed them utterly if we had not made a truce with him, at the entreaty of good men, both clergy and others, until Whitsun next [2 June 1308]. May help come from you, our lord, if it please you, for in you Sir is all our hope and trust. And know, dear lord, that we would on no account have made a truce with him if the warden of Moray [Reginald de Cheyne] had not been absent from the country ...

Earl William found himself menaced on either side. He was under pressure from Lachlan MacRuaridh's galloglass on the west and now he found himself attacked from the south by Robert. Ross's blaming of his neighbour for failing to support him is typical of the reaction of the Scottish opposition, who lacked leadership above all. Robert established a pattern: by forced marches and surprise attacks he outmanoeuvred and caught his enemies unawares, dividing them and forcing them singly into temporary subjection. Robert is most unlikely to have faced down an army of 3,000 men. The earl has greatly exaggerated the size of Robert's army to justify his failure to resist. In fact, at this point in the narrative Barbour estimates Robert's strength at a realistic 700 men. Ross probably paid heavily in tribute in order to secure this truce.

It was now late November, and Robert with confidence turned his back on Ross. He marched eastwards to destroy Inverness and Nairn castles. At this point however, his attack lost momentum. He was unable to reduce Elgin but made a truce with the defenders. He was now in deeply hostile territory, held by the Comyns for generations, and, winter though it was, the Comyns organised the opposition lords of the north for a counter-attack. There closed in on Robert the combined strengths of John Comyn earl of Buchan, David of Strathbogie earl of Atholl – son of the executed earl John – Duncan of Frendraught and John Mowbray.

One can scarcely imagine a worse time for Robert to fall ill, which occurred as he was advancing on Banff Castle. Of the nature of the illness we know nothing; he was unable to ride his horse and had to be carried in a litter. His men could find no effective medicine. The sickness was probably the result of campaigning into the winter, and if so, many of his men will have been affected. Barbour has a good word for Edward Bruce's attempts to rally the troops, but Edward made no attempt to take his brother's place by leading the men into battle. They stayed at Duncan of Frendraught's manor of Concarn for two nights; then, burning the manor and all the corn, they moved on towards Slioch, near Huntly. The galley fleets of the Gaelic lords did not operate on the eastern seaboard. Desertion was endemic in medieval armies, and many following Robert would have seen this as a good time to run away. On Christmas Day the enemy sighted Bruce's force, safe from cavalry attack in 'a certain wooded marsh' near Slioch. Buchan's army retired to collect a sufficient infantry force to flush out the Bruces, and having done so they returned to the spot on 31 December 1307. But there was no engagement that day, and during the night the Bruces withdrew towards the south. Instead of closing in for the kill, the opposition leaders then fell out with one another. Some loss of nerve or lack of leadership seems to have overcome them at this crucial time; Buchan was to die in 1308, and he may have been ill already. They approached the earl of Ross and tried to persuade him to join with them in the attack, but Ross was too terrified of reprisals to abandon his truce. As a result of pressure from Robert to the south and east, and from the MacRuaridhs to the west, Ross's power had collapsed. The MacRuaridhs now refused to pay the earl revenues from Skye and other Hebridean islands hitherto subject to the earldom. Robert's policy of dividing the opposition appears to have tided him over the dire emergency of Christmas 1307.

The following spring Edward II's faithful liegemen in northern Scotland wrote to him, appealing for help. Edward responded on 20 May in typical fashion, thanking them for their good service and ordering them to stay in their commands. In early March 1308 John Mowbray was next to be forced to accept a truce from the Bruces; they were then free to waste the castle and lands of Sir Reginald Cheyne at Balvenie – known then as Mortlach – and of Sir Alexander Comyn at Tarradale. Robert dispatched William Wiseman to the rear to capture the castle of Skelbo on Palm Sunday, 7 April, and to renew his siege of Elgin Castle, held by Duncan of Frendraught. Wiseman was not able to capture Elgin, however, for John Mowbray arrived to relieve it in apparent violation of his recent agreement with the Bruces.

1. (left) Robert Bruce and Elisabeth de Burgh from the Seton Armorial, 1591.

In April 2006, a poll of 1,000 respondents was taken by Stirling University to discover who is considered to be the greatest Scot of all time. William Wallace came first with 36% of the vote, Robert Burns next with 16% and Robert Bruce third with 12%. Seven hundred years after his seizure of the throne of Scotland, Robert retains an attraction and relevance for most Scots.
(*From the Seton Armorial © Trustees of the National Library of Scotland*)

2. (below) These three armorial devices were associated with the Bruces. The first, the blue lion (*argent a lion rampant azure*), was the original arms of the Bruces in the twelfth century; the second shows the arms of the Lordship of Annandale (*or, a saltire and chief gules*). The third shield shows the arms of the earldom of Carrick (*argent a chevron gules*).
(*Courtesy of Jean Munro and Don Pottinger*)

3. (right) The interior of the Bannatyne Mazer. This wooden drinking bowl was meant to be passed around the company at a feast. The base of the interior shows a crouching lion encircled by the six heraldic shields of Walter the Stewart, James Douglas, Walter fitzGilbert, John fitzGilbert, Crawford and Menteith. Until recently this decoration was interpreted as King Robert surrounded by the chief lords of the Stewart affinity. However, the grinning, crouching lion is entirely inappropriate as a representation of the king. Barrow suggested that the cup was made to celebrate the marriage of one of the fitzGilbert family, Leo or Gilbert, with the younger daughter and co-heiress of Sir Reginald Crawford.
(*© Trustees of the National Museums of Scotland*)

4. (above) Lochmaben Castle, Annandale. The Bruces moved the caput or head of their lordship from Annan to Lochmaben some time around 1200. The stone castle was built by Robert Bruce V, Robert the Noble. However on capturing the Bruce Castle in 1298 Edward I decided to dismantle it and, using the stones from the original, built the castle illustrated nearby.
(© *Trustees of the National Library of Scotland*)

5. (right) Edward I makes his son Edward the Prince of Wales. Edward I's high expectations of his son were disappointed. An important factor in Robert's success was the difference, much remarked upon by contemporaries, in the personalities and capabilities of these successive English monarchs.
(*BL Cotton Nero DII, f. 191v,* © *British Library*)

6. (above) Sixteenth-century reconstruction of an Edwardian parliament by Sir Thomas Wriothesley. The illustration shows the English king flanked by Alexander King of Scotland and Llywelyn Prince of Wales. It is fantasy, since there was no such meeting; yet as an expression of Edward's ambitions, it may not be too wide of the mark. (*Wriothesly MS, quire B The Royal Collection © HM Queen Elizabeth II*)

7. (left) King John of Scotland and his wife Isabella de Warenne. John abdicated as king of Scotland by a deed of 10 July 1296, and was ceremonially un-kinged by Edward I. The arms of Scotland were ripped from his surcoat. Henceforth he bore the nickname 'Toom Tabard', 'the empty surcoat'. (*From the Seton Armorial, 1591 © Trustees of the National Library of Scotland*)

8. (left) Edward I's army slaughters the inhabitants of Berwick, 1296. The Lanercost Chronicle records the slaughter of the townsfolk. Corpses were thrown into the sea or buried in mass graves. (*MSS No. ADD.47682 Folio 40 © British Library*)

9. (right) Stone of Destiny, Jacob's Pillow or the Tanist Stone. There is no doubt that Edward I removed the genuine Stone of Destiny from Scone Abbey. He paid Walter of Durham, his painter, to make a wooden throne to contain it, and this was completed by 1300. Robert was enthroned in the absence of the Stone, but as soon as he had an heir in 1324 he asked for its return, and renewed his request in 1328. On that occasion however the Abbot of Westminster or the London mob prevented its removal. In 1950 it was removed by nationalist students to Arbroath Abbey, but returned to Westminster by the authorities. On St Andrew's Day 30 November 1996, it was officially restored to Scotland, where it is kept with the Scottish crown jewels in Edinburgh Castle. (© *Marianne Majerus*)

fuper misernu + cōnuulat ce nealde + cs nobis fragenti tare li dici + bis nor
latate sunt os aic li cmnt i iscino + tis quam totum temp op uimmus
clamabat noce magna dicētes bn tr cia. bi ergo qui tuebo duit die bca
dicimus te vie sau di uuu q dignat qin npi liebit pie ni scis i scla scloz.

10. The Coronation of Edward II. English and French kings were crowned, anointed and enthroned, with sceptre and orb as this manuscript illumination shows. Prior to 1329, however, Scottish and Irish kings were enthroned but lacked the rite of coronation. The winning of rites of coronation and unction for Scottish kings was a major diplomatic triumph for Robert. (© *Corpus Christi College, Cambridge*)

11. (above) Dunstaffnage Castle, the chief stronghold of the MacDougalls. Alexander MacDougall and his son John of Argyll were Robert Bruce's bitterest opponents. Their stronghold was eventually reduced by the Bruces in 1309, but the MacDougalls continued their opposition from Ireland and Man.

12. (left) Coin showing the head of Robert I. For any medieval monarch coinage was crucial as a public demonstration of royal power. Robert however was unable to mint his own coins until his capture of the Berwick mint in 1318. Consequently coins bearing his image are rare. Pennies, halfpennies and farthings were minted in Robert's name. (*Courtesy of www.londoncoins.com*)

13. Equestrian statue of Robert at Bannockburn. Pilkington Jackson's striking and impressive statue of the hero king stands on the site of a battle which was a pivotal event in the War of Independence. At a stroke, Robert gained three important castles and a variety of English prisoners, valuable for ransoms and exchange for family members held captive. (© *Marianne Majerus*)

14. The Monymusk Reliquary. For many years this eighth-century house-shaped shrine or pyx was thought to be the *Brecchennach*, a relic of St Colmcille which was believed to lend the Scottish army potency in battle. The *Brecchennach* featured as a sacred talisman of the Scots, but David Caldwell showed that its identification with this object is not to be taken for granted. He also suggests that the *Brecchennach* may have been a banner. Nevertheless, it is likely that the *Brecchennach* and this reliquary were both present at the battle of Bannockburn, as sacred objects would have been collected beforehand to ensure the intervention of the saints on the Scots' behalf. (© *Trustees of the National Museums of Scotland*)

15. The Declaration of Arbroath, April 1320. Written in the papal cursus (or approved metre) and employing phrases borrowed from classical authors as well as many quotations from the Vulgate, the famous letter of the Scottish lords to Pope John XXII was carefully crafted to push all the right buttons at the papal chancery. (*The Nation of Scots and the Declaration of Arbroath*, © *National Archives of Scotland*)

16. Victorian brass marking the tomb of Robert Bruce. The discovery and exhumation of Robert's body in Dunfermline in 1819 may have been somewhat challenging to the authorities. After all, Scotland was then a province of the United Kingdom that had been subdued only in the last century. The discovery of the tomb thrilled contemporaries as it appealed to fashionable interest in the romantic aspects of chivalry. Michael Penman disputes the identification of the tomb. (© *University of St Andrews*)

17. (right) and 18. (below) Lead container that holds Robert's heart and the carved device at Melrose Abbey over the place where Robert's heart is buried. The heart of Robert Bruce, famously borne into battle by Sir James Douglas, was twice exhumed from its resting place in Melrose Abbey. In 1921 it was discovered by archaeologists, who found an embalmed heart in a leaden cone-shaped casket. They sealed it in a lead container and reburied it. It 1996 it was discovered again and reburied on 24 June 1998. (© *Historic Scotland*)

19. Cast of the skull thought to be that of Robert Bruce. A plaster of paris cast was taken during the exhumation of 1819, and many copies of this exist. The cast has been the principal evidence in the debate over whether the king died of leprosy or some other condition. (*Courtesy of the Scottish National Portrait Gallery*)

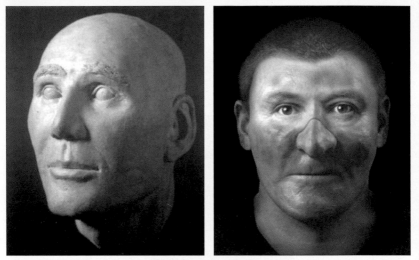

20. (right) and 21. (left) Reconstructions of the head of Robert Bruce, each of which is based on the plaster cast of the skull exhumed in 1818–19. That on the right is a physical reconstruction created by Brian Hill of the Newcastle Dental Hospital in 1996 by applying standard soft tissue depth measurements to the cast. The facial depiction on the left is based on a 3-D scan of the cast by a team headed by Caroline Wilkinson of Face Lab (Liverpool John Moores University and University of Glasgow). The project was the subject of a 2016 BBC television programme *'Ceann an Rìgh* (The King's Head)'. There is, however, some uncertainty as to whether the skull exhumed is indeed that of Robert Bruce.

22. A 3-D digital model of the original tomb of Robert Bruce created by a team of experts from across the heritage sector. Details of the tomb of marble and alabaster, with gilding, are referred to in the contemporary Exchequer Roll. The tomb was destroyed during the demolition of Dunfermline Abbey following the Reformation. In the early nineteenth century fragments of carved and gilded marble were discovered during the building of the present parish church. Using the fragments extant, Dr Iain Fraser (RCAHMS) identified the original form of the monument. The model formed the centrepiece of an exhibition mounted entitled 'The Lost Tomb of Robert Bruce', part of the commemorations of the 700th anniversary of the battle of Bannockburn. (© *Historic Environment Scotland. Image courtesy of CDDV*)

In May of 1308 Robert, not yet fully recovered from his illness, decided to confront the ailing John Comyn earl of Buchan, and John Mowbray. He must have received an accession of strength during the spring, but from where? It seems that, despite the power of the Comyns, not all northern gentry and freeholders opposed Robert. Earlier in the year John Mowbray had had to punish 'freeholders and others whom he knew to be of ill repute', apparently for their support of the Bruces. The growth of Robert's force in this unfavourable territory lends support to Duncan's assertion that Robert possessed 'the capacity to by-pass the reluctant traditional leaders of the community and to appeal to and command other social ranks'.

Robert advanced from Inverurie towards Old Meldrum. There, in an action known as the battle of Inverurie, his vanguard was attacked and worsted by the enemy. When the main enemy force came in sight Fordun reports that 'he ordered his men to arm him and set him on horseback. When this was done, he too, with cheerful countenance, hastened with his host against the enemy to the battle-ground, although by reason of his great weakness he could not go upright, except with the help of two men to prop him up.' Comyn and Mowbray were put to flight and their army scattered and 'pursued as far as Fyvie twelve leagues away'. In the wake of this victory Robert set about a systematic destruction of the earldom of Buchan, known to history in Barbour's phrase as 'the herschip of Buchan' and designed to weaken permanently the Comyn power base:

> Now let us go to the king again
> Who was well pleased with his victory
> And had his men burn all Buchan
> From end to end and sparing none.
> He harried them in such a way
> That a good fifty years afterwards
> People bemoaned 'the herschip of Buchan.'

From detailed accounts of the destruction that befell the north of England in the following decade, we can picture the destruction of Buchan: the burning of barns and mills, the burning and trampling of standing crops, the killing and driving off of the tenantry and the burning of their villages. The prominent symbols of Comyn lordship in the area would all have been targeted and destroyed: Dundarg and Slains castles, as well as Deer Abbey would all have been severely damaged. After this Robert is said to have 'taken into his peace' the people north of the Mounth: that is to say, he accepted a sum of money to spare them from further destruction and take them under his protection.

The campaigning season proper began, and Robert set his sights on Aberdeen, the northernmost significant port. This would bring him the additional revenues of tolls on commerce and lucrative customs on wool and hides. It would also enable him to open communications with other North Sea towns and kingdoms. Accordingly Robert besieged Aberdeen late in June and around 1 August it fell to him. Commercial relations with towns and cities across the North Sea were now possible; it will be remembered that on the taking of Berwick, Wallace had wasted no time in inviting traders to visit liberated Scotland. Markets had to be found for the produce of Robert's territories – wool, hides and timber – and Robert's forces were in sore need of weaponry and armour. His nobles too would have been clamouring for those luxury goods that differentiated them from their followers: high-quality clothing, furs and wine. More important in the long-term was the diplomatic window on the wider world that Aberdeen provided. Robert was enabled to open diplomatic relations with King Philip the Fair of France. Within a year of the capture of Aberdeen Philip had abandoned recognition of John Balliol and had written to Edward II describing Robert as King of Scots.

Possession of this first port enabled the Scots to forge crucial alliances with seagoing peoples. Robert received only diplomatic support from France, but the towns of the North Sea could supply him with war materials in return for Scottish wool. German merchants from the Hanseatic cities of eastern Germany, known as Eastlanders, and Flemish traders had resented the interruptions war had brought to the Scottish trade, and they were keen for it to resume. Since 1303 France and England had been at peace, which had left each of these large kingdoms free to attack its smaller neighbours. While England attacked Scotland, France was free to pressurise the Flemish towns, particularly Ghent and Bruges, which were centres of the European cloth-making industry. On the seas, the Scots and Flemings made common cause, co-operating in attacks on English vessels, and running the English blockade of Scottish ports. Through Aberdeen, the territories under Robert's sway traded wool for arms and foodstuffs supplied by the Flemings and Germans. The North Sea trade between independent Scotland and the continent had already been an irritant to Edward I; to Edward II, it was to become an open wound.

As early as April 1305 Edward I had suspected the Flemings of sustaining Scottish revolt. However, privateering on the North Sea by the Scots, Flemings and Eastlanders began in earnest from about 1308, just before the capture of Aberdeen. In that year the English tried to impose a blockade on independent Scotland, but given the distances involved this was almost impossible for them to enforce. In October 1309 Edward II complained to the count of Flanders and the city of Bruges that Flemish merchants had been trading with the Scots and their partners, the Eastlanders. Robert issued formal 'letters of marque', authorising Scottish crews to attack English vessels. Typically the privateers would commandeer or rob an English ship of its cargo of wool, and take the wool to Aberdeen. There they would remove the seal of the English customs known as the cocket, the proof that duty had been paid, and replace it with either the Scottish cocket or with the seal of a Flemish trader operating in England. This then enabled the privateers to sell the stolen English wool legitimately on the continent. Early in 1311 the notorious Flemish privateer John Crabbe robbed two ships leaving Newcastle with eighty-nine sacks of wool, and disposed of them in exactly this fashion.

After the capture of Aberdeen, Robert turned south-west to confront Argyll in August 1308. At some point in the summer James Douglas rejoined the king. With Buchan dead, John of Argyll was certainly the most virulent in resistance to the Bruces, but he had been confined to bed with illness for months. He will have striven to build a coalition against Bruce, but most lords, himself included, were parochial in outlook and sought first and foremost the security of their own lands and incomes. On the approach of Bruce, John assembled a significant force of men and galleys and prepared an ambush on the slopes of Ben Cruachan. The exact site of the battle is in dispute – it was formerly known as the battle of Brander Pass – but John's force waited high on the slopes of the mountain to attack Robert's army as it passed between the mountain and either Loch Awe or the sea at Loch Etive. Robert however, had anticipated the ambush and secretly sent Douglas higher up the slopes still with a force of archers. John directed the Argyll men from a galley on the sea loch, but when his men attacked by rolling boulders down the hill as Robert's main force passed below, they found themselves caught between Robert's and Douglas's forces. They were forced to take flight and they scrambled downhill for the bridge over the River Awe, intending to break it down once across. But Robert's men were hot on their heels and caught up with and slaughtered the enemy and drove off their cattle. Barbour, Fordun and other chroniclers state that Dunstaffnage Castle was then captured, but it is now considered that this occurred the following year; instead Robert extracted tribute from Argyll in return for a truce, to last until the English king came to their aid. Afraid that his acceptance of Robert's terms would be interpreted as desertion, John of Argyll wrote afterwards to Edward II explaining the impossibility of his position in face of Robert's strength, assuring him of his loyalty and urging him to lead an army into Scotland. Unsurprisingly John makes no mention of his defeat, and he wildly exaggerates Robert's strength, the better to explain his actions:

> Robert Bruce approached these parts by land and sea with 10,000 men they say, or 15,000. I have no more than 800 men, 500 in my own pay whom I keep continually with me to guard the borders of my territory. The barons of Argyll give me no aid. Yet Bruce asked for a truce, which I granted him for a short space, and I have got a similar truce until you send me help.
>
> I have heard, my lord, that when Bruce came he was boasting and claiming that I had come to his peace, in order to inflate his own reputation so that others would rise more readily in support of him. God forbid it. I certainly do not wish it, and if you hear this from others you are not to believe it; for I shall always be ready to carry out your orders with all my power, wherever and whenever you wish. I have three castles to keep as well as a loch twenty-four miles long, on which I keep and build galleys with trusty men to each galley. I am not sure of my neighbours in any direction.
>
> As soon as you or your army come, then, if my health permits I shall not be found wanting where lands, ships or anything else is concerned, but will come to your service.

In far away Westminster, preoccupied and infatuated, Edward II failed to take the hint, and that Christmas, Edward lost yet another stronghold, Forfar, to Robert.

In other theatres of combat Robert's lieutenants had been active, both on his behalf and in their own interests. When Robert had marched northwards in September 1307 James Douglas had begun to establish himself deep in the Forest of Selkirk. From there he made further efforts to regain his patrimony. With relish Barbour describes how the wily Douglas planned another assault on Douglas Castle. Disguised as a thresher, secretly armed and accompanied by only a few men, he attended the Palm Sunday service at St Bride's Kirk, the chancel of which still stands; the mention of Palm Sunday dates the episode to 7 April 1308. The whole of the garrison except a cook and a porter were present in church 'to carry their palms'. Prematurely one of his men gave out the traditional battle cry 'Douglas!', but Douglas drew his sword and laid into the men of the garrison. In a short time two-thirds of the garrison lay dead or dying. Thirty prisoners surrendered, and Douglas took the castle easily. He entered to find the table laid for the feast. His men ate their fill and then ransacked the building for weapons, armour, treasure and clothing. Before leaving, he beheaded his prisoners and threw their bodies into the cellar. Into the cellar too he emptied all the food he could not carry off:

> He made a foul concoction there,
> For meal and malt and blood and wine
> All ran together into a mush
> That was disgusting to see.

Afterwards he polluted the well with salt and the bodies of dead horses. Finally, he set fire to everything that would burn, abiding by Bruce's policy of denying shelter to the enemy. He split his men into several groups, and they disappeared into the forest by diverse routes. To our minds an appalling atrocity, the 'Douglas Larder' as it became known served the purpose of warning the local population against serving with the enemy.

Having regained his patrimony in Douglasdale, James Douglas was henceforth a constant and reliable ally of Robert. In the Forest of Selkirk he had established a de facto lordship, which in time Robert recognised with grants of land and privilege, and it was to there that he shifted his powerbase. From there he made his reputation as the Black Douglas, renowned for a ruthlessness that struck fear into the hearts of the English.

Douglas was among those who joined Edward Bruce for an equally savage attack on Galloway in the summer of 1308: 'Meanwhile, taking advantage of the quarrels between the king of England and the barons, Edward Bruce, brother of the oftmentioned Robert and Alexander Lindsay, Robert Boyd and James Douglas knights, with their following which they had from the outer isles of Scotland, attacked the people of Galloway, disregarding the tribute which they took from them, and in one day slew many of the gentry of Galloway and made nearly all that region subject to them. Those Gallovidians who could escape came to England to find refuge.' Hebridean galloglass were used for this harrying of Galloway, said to be led by Donald of Islay. This Donald was a leading MacDonald chieftain; he is thought to be a cousin of Angus Óg. It seems that one, or possibly two, bitter battles were fought. The first took place on the banks of the River Dee, at which the Gallovidians put up stout resistance. They were led by the Gallovidian chief Dungal MacCann. MacCann was forced to flee to his fortress of Threave, an island in the River Dee. There he was captured and handed over to Edward Bruce, presumably for execution. The second battle seems to have been fought far to the west on the River Cree, when English reinforcements led by Ingram de Umfraville and Aymer de St John set out to counter-attack. Edward Bruce defeated them too, and they fled to Buittle Castle on the Urr Water. Edward then besieged Buittle but failed to take it. In fact, successful as the campaign was in terms of devastating the countryside and exacting vengeance for the deaths of Thomas and Alexander Bruce, Edward failed to capture any major castle in the south-west. Lochmaben, Tibbers, Loch Doon, Dumfries and many more hostile garrisons survived for another three to five years. No doubt Edward, who bore the titles lord of Galloway from 1309 and earl of Carrick from 1313, took all these castles eventually, but Barbour's statement that he won thirteen castles by force must refer to the whole period 1308–13. Strangely there is no mention of Dungal MacDowall in resisting this attack; we might expect him to have taken a leading role in defending Galloway, and he may well have done despite the chronicles' silence, for in April 1309 he received a grant of a Cumberland manor for his good service, 'whereby he has become hated by the enemy'.

The subjugation of northern Scotland was assured when on 31 October 1308 Ross surrendered utterly to Robert, and in return was permitted to retain his lands and titles. Obviously this sort of arrangement necessitated a mechanism for keeping track of the king's grants and commitments, and it is around this time that evidence emerges that Robert's entourage included a royal bureaucracy. A mandate dated 14 October 1308 is witnessed by 'Sir Bernard the king's chancellor'. This cleric was the head of the king's writing office and part of his job was to keep a record of royal orders and grants of land issued. Bernard the Chancellor probably had long experience of royal diplomatic form, correct forms of protocols and address, methods of sealing and so on. He would certainly have been familiar with the texts and arguments put into the mouth of Boniface VIII by Scottish diplomats in the past, and he may previously have served in the chanceries of King John Balliol and the Guardians. Robert subsequently endowed Bernard with the abbacy of Arbroath in 1311.

Bernard's assistance was therefore invaluable when in January 1309 there arrived from the king of England the earl of Gloucester 'and two other earls' to negotiate a truce. It was a high-powered delegation, and well chosen. The house of Gloucester had been the English family most closely associated with the Bruce affinity and Gloucester and his companions were accompanied by papal and French envoys. Such a delegation may even have been intended to negotiate a lasting peace. This however eluded them, probably because Robert was not prepared to concede sovereignty of Scotland. Terms for a truce, however, were brokered by the emissaries of King Philip of France, who had recently become Edward II's father-in-law. These were as follows: both sides were to return to the positions they occupied at the feast of St James the Apostle – 25 July 1308 – and there would be a cessation of hostilities until All Saints' Day – 1 November 1309. It was just the sort of arrangement that played right into Robert's hand. The English might as well have conceded truce to Midsummer 1310, for they could do nothing until the weather and food supplies permitted campaigning.

Robert however could do plenty. There is no evidence that he blatantly violated the agreement, but the truce did not have a neutral effect. In the localities, perceptions, understandings and loyalties were shifting in Robert's favour. Edward II's supporters were leaderless, bickering, increasingly demoralised and isolated. Robert restored nothing to the enemy, and continued to intimidate and bully vulnerable garrisons and communities loyal to Edward. Time and distance ensured that he was not brought to account. Increasingly the English administration was paralysed by magnate rivalry and the king's preoccupation with keeping his favourite, Piers Gaveston, safe from the hands of the magnates.

On 16 and 17 March 1309 Robert held a parliament at St Andrews. Such a gathering of the higher nobility – common people would not have been represented – was a powerful claim to sovereignty, and a clear statement that an alternative government had been established and demanded obedience. The pretext for summoning such an assembly was to consider a reply to a letter from Philip, requesting that Robert contribute forces to the crusade he was planning; Robert was thus advertising that he had received a letter from the king of France, who had previously sponsored the Balliol cause. The careful crafting of such a reply was, of course, far too important to be left to a large assembly. Bernard the Chancellor would take care of the drafting, but the pretext kept up the fiction that the nobles participated in matters of state. The real purpose of parliaments at that time was to project the majesty of monarchy and thus enhance its legitimacy. Parliament was the fullest expression of kingship, solemn and dignified, the occasion of many grants and mandates. Robert could only have held this assembly in time of truce for, as a mark of their loyalty, lords were expected to leave their estates and attend. Heading the list of those in attendance were the great magnates, the earls of Ross, Lennox and also Sutherland. James the Steward of Scotland was there, and Robert had appointed other great officers of state for the occasion: Gilbert Hay, Constable of Scotland, and Robert Keith, Marischal. Robert's chief lieutenants were there: Edward Bruce, now bearing the title lord of Galloway; James Douglas; and with Donald of Islay rather than Angus Óg representing the MacDonalds. Donald may have ousted Alexander from the chieftainship, and Angus, it seems, had fled to the service of Edward II. Lesser stalwarts were there too: Lindsay, Boyd, Gillespie MacLachlan of the MacRuaridhs and three representatives of the Campbells. Sullen and disaffected, old Alexander MacDougall too had been compelled to attend, but before the year was out he would rejoin his son in the service of Edward II. Present were a number of prominent 'newcomers' to Robert's camp. Robert's nephew, the young Thomas Randolph, lord of Nithsdale, was among them. Earlier he had sounded off to the king about unchivalrous methods of warfare; evidently he had atoned for his contempt. Another noteworthy recent addition was John Stewart of Menteith, to whom Edward I had granted the earldom of Lennox; this title he had surrendered to Robert in return for lands in Knapdale – awarded at the expense of the MacSweeneys – and Arran. Many of the hierarchy would have attended the parliament, including bishops of Dunblane and Dunkeld, and possibly those of Ross, Moray and Brechin. A senior bishop of the Scottish kirk, Robert Wishart of Glasgow, was then a prisoner, yet his seal was appended to the document as though a representative of his were present; William Lamberton of St Andrews may have attended in person, even though Edward II still considered him loyal.

Robert might have used the occasion of the parliament to demand a grant of taxation of these worthies, but it is unlikely that he would have tried to impose such a burden while acutely dependent upon their support. Money might have been forthcoming from the Scottish Church, however. Some £7,000 of clerical subsidies was outstanding from Scotland and had never been paid to collectors, and Robert may have been formally granted this by a council of the clergy that met at the same time as the parliament. This was papal taxation which had been promised by the pope to the king of England. The chances are Robert already had his hands on the money and required only ratification of the status quo.

Opportunity was taken at this assembly to publish a proclamation by a general council of the Scottish clergy in fulsome support of Robert's kingship. This document may have been intended for an international audience, at the general council of the Church which had been summoned for Vienne in 1311. It contained arguments for the independence of Scotland, produced in 1299 and 1301, and authors of these earlier statements of Scottish independence may well have been present at the council. Rehearsing the events of the Great Cause, the Declaration of the Clergy states a myth which Robert was desperate to foster and perpetuate, that 'When there arose a subject of dispute between John Balliol, lately installed as king of Scotland … by the king of England, and the late Robert Bruce of honourable memory, the grandfather of Robert who is now the king, concerning which of them had the better title by right of birth, to inherit rule over the people of Scotland, the faithful people have always believed without hesitation, as they had understood from their ancestors and elders, and held to be the truth, that Robert the grandfather was the true heir, and was to be preferred to all others.' Of course 'the faithful people' represented at the parliament and church council had no such memory; nevertheless they had found a leader who, they believed, might deliver them from foreign occupation and safeguard their Church from subjection to the Archbishop of York, and so they were willing to accept this rewriting of history. The whole point of the declaration, and of the 1309 parliament, was that Robert sought acknowledgement as the 'natural', or divinely appointed, ruler.

A second embassy may have been received during this truce. In August 1309, Richard de Burgh, the earl of Ulster, was sent to western Scotland to reason with his son-in-law. He was paid to set out on the instructions of Piers Gaveston, who was then lord lieutenant of Ireland, and with an impressive following of Irish magnates, men-at-arms, hobelars (troopers mounted on a 'hobin': a pony or hackney) and 3,000 foot. His mission was perhaps to intimidate as much as to persuade. The expedition, intended to be the western arm of a general invasion, was postponed and then diverted to defence of the Isle of Man. That same month Bruce was in the far north at Loch Broom, where he can only have been collecting men and ships from his MacRuaridh allies for another assault on Argyll. A charter dated 20 October shows that he was again at Dunstaffnage. On this occasion he had indeed captured the castle. Alexander MacDougall, now evicted from his ancestral pile, fled to England and eventually joined his son John of Argyll in Ireland.

The truce with Edward II was now drawing to a close. Cumberland gentry were ordered to go to their border demesnes, either in preparation for the resumption of hostilities, or to protect them against raiding that was already taking place. On expiry of the truce in November 1309, Robert increased the pressure on garrisons and communities loyal to Edward II but, as was his wont, he was prepared to be bought off. In December 1309 Edward advised his commanders at Ayr, Perth, Dundee and Banff, probably in response to increasingly desperate pleas for assistance, to do likewise by taking what truce they could until Whitsun, 7 June 1310. That was the earliest conceivable date by which an English army would appear in Scotland. These castles could at least be provisioned by sea, but others inland were more vulnerable to siege, and to the pleas of their garrisons Edward's government turned a deaf ear. Even commanders at Berwick and Carlisle agreed a truce until 14 January 1310, and money was paid to Robert as part of these deals. Edward's commanders succeeded in getting a general truce, intended to title them to the campaigning season, but it was practically worthless. Early that summer a delegation of loyal Scottish magnates wrote to Edward II and advised him that unless he set out for the north in person all would be lost in Scotland. In July orders were at last issued for a general muster of the English host: 'Since the king's enemies the Scots, to whom he had granted a truce, contrary to the form of that truce, daily take from him castles, towns and lands, as he understands from men in his service in these parts, he has resolved to be at Berwick in person at the Nativity of Our Lady next [8 September] with horses and arms as powerfully as he can.' But it was not the pleas of the loyal Scots that had forced Edward to attend to his duty, rather it was outrage at royal misrule in England.

Edward had made lavish grants to his hated favourites. He had over-exploited the royal prerogative of 'prise', which allowed the king arbitrarily to seize goods as the itinerant court needed them and to defer payment for them. Heavy taxation had been levied on the pretext of Scottish war, with nothing yet achieved. It was scarcely surprising that a committee of the baronage, known as the Lords Ordainer, had been appointed to take government out of the king's hand for the time being and to regulate his household. Edward deeply resented what he saw as usurpation of his rights. He intended his Scottish campaign of 1310–11 to take the wind out of opposition sails, and to undermine reform at home. The campaign also had the virtue that he could keep his beloved Piers Gaveston by his side and safe from the hands of magnates.

Since the campaign suited all these domestic purposes, Edward at last showed a resolve to confront Robert. All did not go well, however, and elaborate plans for a landing in Argyll had to be called off on account of unseasonal weather. As a result of Gaveston's presence, many of the English magnates boycotted the campaign, and Edward rode north with only three earls at his side: Gloucester, Warrene and Gaveston himself as earl of Cornwall. At the end of September 3,000 infantry mustered at Berwick, most of whom were Welsh. The cavalry comprised the royal household of 50 knights and 200 squires or men-at-arms, plus the contingents of the earls – who traditionally did not accept royal wages and therefore do not figure in the accounts.

In the face of such odds Robert kept well to the north. On 4 September he was rumoured to be at Perth, where he had made a truce until Michaelmas with the beleagured garrison. Douglas remained in the Forest of Selkirk, avoiding confrontation when the English came looking for him. On 1 September Edward advanced from Wark into the valley of the Tweed, in businesslike fashion. It being late in the year, he was able only to consolidate his grip on accessible parts of southern Scotland, replenishing and reorganising the garrisons of southern Scotland. He visited Roxburgh and the peel of Selkirk, vital for checking Scottish activity in the forest. From the main army, raiding parties sallied into its thick cover. The author of the *Vita Edwardi Secundi* recounts what happened to one such party:

> One day, when some English and Welsh, always ready for plunder, had gone out on a raid, accompanied for protection by many horsemen from the army, Robert Bruce's men, who had been concealed in caves and in the woodlands, made a serious attack on our men. Our horsemen, seeing that they could not help the infantry, returned to the main force with a frightful uproar; all immediately leapt to arms and hastened with one accord to help those who had been left amongst the enemy; but assistance came too late to prevent the slaughter of our men ... Before our knights arrived up to three hundred Welsh and English had been slaughtered, and the enemy

returned to their caves. From such ambushes our men often suffered heavy losses.

Later in the month, a letter from Edward's spies informed him that Robert's army was located on a moor near Stirling. It seems that as early as this Robert had decided that, if he had to make a stand and offer battle, he would fight in that location. However, in 1310, it did not come to that.

Edward's army then proceeded by way of Biggar to Linlithgow – the vital staging-post between Edinburgh and Stirling – and across Lothian to Renfrew. Then Edward retired to Linlithgow and Edinburgh, and thence by sea to Berwick by the beginning of November. Such were the difficulties of finding forage for animals in the winter that further campaigning was not possible. The infantry returned home, their forty days' service completed, and the royal court settled down into winter quarters at Berwick. At this point Robert's forces returned to harass the garrisons.

Remaining over the winter on Scottish soil was not so much a statement of Edward's determination to reduce Scotland to his obedience as an admission of his fears associated with returning to England: fears of facing further sanctions imposed by the magnates or parliament, or of banishment of his favourite, Gaveston. The English expedition had been hamstrung by the refusal of the English earls to participate fully in the war. Even Gloucester and Warrene made the political point of wintering just across the border, on English soil and so not technically on the king's service. Edward's new and vociferous opponent, Thomas of Lancaster, arrived to do homage for two of the five earldoms which he had inherited, but refused to cross the Tweed – that is, to leave the kingdom – to perform the service. The king of England was humiliated into making the crossing himself.

Against this background, the English chronicles are surely correct to take the view that Edward was considering making a deal with Robert which would allow him to face down this domestic opposition. He did make contact with Robert at this time; from a letter written the following February it seems that two royalist nobles, Robert Clifford and Robert fitz Payne had their king's permission to meet with Robert at Selkirk on 17 December 1310. We do not know whether the meeting took place. Subsequently, Gloucester and Gaveston were to have met Robert near Melrose Abbey, but Robert was warned of treachery and did not show up. Either of those arrangements might have been for straightforward parley with the enemy. But a third suggests that Edward II was trying to reach a private arrangement with Robert behind the backs of his baronage. In February a high-ranking clerk of the English chancery, John Walwayn, was arrested and thrown in prison 'because he suddenly went towards those parts to speak with Robert Bruce'. That same month Edward sent Gaveston with 200 men to strengthen the Perth garrison, which, together with Dundee, now marked the farthest limit of the English occupation. Gloucester and Warenne meanwhile penetrated the Forest of Selkirk, where Douglas found it easy to avoid confrontation.

Robert did not confront the powerful English earls, but instead punished the weaker and more vulnerable of his adversaries in the west. That December, rumour at the English court had it that he had assembled a galley fleet in the Western Isles and intended to attack Man. In February he was said to be marching towards Galloway. As winter turned to spring Edward became desperate to raise an army, but in the teeth of stout opposition from the English magnates this was virtually impossible. John of Argyll had visited the court over the winter, and appears to have persuaded Edward, now clinging to any straw to avoid a humiliating return to England, that he could raise a large army in Ireland. Accordingly orders for the raising of improbably large forces in Ireland were issued, with John at their head, and a fleet of sixty-two English and Irish ships were to ferry this army to Ayr. Edward put great store by this plan, calling it 'one of the greatest movements of the Scottish war'. The ports, however, refused to supply the ships, and the plan was largely abandoned.

John of Argyll did succeed in mustering some sort of force however. Three letters to Edward II, from a fleet anchored at Bute and Kintyre, have recently been re-dated to September 1310. The letters are from Hugh Bisset, Angus Óg MacDonald and John MacSweeney. Bisset commands this fleet, and he seeks the king's instructions. Angus Óg had been alienated from Robert's service by the dominance among the MacDonalds of his rival Donald of Islay and, for the moment, Angus had switched his allegiance to Edward II. He asks Edward to command the co-operation of Alexander MacDougall of Argyll who, we can well believe, was slow to work with any MacDonald. John MacSweeney was the head of a galloglass kinship which had recently been ejected from its ancestral lands in Knapdale. Castle Sween was presumably their ancestral pile. In July 1310, Edward II had granted the land of Knapdale to John and the two other sons of Sweeney if they could recover it from John Stewart of Menteith, enemy and rebel, who had come into Robert's peace by 1309. MacSweeney complains to Edward II that John of Argyll, the king's admiral, has captured Argyll but on behalf of John of Menteith. The letters demonstrate the vulnerability of Robert's western flank to interference from Ireland. MacSweeney clearly believed that John of Argyll had the power to deliver Knapdale into his own hands, and begged Edward II to write to him and make him do so. The MacSweeney descent on Knapdale is also somewhat imaginatively celebrated in a Gaelic praise-poem, which describes the voyage of his mailed galloglass to retake Castle Sween. Here is a taste of it:

> Who is this by whom the fleet is sailed against the Castle of Sweeny of Slieve Truim?
>
> A sinewy man who could not avoid arrows, one of the two piercing lances of the region of Conn.

It is John MacSweeney who is the commander of their fleet on the
surface of the sea, a hardy leader;
　　The masts of his ships are exceedingly precipitous in height, the
wave will test them in an ocean of summits.

John has made a happy landfall in the bosom of Knapdale, at the
end of an ocean voyage;
　　The thick-cropped, fortress-possessing, handsome eyebrow,
with many masts and heroes, a vigorous man with a warrior's moon.

In the poem, MacSweeney is welcomed to Knapdale by poets, and
the castle is joyously surrendered to its rightful lord. In reality,
although MacSweeney claimed in his letter to have seen and
visited his lands, he gained no permanent foothold. The episode
illustrates how enormously difficult was Robert's task of dislodging
the MacDougalls and their allies from their ancestral lands. It is
hard to believe that MacDougall influence was fully extirpated
from Argyll during Robert's reign, even though by 1318 the king of
Argyll is reported to be a MacDonald. The poem, a narrow window
on the Gaelic west, is also instructive in that it reminds us that
this whole western dimension of Robert's long war goes virtually
unrecorded in the English royal records upon which we are so
heavily dependent.

Edward II, then, obtained some service in the west in 1311; from
England, however, he obtained virtually none. He tried to raise troops
through a totally novel and unparliamentary levy of one foot soldier
from every village in England, but to little effect. With no troops and
no money there was nothing he could do at the end of July 1311
but summon the English parliament and leave Berwick with a bad
grace. In August 1311 Edward was forced to accept the *diktat* of the
Lords Ordainer, known as 'the Ordinances', which imposed upon his
household a series of unpalatable reforms and restrictions. Edward
II's worst fears were realised when Gaveston was seized and executed

by the English magnates on 19 June 1312. Thus the English baronial opposition had played into Robert's hands. It would be interesting to know whether Robert had any contact with them, but at this date that seems unlikely. He had, rather, judged wisely and allowed events to take their course. In seeing off Edward, Robert had not merely survived the great test of English invasion, he had triumphed in all but name. The lords of the Scottish opposition had longed for Edward to lead an army into Scotland; when that army had come and gone, many would have read the writing on the wall.

7

The road to Bannockburn
(1311–14)

In the aftermath of Edward II's withdrawal from Berwick, two powerful themes begin to dominate the narrative: the raiding of England, and the capture of Scottish towns and castles. The two are more closely connected than they might first appear. The raiding of England and the extraction of tribute from her terrified and defenceless northern communities provided Robert with the funds to pay his soldiery to undertake prolonged sieges of castles and walled towns. Scottish subjects were custom-bound to serve their king unpaid for only forty days; for anything beyond that the king had to pay. Lucrative raiding opportunities must also have provided a carrot, enticing Scottish aristocrats to adhere to the Bruce cause; the stick keeping them in line was the destruction of not just enemy-held castles but virtually all castles, privately held or royal. As we have seen, it was a matter of policy for Robert to deprive Scottish nobles of the luxury of choosing between allegiances from within the safety of private castles. Thus Robert's civil war against the opposition nobles was intimately connected with his patriotic war against the English.

On the departure of the English court from Berwick, Robert seized the initiative and mounted two devastating raids on the north of England. The first, which lasted from 12 to 20 August 1311 is narrated by the English *Lanercost* chronicler: 'having collected a great army, he [Robert] entered England at Solway on the Thursday before the feast of the Assumption; and he burned all the land of Gilsland and the vill of Haltwhistle and a great part of Tynedale, and after eight days he returned to Scotland, taking with him a great booty of animals; nevertheless he had killed few men apart from those who wished to defend themselves by resistance.' The following month, Robert again invaded England:

> About the feast of the Nativity of the Blessed Virgin [8 September], Robert returned with an army into England, directing his march towards Northumberland, and passing by Harbottle and Holystone and Redesdale, he burnt the district around Corbridge, destroying everything; also he caused more men to be killed than on the former occasion. And so he turned into the valleys of the North and South Tyne, laying waste those parts which he had previously spared, and returned into Scotland after fifteen days; nor could the wardens whom the king of England had stationed on the marches oppose so great a force of Scots as he brought with him.

These expeditions were of a different order to the cross-border cattle raids that Douglas and others had inflicted on the western march since 1307. Robert was apparently leading large infantry forces and systematically laying waste enemy territory, as he had done at the herschip of Buchan. For his followers the plundering was a useful reward that increased loyalty, but the troops could not keep everything they captured. Traditionally one third of the plunder and any prisoners taken had to be handed over to the lord. Extraction of money seems to have been Robert's main objective at this stage, for he showed himself quite willing to be bought off. Following these raids the Northumbrians sent envoys to negotiate a truce, and they agreed to pay £2,000 until 2 February 1312. The men of the earldom of Dunbar, still of the king of England's peace, also paid a heavy fine for a truce to that same date.

The money was needed to prosecute sieges of the east-coast towns of Perth and Dundee, and for increasing military pressure on Berwick.

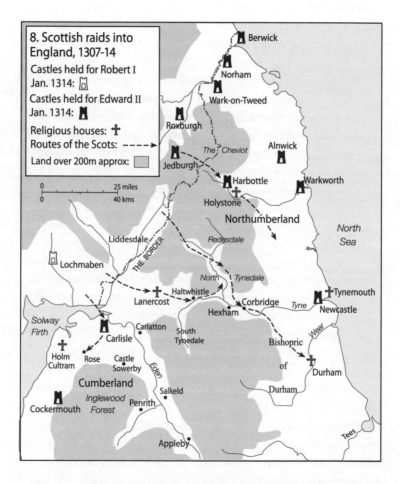

8. Scottish raids into England, 1307–14

Castles held for Robert I Jan. 1314: 🏰

Castles held for Edward II Jan. 1314: 🏰

Religious houses: ✝

Routes of the Scots: ⟶

Land over 200m approx: ▨

0 — 25 miles
0 — 40 kms

Berwick
Norham
Wark-on-Tweed
Roxburgh
The Cheviot
Alnwick
Jedburgh
Harbottle
Warkworth
Holystone
Northumberland
North Sea
Liddesdale
Redesdale
Lochmaben
THE BORDER
North Tynedale
Lanercost
Haltwhistle
Tynemouth
Corbridge
Hexham
Newcastle
Tyne
Carlatton
South Tynedale
Wear
Carlisle
Solway Firth
Holm Cultram
Rose
Castle Sowerby
Bishopric
Eden
Durham
of
Cumberland
Inglewood Forest
Salkeld
Durham
Cockermouth
Penrith
Appleby
Tees

Barbour treats the recovery of castles and walled towns in a special way. As has been pointed out, chronicles were written for entertainment, and some of the most entertaining passages in Barbour are those relating to the capture of the castles of Scotland from 'English' garrisons. More than any other aspect of the narrative they demonstrate how the Scots overcame the vast material wealth and superiority in numbers of their adversaries by deploying *slight*, that is, native wit and cunning. Robert could rarely resort to long sieges, which were expensive and would leave his forces stationary and vulnerable to attack; nor did he have in sufficient number the catapults, battering rams or other machinery that would facilitate taking by storm. Trickery was the Scots' only resource. The pattern was already well established: as early as Christmas night 1308 the castle of Forfar was captured by stealth. 'Philip the Forester' and some others used ladders to scale the wall while the guards slept, and they killed everyone within and handed over the castle to Robert. He then demolished the castle wall and poisoned the well. At Douglas Castle in Lanarkshire in May 1307, as we have seen, they tempted the garrison out with the prospect of robbing a line of packhorses; at Linlithgow in August 1313 they hid in a hay wain which they lodged in the gates of the peel to prevent their closing, springing out to surprise the guards and capture the fortification. Frequently the episode is set on a feast day – Christmas Night, Palm Sunday and Shrove Tuesday are all mentioned – when the sentries were lax or distracted or drunk. Usually Barbour gives a key role to a named folk hero: Tom Dickson planned the ambush of the Douglas Castle garrison in St Bride's Kirk, William Bunnock drove the hay wain in the capture of the peel of Linlithgow, and Syme of Ledhouse made the ingenious rope ladders for scaling the walls of Roxburgh in February 1314. A rivalry emerges between Robert's lieutenants Douglas and Thomas Randolph – who was created earl of Moray in 1312 – as to who could gain most glory in the taking of castles.

In December 1312 Robert made his first attempt to capture Berwick: the first of many. Berwick was at once the largest and richest town in Scotland; the administrative and military centre of the English occupation; the locale of the English supply operation; and the key strategic position that controlled access to the rich Northumberland coastal plain. Bruce's night-time attempt to scale the walls by way of rope ladders was, however, foiled by a barking dog 'just as old geese saved Rome by their gaggle'. Robert was forced to turn to lesser targets, but in the meantime the depredations of the enemy garrisons of Lothian were doing his work for him. Neglected by Edward II, low on morale and desperate for provisions, they raided the surrounding countryside mercilessly, causing loyal Scottish gentry such as Adam Gordon to protest to Edward II that the sympathies of country people were being alienated by rampaging garrisons.

Robert had Dundee under siege from February 1312. Edward II was anxious to keep the town at all costs, and he forbade an agreement which the commander, William de Montefichet, had reached with Robert, that Dundee should be surrendered in exchange for return of English prisoners. Instead, ships and barges along the east coast were collected to ferry heavily armoured infantry to Dundee, but at last, in April, Montefichet was forced to surrender, and his garrison was permitted to leave for Perth. Robert's possession of Dundee, however, made the supply of Perth by sea all the more difficult for the Scottish opposition and English.

The chronicles agree that Robert invaded England next in mid August:

> Having assembled a great army, he invaded England about the feast of the Assumption of the Blessed Virgin [15 August 1312] and burned the towns of Hexham and Corbridge and the western parts, and took booty and much spoil and prisoners, nor was there anyone who dared to resist. While he halted in peace and safety near Corbridge, he sent a part of his army as far as Durham, which, arriving there suddenly on market day, carried off all that was found

in the town, and gave a great part of it to the flames, cruelly killing all who opposed them.

The next day 'despairing of help from the king of England', the men of the bishopric of Durham and those of Northumberland each agreed to pay the Scots £2,000 for peace until Midsummer 1313. The deal with the men of Durham was struck at Hexham on 16 August. The communities of Westmorland, Copeland and Cumberland 'redeemed themselves in a similar way' and, though they did not have the cash to give straightaway, they surrendered the sons of the chief lords as hostages. In the English counties the normal machinery of regular taxation seems to have been employed to collect these blackmail payments, but the rate at which Robert exacted this tribute from England was ruinous. The £2,000 which Northumberland paid to Robert in 1311 was double the amount it had yielded to the king of England in 1296, and Northumberland was made to pay the same amount the very next year.

Coffers replenished, Robert redoubled his efforts to capture Perth. This was a difficult task, for Perth was protected on the landward side by the River Tay and by a ditch. The defenders were led by Sir William Oliphant, Montefichet, and the earl of Strathearn. Oliphant was the same man who had valiantly defended Stirling Castle to the last in 1304; this is at once an indication that Robert was up against experienced veterans of siege warfare, and a salutary reminder that many patriotic Scots did not approve of the Bruce regime. The siege also illustrates that aristocratic families were often divided in their allegiances: while Strathearn was defending the town, his son and heir was at Robert's side attacking it. Barbour describes how Robert tested the bed of the ditch with a long pole to find out where it was shallowest, and at last found a place where men could wade across, though the water was shoulder high. At the end of December he had his men pack up their equipment and feign retirement from the siege, but eight days later they crept back in dead of night with a small force carrying ladders. It was the night of 7/8 January 1313. They listened carefully, but heard no noise from sentries. Then 'to show an example to his men', the king shouldered his ladder and slipped into the icy water, and, using his spear to prod the bed of the moat, waded across the ditch. In admiration, Barbour puts the following words into the mouth of a French knight witnessing Robert's actions:

> Ah, Lord, what shall we say
> Of our French lords,
> Always stuffing their bellies with good food,
> Willing only to eat and drink and dance,
> When such a knight, so noble
> As this one, by his chivalry
> Has put himself in such danger
> To win a wretched hamlet.

The king, Barbour says, was the second man to scale the town wall. The French knight may be a device, employed by Barbour to reflect upon the king's bravery, but Robert's energetic participation in the attack on Perth is borne out by other sources. Taken entirely by surprise, the townsfolk put up no fight, and, though there was widespread spoliation, few were slain as a result. The walls and towers of the town's defences were then destroyed. Strathearn, arrested by his own son and heir, was taken into the peace of King Robert, another earldom brought onside.

In the summer of 1313 Robert had only to make threatening noises for northern England to pay up. In the run-up to midsummer, when the truce would lapse, the Northumbrians wrote to Edward II pleading for aid. Their king replied characteristically by ordering the men of Northumberland to do their best to defend the county against the Scots. In June it was reported that the Scots were ready to attack in three places on the March, and on 5 August the bishop of Durham excused himself from parliament saying that Robert Bruce 'has of late caused a great host to be assembled'. To stave off disaster, the northern English counties negotiated for a third year, and Northumberland, Westmorland, Cumberland 'and other borderers' offered large sums for a truce, to last until 29 September 1314. We know that on this occasion Cumberland was forced to pay 2,000 marks (£1,466), because Edward II subsequently ordered that collection of the money should be audited. From this audit we see how the burden was allocated to the different wards and lordships of that county; the generous sums allowed for maintenance of the hostages – sons of local knights; the hefty expenses claimed by the collectors, who were local gentry; and the sweeteners paid. These last included twenty measures of oaten flour to King Robert and £12 in cash, a salmon and two measures of wine to Brother Robert de Morton, King Robert's attorney.

To us it is remarkable that, as an alternative to providing protection, Edward II was prepared to countenance the buying of private or local agreements with his enemy. 'No deals with terrorists' is a dictum to which all modern states subscribe. Edward II may similarly have considered that his royal dignity was being compromised by agreements between local communities loyal to him and hostile Scots. Yet he tolerated and even encouraged them for two reasons. Firstly, since the local commanders or local communities paid for them, they were cheaper than campaigning, and secondly, they saved him from having to compromise on domestic issues in return for parliamentary taxation which he needed to mount a campaign. But, as Edward discovered, this method of staving off enemy attack undermined perception of him as king: it sapped faith and confidence in his lordship, and ultimately encouraged local communities to accept the alternative of Robert's lordship. In 1315 the people of North Tynedale 'gave themselves up completely to the King of Scotland'. As one historian has remarked, by the late 1310s a fifth of Edward's kingdom was paying tribute to Robert. Short-sighted and temporising

Edward II's policy may have been, but he might have recovered all his compromised lordship with a single victory on the battlefield.

Robert did not confine his raids to England. In February 1313, Robert assisted his brother, the new lord of Galloway, in inflicting further punishment upon the Gallovidians. The castles of Buittle, Dalswinton and Dumfries were all taken and destroyed. On 17 May 1313 Robert landed at Ramsey on the Isle of Man 'with a multitude of ships' and besieged the castle of Rushen for five weeks. The enemy commander at Rushen was the Gallovidian Dungal MacDowall. In unleashing this attack, Robert seems to be pursuing a blood feud, typical of a Gaelic warlord. As we have seen, Dungal had captured and handed over for execution Robert's brothers Thomas and Alexander in 1307; he had survived Edward Bruce's assault on Galloway in 1308; in February 1313 he had been driven out of Dumfries Castle and fled to Man; and now, as castellan at Rushen, he seems to have attracted the enmity of Bruces once again. The five-week siege required a widespread search for foodstuffs, and Robert sent galleys to Ulster on the last day of May. 'The Ulstermen resisted them and manfully drove them off. It was said, nevertheless, that Robert landed by licence of the earl [of Ulster] who had taken a truce.' While the earl's position as father-in-law to Robert seems often to have given rise to such suspicions, it is likely that no love was lost between the two men. Robert may have wished to use the opportunity to repay his father-in-law for his troublemaking visit to Argyll in 1309. Rushen fell to the Scots on 12 June, and Robert had it demolished. Dungal seems to have fled to join other Scottish émigrés in Ireland, to which place the vengeance of the Bruces would pursue him yet.

In the North Sea theatre of war, the Scottish privateers continued their co-operation with Flemish and Eastlander merchants against English vessels. As Robert captured further east-coast ports – Dundee in 1312, Perth in 1313 and Edinburgh in 1314 – the English blockade became progressively unenforceable. English ships began to sail in convoys for safety. Tension between the English government and

Robert, Count of Flanders, mounted as the English demanded sterner measures against the privateers, and the count protested his inability to hinder legitimate trade. In 1311 the English seized three Flemish-owned vessels near Aberdeen in Scotland for supplying the Scots. In reprisal, English merchants in Flanders were arrested. English vessels supplying Scottish castles also fell prey to the privateers. From 1311 protracted talks between the two governments tried to repair relations, but these were abandoned in 1313. Incidents continued to occur: in the estuary of the Schelde three Flemish-owned ships sailing from Hull to Flanders were attacked, with English merchants claiming to have lost £4,000 in wool, cash, and other commodities in the shipment. Five English merchants travelling with the convoy were taken as captives to Aberdeen and sold to the Scots. In return for stolen wool, the Scots acquired arms and foodstuffs. On 1 May 1313 Edward II wrote to Count Robert complaining of the activities of the now notorious John Crabbe, and alleging that a convoy of thirteen Flemish ships laden with arms and foodstuffs had lately departed for Scotland from the port of Zwyn. Edward II then played a trump card: he denied the Flemish towns direct access to English wool, by establishing a staple, or exclusive trading post, at St Omer in Artois, outside Flanders and in the French sphere of influence. English wool would henceforth be taken heavily guarded and in convoy to this staple port, and Flemish merchants would have to pay a higher price for their raw material. Even so, privateering on the North Sea continued: at Michaelmas 1314 another English ship was captured, and a wool merchant of Beverley and his son were abducted.

In 1312 Robert repaired diplomatic relations between Scotland and Norway. Influential in the North Sea and more especially in the Western Isles, Norway remained important to Scotland's wider interests. Robert's sister Isabel had married King Eric II. Eric had died in 1299, but Isabel continued to live there as dowager queen until 1358. By an agreement sealed at Inverness in October 1312

Robert undertook responsibility for payment of the annual 100-mark tribute due to Norway. In 1266 Alexander III had promised to pay this sum annually in return for Norway's ceding of the Western Isles to the kingdom of Scotland. With money extracted from northern England, Robert could afford to square up to this foreign commitment, proving to North Sea traders that Scotland was a safe and reliable country with which to do business.

Commercial and diplomatic relations were only one of a number of problems distracting Edward II from the task of shoring up his deteriorating military position in Scotland. A new development however sent Scotland to the top of his priorities. At an assembly at Dundee on 21–24 October 1313 Robert issued an ultimatum to those Scots who still refused to acknowledge his kingship. Although hostilities would continue, those who submitted to him within one year might be allowed to retain their lands and titles. Having taken Linlithgow, and severed communications between Stirling and Edinburgh, he was now in a powerful position to threaten Lothian, and considered that by this well-advertised ultimatum he might tear the heart out of the Scottish resistance. This decree – so tempting to the remaining opposition lords – ensured that the king of England would at last bestir himself and lead an army into Scotland, and in November the English administration set the wheels in motion for a full-scale invasion of Scotland the following summer.

As 1314 opened, the English remained in control of four main garrisons – Edinburgh, Roxburgh, Stirling and Berwick – and still had possession of several lesser strengths. Early in 1314 the earl of Moray set about besieging Edinburgh Castle. Barbour relates that the castle was well provisioned, but that the garrison commander, the Gascon Sir Piers Lubaud, came under suspicion of wanting to betray the castle. His men clapped him in irons and imprisoned him, and appointed an English constable to take charge. The siege wore on until March and still Moray had made no progress, as the garrison did not want for food. Hearing of Douglas's success at Roxburgh however, he offered a reward to any of his men who might be able to scale the cliff and the castle wall, and one man came forward. This folk hero was William Francis, who in his youth had been in the castle and had learned to climb down the rock at night to visit a girlfriend in the town. Accordingly, on the night of 14 March, Moray and thirty of his men set off to follow William Francis's ascent of the rock:

> The night was dark, as I heard tell,
> And soon they came to the foot of the rock
> Which was high and sheer.
> Then before them William Francis
> Climbed in the clefts
> Always the first among them
> And they followed him at the back;
> With great difficulty, sometimes to, sometimes fro
> They climbed in the clefts
> Thus until they had climbed half the crag.

At the foot of the wall they used a ladder, and gained the parapet. After a bloody battle the assailants took possession of the castle. They discovered Piers Lubaud in the dungeon. Piers did homage to Robert and became his liegeman. True to form, Edinburgh Castle too was demolished to deny it to the English occupation, 'lest the English ever afterwards might lord it over the land by holding castles'.

Moray's capture of Edinburgh had been inspired by Douglas's success in taking Roxburgh. Barbour states that Douglas had rope ladders, similar to those used at Berwick two years previously, made specially for the task. These ladders were 'of wonderful construction', and much admired by the English chronicler who inspected them in person and at close quarters at Berwick. On Shrove Tuesday – 19 February 1314 – Douglas and his company crawled up to the wall and used a lance to place a grappling crook in the embrasure. The clatter was heard by the sentry, but too late, for the Scots had mounted the wall. They surprised the large garrison, who were making merry in the hall, and killed until it was clear that they had the upper hand. A small party led by the warden, Guillemin de Fiennes, retreated to a tower where they continued resistance. But the next day Fiennes was wounded fending off an assault, and, in return for life and limb for the defenders, he surrendered the tower. Edward Bruce was sent especially to destroy the castle; he and his men 'knocked to the ground the whole of that beautiful castle, just as they did other castles'.

In March Robert began putting pressure on Stirling to surrender, and in mid May Edward Bruce made an arrangement with the commander of Stirling: unless the English army came within three leagues the castle, within eight days of 24 June, the castellan Sir Philip Mowbray would surrender it. Edward Bruce's prominence at this time, indeed the prominence of all three of Robert's lieutenants – Edward, Douglas and Moray – might suggest that Robert was once more temporarily ill. Edward Bruce had also invaded the Western March in the middle of April 1314, and stayed three days at the manor of Rose, which belonged to the Bishop of Carlisle. He pillaged and burnt a number of towns and two churches, taking many prisoners and driving off a great number of cattle from Inglewood Forest. This was because the men of that march had failed to keep up their payments of tribute.

Only the threat of a complete collapse of the English position in Scotland had stirred the English king into action, and some of his nobles into grudging co-operation. Two of the four key Scottish castles had already fallen that spring: Roxburgh in February 1314, Edinburgh in March. For the coming campaign Edward II called up 10,000 infantry – including 3,000 Welsh – with additional writs of array demanding masons, carpenters and smiths. Clearly he was expecting to besiege and retake castles that had fallen to Robert. A further 10,000 troops were ordered up, chiefly from northern England, which had been laid waste and taxed to ruin by the Scots. Though

Edward knew well that 20,000 men would not turn out, this doubling of the call-out is indicative of his determination to overwhelm the Scots. Full wardrobe books survive for many of Edward I's Scottish campaigns, but one could not be compiled for the Bannockburn campaign since the records were lost in the rout. We are therefore forced to estimate. For the main thrust of attack along the Eastern March perhaps 10,000 infantry mustered for battle. The army lacked the full quota of cavalry as the earls of Lancaster and Warwick and their allies again refused to serve in person and sent only knights to perform the strict terms of their service. But the royal household provided the kernel of the heavy cavalry force, and, in addition, the 'royalist' earls of Gloucester, Hereford and Pembroke brought their contingents of knights and men-at-arms. Other powerful magnates present included Robert Clifford, Henry Beaumont, Pain Typtoft and John Segrave. Scots who rode with Edward included Robert Umfraville, earl of Angus; John Comyn, son and heir of the murdered John Comyn; Sir Edmund Comyn of Kilbride; and Sir Ingram de Umfraville. An English chronicler states that Edward had 2,000 horse; allowing for the chronicler's exaggeration 1,000 seems reasonable. Sensible provision was made for the presence of a large English army. A Genoese merchant banker was employed to ensure that enough grain was stored at the twin provision depots of Berwick and Carlisle. As in 1311 there was to be a simultaneous campaign on the western approaches to Scotland: the earl of Ulster was to lead 27 Anglo-Irish lords, 25 Gaelic Irish chiefs and 4,000 foot. John of Argyll – who must have savoured the prospect – was to lead the fleet. While it is not at all clear how this arm of the campaign proceeded, the earl of Ulster at least linked up with the royal army.

What could Robert pit against this formidable array? The Scottish cavalry were led by the hereditary marischal, Sir Robert Keith. They were vastly inferior in numbers and quality. At a stretch there might have been 500 Scottish horse, but it seemed they played no part in the battle. While the English knights rode large specially bred chargers called *destriers*, many of the Scots were probably mounted on light 'hackneys' or 'hobbies'. It is estimated that Robert mustered 5,000–6,000 infantry. He was at least contemplating the possibility of a pitched battle.

The relief of Stirling became urgent as the English royal army approached Scotland. At Newminster in Northumberland on 27 May, Edward II stated that the Scots could be expected to assemble 'in strongholds and morasses between us and our castle of Stirling'. An English chronicle relates that the host proceeded by forced marches: 'Brief were the halts for sleep, briefer still for food; hence horses, horsemen and infantry were worn out with toil and hunger.' Entering Scotland, resplendent with heraldic banners and trappings, the English vanguard, led by the earls of Gloucester and Hereford, was a colourful and awe-inspiring sight:

> The sun was shining bright and clear
> And arms that were newly polished
> Flashed in the sun's rays
> In such a way that the whole land was aflame with
> Banners fluttering right freshly
> And pennants waving in the wind.

The great host proceeded to Edinburgh, and occupied the town. The slighted castle afforded little comfort, but the harbour at Leith was useful for unloading provisions. The following day the vanguard set out towards Falkirk and Stirling.

Despite the lack of an English royal wardrobe book, the sources for Bannockburn are plentiful by comparison with other major battles. That blessing creates the difficulty of reconciling what are often conflicting accounts, as the various eyewitnesses recorded different aspects and episodes of the battle. We have three good chronicle accounts from the English, at least two of which were based upon eyewitness accounts. However, in the topography described there are two forests – Torwood and New Park – two approach roads – the road running north towards Stirling from Denny, which corresponds to the modern A80, and the road from Falkirk and Larbert, corresponding to the modern A9 – and two churches – the church of St Ninian, a mile south of Stirling Castle, and the chapel at Larbert, two miles north of Falkirk; deciding upon the precise meaning of references to places is thus fraught with difficulty. We have a rough idea of the general whereabouts of the battle: Barrow and Duncan share a very similar idea as to the location of the main engagement on 24 June. Artefacts from the period, possibly connected with the battle, have been discovered in that vicinity; recently, during the course of a BBC archaeology programme, two pieces of stirrup were discovered, and in 2004 a 'bodkin', or armour-piercing arrowhead was unearthed. The archaeologists have done well: the field was picked clean immediately after the battle by the Scottish camp followers. In the run-up to the 700th anniversary of the battle, strenuous efforts were made to locate the site of the main engagement, but still no consensus has emerged among the authorities. The only thing that would definitely establish the site of the engagement would be the discovery of a mass grave.

In the Barbour narrative the course of the battle is central, representing the key vindication of the hero-king's struggle, and Barbour has not resisted embroidering the narrative with anecdotes and material to entertain a courtly audience. Consequently his account of the battle occupies three books of *The Bruce*. Robert assembled his host at the Torwood, which was a forest stretching either side of the road to Stirling, between the Tor Burn and the River Carron. Understandably, Robert appears to have been racked by indecision: to fight or flee? And if to fight, where and how? At first he decided to make a stand on the Tor Burn. He divided his army into three: Moray was to lead the vanguard, Edward Bruce the second division and he himself the third. Barbour records a fourth division led by Walter the Steward and Douglas, but since the English chronicles all record three it seems that Barbour invented a fourth to

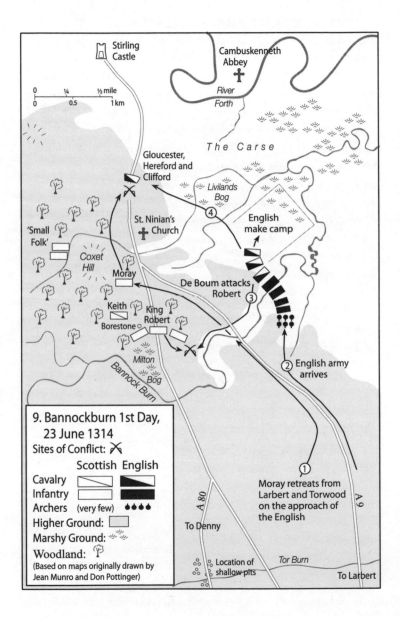

Stirling Castle

Cambuskenneth Abbey

River Forth

0   ¼   ½ mile
0   0.5   1 km

The Carse

Gloucester, Hereford and Clifford

Livilands Bog

'Small Folk'

St. Ninian's Church

English make camp

④

Coxet Hill

Moray

De Boum attacks Robert

③

Keith

King Robert

Borestone

English army arrives

②

Milton Bog

Bannock Burn

9. Bannockburn 1st Day, 23 June 1314

Sites of Conflict: ✗

Scottish English

Cavalry

Infantry

Archers   (very few) ●●●●

Higher Ground:

Marshy Ground:

Woodland:

(Based on maps originally drawn by Jean Munro and Don Pottinger)

①

Moray retreats from Larbert and Torwood on the approach of the English

A 80

To Denny

Location of shallow pits

Tor Burn

To Larbert

A 9

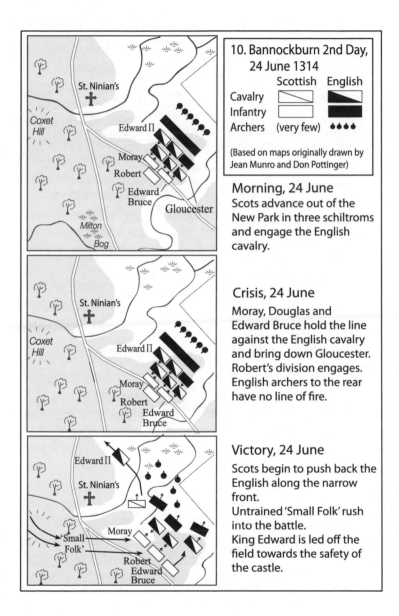

10. Bannockburn 2nd Day, 24 June 1314

	Scottish	English
Cavalry		
Infantry		
Archers	(very few)	●●●●

(Based on maps originally drawn by Jean Munro and Don Pottinger)

Morning, 24 June
Scots advance out of the New Park in three schiltroms and engage the English cavalry.

Crisis, 24 June
Moray, Douglas and Edward Bruce hold the line against the English cavalry and bring down Gloucester. Robert's division engages. English archers to the rear have no line of fire.

Victory, 24 June
Scots begin to push back the English along the narrow front.
Untrained 'Small Folk' rush into the battle.
King Edward is led off the field towards the safety of the castle.

give roles to all his heroes. Robert positioned all his forces in or near woods to keep them safe from cavalry attack. His own division he took to the woods of the New Park, while Moray was ordered to stay in the Torwood, with instructions to 'keep the road beside the kirk'. Duncan takes this to mean the chapel at Larbert. For the present, Moray was to block the main approach road, the A9 route. Robert had selected a battlefield, probably the area spanning the A80 just north of the Tor Burn, where he ordered his men to dig a trap for the English cavalry: a honeycomb of shallow holes, 'a foot in diameter and as deep as a man's knee', each concealed with twigs and grass. This device has been likened to a minefield; it would certainly have disrupted a cavalry charge.

The English spent the night at Falkirk, and on the Sunday 23 June 'after dinner' they came within sight of the Torwood. They were anxious to reach Stirling Castle either that day or the next, before Mowbray delivered it up for lost, so there was a tendency for leading groups to press ahead. There were two encounters that evening, which took place as the main body of the English army was still arriving. In the first incident, a group of young aristocratic hotheads, spying some Scots 'straggling under the trees as if in flight', galloped off around the Torwood to cut off their retreat. What they had seen was Moray, retiring from his position at the chapel of Larbert to join King Robert in the New Park. Probably he had seen the English host from afar and decided upon withdrawal. The English must have seen further activity around the New Park, for they rode off in that direction, confident that the Scots were in full retreat before them. Great was their surprise then, when the Scottish king himself galloped out towards them, at the head of a force of cavalry:

> He rode upon a little palfrey,
> Low and bonny, and directing
> His company with an axe in his hand
> And on his bascinet he wore

> A hat of boiled leather
> And on top of that
> As a sign that he was king,
> A high crown.

At the head of the English aristocrats rode Sir Henry de Boun, a knight of Hereford's retinue and possibly a relative of that earl. Levelling his lance, he rode full tilt at the king, but missed, and as he passed Robert stood up in his stirrups and brought his axe down on de Boun's head. With the force of the blow, Barbour tells us, the axe-shaft broke in two, and Barbour has the king complain nonchalantly that he had ruined a bloody good axe. The English knights fled. Robert's victory in this one-to-one combat is attested by two English chronicles, and such a personal feat of arms at the very commencement of battle sent Scottish morale soaring. It was in itself a vindication of Robert's right as king. Enormously encouraging, news of the encounter will have spread rapidly throughout the Scottish ranks.

Shortly before or after this, Robert Clifford, who also saw Scots close by the woods, led a contingent of cavalry to skirt around the woodland and cut off what he thought was the Scots' retreat. Clifford was accompanied by the earl of Gloucester, Henry Beaumont and, among others, to our good fortune, by Sir Thomas Gray, whose son included his father's eyewitness account in his narrative, *Scalachronica*, written in 1355–57. These knights galloped around the wood until out of the sight of the main body of the English army, and took up a position to block a retreat towards Stirling. Suddenly, out of the woods, came a rush of Scottish infantry, bunched closely together in a tight schiltrom formation, and carrying pikes. Moray had seen that the English contingent was isolated. The English cavalry had halted too close to the trees to form up and charge, expecting the retreating Scots to come from another direction. The horses were the main targets of the Scottish pikemen, and, maddened by their wounds, the chargers reared up and threw their riders. Sir

William Deyncourt was killed. Sir Thomas Gray was taken prisoner. Gloucester was unhorsed – an omen of what would happen on the morrow. Robert Clifford was routed, and he led the remainder of the contingent back to rejoin the main army. Thus a second and stronger group of cavalry rejoined the main body of the troops with wounds, excuses and tales of the valour of the Scots.

Both actions took place in the evening, and the light was now fading. The English, tired when they had arrived, were now thoroughly demoralised; the Scots were buoyant. The summer night was heavy with expectations, full of possibilities and riddled with politics. Robert should never have fought the Battle of Bannockburn: in the face of such a host he should have prudently retired to the hill country to keep his forces intact and wait for the English to starve. Yet these incidents meant that, psychologically, the battle was already won. He had decided against pushing his luck, however, and Sir Thomas Gray tells us that he was preparing to withdraw under cover of night to the high country of Lennox when he received a defector from Edward's camp. This was Sir Alexander Seton, who had supported Bruce in 1308, but had returned to the faith of Edward II after 1310. He brought news of the demoralised state of the English camp, and Robert changed his mind once more, determining to gamble everything on the outcome of the morrow's battle. Seton was not the only defector. David Strathbogie earl of Atholl deserted the Bruce camp to defend the honour of his sister Isabel. Edward Bruce was affianced or perhaps even married to her, but he had deserted her for Isabel of Ross. Atholl defected to the English, further diminishing the Scottish cavalry and carrying off Robert's stores from Cambuskenneth Abbey.

The text of Robert's crucial eve-of-battle speech to his lords does not survive, but echoes of it have come down to us in several versions. Barbour gives the king a speech of 150 lines, in which he commences by asking his men whether they should fight or flee. They opt enthusiastically for the former. Then Robert reassures them that in three ways they have the edge. 'The first is that right is on our side and God will always fight for the right.' Secondly, the arrival of the enemy host affords a tremendous opportunity for the Scots to plunder. Thirdly, the enemy fight only to destroy them, but the Scots fight for survival itself:

> And for our children and our wives
> And for our freedom and our land
> We are bound to stand in battle.

Later Robert presents the stark choice that lies before them:

> You bear honour, reputation and riches
> Freedom wealth and happiness,
> If you carry yourselves like men;
> And exactly the opposite
> Will befall you if you let cowardice
> And wickedness take over your hearts.

In one part of the Barbour text the king acknowledges the personal loyalty and profound trust that his men are demonstrating by their presence:

> You could have lived in serfdom,
> But, because you have yearned to have freedom,
> You are gathered here with me.

There is also practical advice: to charge with speed towards the enemy and not to be too quick to plunder or take prisoners until the day is indisputably won. In another version – quite possibly the 'official' version, penned after the event by the Scottish chancery, especially for inclusion in chronicles – these ringing words are put into the mouth of the king:

We have lost brothers and friends and kinsmen.
Your relatives and friends are captives,
And now prelates are shut up in prison with other clergy
And no order of Mother Church remains safe;
The nobles of the land have passed away in the bloodshed of war ...
They [the English] glory in their wagons and horses; for us
The Name of the Lord and victory in war is our hope.
Happy is this day! Saint John the Baptist was born on it;
And Saint Andrew and Thomas who shed his blood
Along with the saints of the Scottish fatherland will fight today
For the honour of the people, with Christ the Lord in the vanguard!

The mood in the English camp contrasts deeply with that in the Scottish. For the tired English troops there was a lot of work to be done in the dark. The infantry bivouacked in the carse – the marshland near the river – and stayed under arms the whole night, expecting Scottish attack. The horses, however, had to be moved onto firm ground across the Bannock Burn, and makeshift bridges were constructed from the thatch, doors and shutters of nearby dwellings.

At daybreak each army heard mass for the feast day, and the troops confessed to priests and then breakfasted. It was the custom that men were knighted on the morning of battle, and Robert used the occasion to confer that honour upon Walter Steward and James Douglas. Then the Scottish troops arrayed in their three divisions with banners displayed, and emerged from the forest of New Park. Only the composition of the king's division is described and it is said to have included men of Argyll, Carrick, Kintyre and the Isles. There was, then, a large galloglass element in Robert's division, and it is surprising that the men of Carrick fought alongside the king rather than their earl, Edward Bruce. An English chronicle describes the Scots in these terms: 'Not one of them was on horseback, but each was furnished with light armour not easily penetrable by a sword. They had axes at their sides, and carried lances in their hands. They advanced like a thick-set hedge and in a phalanx such as cannot easily be broken.' Chronicles from either side agree that at some distance the Scots knelt to pray a Pater Noster before advancing. 'Yon folk are kneeling to ask mercy' remarks Edward II in the Barbour narrative, and by his side the Scot Sir Ingram de Umfraville replies, 'They ask mercy, but not from you. They ask God for mercy for their sins. I will tell you something for a fact; yon men will win all, or die; none will flee for fear of death.' It is likely that the Scots had brought with them the relics of local saints, including the Breccbennach of Colmcille, which was believed to transmit potency in battle.

By contrast with the Scots, the English infantry remained in a single body. The English too had their talismans, but they lacked some that they had brought on earlier campaigns, namely the banners of St Cuthbert and St John of Beverley. The battlefield put them at a significant disadvantage. Cavalry needed space to manoeuvre, but the available space was confined by the Bannock Burn, marshes to the south-east and trees to the north-west. Moreover, the Scots had the advantage of attacking downhill.

Formalities over, the conflict began with archers exchanging volleys. Archery had not yet reached its heyday in England; nevertheless, had the English been able to mass their archers in sufficient numbers they would swiftly have thinned out the ranks of the Scottish schiltroms. But the narrowness of the field, coupled with the size of the host made it impossible to group them effectively. Nevertheless the archers had some impact; an English chronicle states that 'the King of England's archers quickly put the others to flight'.

Then the Scottish infantry advanced, two schiltroms abreast of one another, and a third, the king's, behind. The pause for prayer can only have been for a swift Paternoster because a major factor in the opening phase of the battle seems to have been the rapidity of the Scottish advance over firm ground. English chronicles state that the Scots 'came quickly lined in schiltroms'. Barbour records that the English were clearly taken by surprise. The *Vita Edwardi Secundi* states that while the earls of Gloucester and Hereford bickered 'the Scottish forces were approaching rapidly'. Clearly the English were given neither space nor time to organise their superior numbers and their cavalry charge could gather no momentum. Gloucester led the English, stung into action, the *Vita Edwardi Secundi* reports, by an accusation of treachery levelled at him by Edward II the previous night, and his cavalry smashed into the phalanx led by Edward Bruce and in which Douglas served: 'When both armies engaged and the great horses of the English charged the pikes of the Scots, as it were into a dense forest, there arose a great and terrible crash of spears broken and of *destriers* wounded to the death; and so they remained without movement for a while.' Many of the *destriers* refused to charge into the forest of pikeheads and threw their riders. The Scottish spearmen targeted the horses of the enemy, and Gloucester's horse was killed under him. At all events the earl rolled to the ground where 'borne down by the weight of his body armour he could not easily rise'. His death was a pivotal event in the battle. There was no need for it to have been decisive, but such was the critical role of great magnates that this event took all the steam out of the English attack. Other magnates too were knocked or dragged from their horses: Robert Clifford, Edmund de Mauley, Pain Typtoft, and William Marshall. At this point, Barbour recounts that Robert directed Sir Robert Keith to use his cavalry, ride down the English archers who were beginning to mass and make an impact. Professor Brown challenges that. He points out the episode is not contained in other sources, and that the English chronicles all say that the Scots fought on foot. He suspects that Barbour has invented it to give a role to Keith, whose descendants were still powerful when Barbour was writing *The Bruce* in the 1370s. There were some Scottish cavalry present at Bannockburn as we know from the pursuit after the battle. The overall impression, however, is that great numbers of English foot archers were crammed behind their own cavalry, with no space to deploy and probably no line of sight. The English chronicles are consistent in reporting that the great mass of English infantry never engaged the Scots, so narrow was the front. Meeting their own men wounded and fleeing, the English infantry themselves began to flee.

Even now, the battle was not necessarily lost for the English, but for a chance intervention. 'Yeomen and boys and men on foot', carters and labourers of the Scottish army, who had been guarding the baggage train heard the din and, witnessing confusion in the English ranks, and believing the battle won, swept onto the field. They were anxious to secure a share of the pickings; yet these *poveraille*, or 'small folk', were mistaken for a Scottish reinforcement. It was this perception that secured victory for the Scots. Among the English the rout became general, and horsemen and infantry stumbled into the Bannock Burn and were drowned. Edward II had appointed the earl of Pembroke and Giles d'Argentan on either side 'to the king's reins', that is, to lead him out of trouble. Giles d'Argentan refused to desert the field and rode off to an honourable death in battle. Illustrating the heraldic practice of maintaining rankings of knightly reputations, Barbour reports that d'Argentan was the 'third best knight' of his time. It was left to Pembroke, to lead Edward to safety, though the English king left much against his will. The English chronicles agree that Edward showed no lack of personal courage or keenness for the fight, and this is to be remarked upon, for they are seldom generous to him. One chronicle has Scottish knights on foot tugging at the covering of Edward's horse to prevent his escape, while the English king, vigorously wielding his mace, knocked them to the ground.

Robert gave the signal that prisoners might be taken for ransom, and the Scots fell upon a bonanza of plunder: horses, armour and weapons thrown away by fleeing knights, harness – 'two hundred pairs of red spurs were taken from dead knights' – tents and pavilions, rich apparel and all the costly trappings of the English royal and three comital households were all for the taking. An English chronicle remarks that had the Scots been less greedy for plunder they might have had many more prisoners. But the value of prisoners' ransoms was never underestimated by the Scots. King Robert claimed all the leading prisoners, as was his prerogative, and in the bag were the earl of Hereford, the earl of Angus, Ingram de Umfraville, Maurice Berkley, John Giffard, Antony Lucy – a powerful knight of the English West March – John Segrave and many others. One chronicle lists seventy-five names of captured gentry, and even that will be a partial listing. All would be forced to pay ransom according to rank.

Edward II, meanwhile, led by Pembroke, arrived at Stirling Castle and sought admittance. However, his garrison commander, Sir Philip Mowbray, refused to lower the drawbridge. Aware that the castle would now have to be surrendered, he honourably saved his king from captivity, and honourably delivered the castle to Robert in accordance with the agreement he had reached with Edward Bruce. It is to be lamented however that Mowbray did not *dis*honourably bring about the end of the war at a stroke by admitting Edward, making him prisoner and gifting to Robert the only thing that the English might trade for peace: their king. Such was the course taken by the constable of Bothwell castle, Walter fitz Gilbert, who after the battle admitted the earl of Hereford and retinue, made Hereford his prisoner and then, changing sides, delivered both earl and castle to Robert. Mowbray's decision not to deliver Edward into captivity enabled war to drag on year after year, neither side able to inflict decisive defeat on the other. For the present, then, Edward II fled around the western edge of the Torwood, to the castle of Patrick, earl of March, at Dunbar, Douglas pursuing him doggedly with a force of sixty horse. Finally, Edward took ship for Berwick and safety. Pembroke, his rescuer, also succeeded in bringing his Welsh retainers through ninety miles of hostile countryside to safety in Carlisle.

It was a magnificent victory, to which Robert responded with magnanimity towards many of his opponents. The bodies of

Gloucester and Clifford were restored with honour to their families. Perhaps we should not be surprised that Raoul de Monthermer, Gloucester's step-father, was allowed to go home without paying ransom, for the house of Gloucester had been loosely associated with the Bruces for many years. Robert was reportedly saddened by the death of the earl. His body was brought from the battlefield and placed in a kirk under guard before being handed back. Marmaduke de Thweng, veteran of many Scottish campaigns, was also released free of ransom. Robert ensured that the widow of Edmund Comyn of Kilbride, who had fought against him, was provided for 'until she could recover her rightful dower according to the assize of the land'. These of course were all adversaries of high rank, and Robert probably took no such interest in the fates of lesser captives. Such were the conventions of the age.

The repercussions of Bannockburn were seismic. In terms of British military history it was revolutionary: for the first time an infantry army had overcome an army led by heavy cavalry, and English chroniclers were not slow to draw parallels with the battle of Courtrai in 1302, when the Flemish townsfolk had put to flight the flower of French chivalry. The English government collapsed. The royalist administration headed by Pembroke was utterly discredited and the dour leader of the baronial opposition, Thomas of Lancaster, five times an earl, took control of the government in the king's name – to the king's undisguised distaste. In Scotland only the garrisons of Berwick and little, isolated Jedburgh remained faithful to Edward, and though his government of Scotland continued to exist it was reduced to managing these garrisons and the immediate vicinity of Berwick.

The Scots enjoyed their windfall of riches, estimated at £200,000 by the *Vita Edwardi Secundi*, a figure that must be dismissed as a wild exaggeration. They also sustained losses: Barbour notes that the Scottish knights William Vipont and Walter Ross died in the battle. But, at a stroke, three major castles tumbled into Robert's lap: Stirling, Bothwell and also Dunbar, which earl Patrick of March surrendered on the departure of Edward II. Prisoners' ransoms brought huge sums of money to individual Scottish lords. Robert, however, had relatives to redeem, and the following year he was able to exchange the earl of Hereford for four prisoners whom the English had held since 1306: Elisabeth his queen, his sister Mary, his daughter the lady Marjorie, and his old mentor, Robert Wishart, Bishop of Glasgow, now blind with age. Money poured into the royal coffers from the ransoms of other prisoners: the earl of Angus, John Seagrave, Maurice de Berkley and Antony Lucy were all redeemed by ransom.

Yet, a great deal remained unchanged by Bannockburn. Robert's victory did not dissolve Edward II's claim to be rightful king of Scotland, nor did it bring him any nearer to a negotiating table. The English remained the stronger side by far, and had no reason to give in on account of one defeat. The very next year, and every year thereafter, if they so chose, they could march a powerful army to Stirling or beyond. Nor did it vanquish the Scottish opposition to Robert. In Argyll and Ireland, the irredentist John of Argyll continued to make trouble for the Bruces, and since 1313 he had been joined in the Irish Sea theatre of war by the Gallovidian knight, Dungal MacDowell. It would take more than a single victory, however momentous, to reconcile these diehard warriors to a Bruce regime.

8

Triumphs and disasters
(1314–18)

Famine, war and Ireland

The Battle of Bannockburn initiated a unique period in the history of the British Isles as Scotland enjoyed a brief military hegemony from that event until the end of Robert's reign. In this period the Scots came close to conquering Ireland and to dominating the Irish Sea. They challenged English control of the North Sea and there are signs too that the Bruces were fomenting rebellion in Wales. Yet Scotland was stronger than England only in the sense that she was better led. England on the other hand had been weakened on two counts. Firstly, she was preoccupied by the hostility that smouldered between Edward II, still grieving and resentful over the murder of Gaveston his lover, and his barons, led by Thomas of Lancaster. Secondly, and more fundamentally, England was profoundly weakened by the onset of the Great European Famine of 1315–18, caused by torrential rains which ruined successive harvests, and thereafter by widespread animal pestilence. As the more populous, and more tillage-dependent of the two warring kingdoms, the famine affected England more severely. In these conditions it was virtually impossible for the English to assemble the provisions necessary to sustain the large concentrations of men and beasts needed for a military campaign. Much less is known about how the Scottish economy fared during the famine at this time, but Scotland was a less densely populated country than England; was less dependent upon sensitive wheat and more so upon rain-tolerant oats; and, in any case, was much more pastoral than arable. The Scots deployed relatively small forces in their raids, preying upon the enemy and living off his lands. While conditions varied enormously between regions, Scotland therefore will not have seen the widespread agricultural distress that the rains caused in England. Ironically, while famine in Britain was the ally of the Scots, famine in Ireland was their Achilles' heel. The Irish campaigns of 1316 and 1317 ended with the Scottish army retreating and suffering from starvation. Nevertheless, it is undeniable that these historical accidents – the famine and the bitter divisions among the English nobles – account for much of Robert's success in these years.

War rolled grimly on, and no time was wasted in following up the victory at Bannockburn. The Northumbrians were horrified at the news of defeat in Scotland and knew exactly what to expect; witness the reaction of two royal officials trying to levy taxes at Morpeth when they encountered remnants of the defeated English army returning from the battle:

> Richard and Robert began to tax the goods of the said men [of Northumberland] in the seventh year [of Edward II], and they sat at Morpeth in the said county; and suddenly there arrived Stephen Seagrave and many others with him and they told them that the lord king was retreating from Stirling with his army and was coming towards England, and at this they were terrified. They fled and, like others of the county, stayed in enclosed towns and castles and forts. And immediately afterwards before 1 August, there came Edward Bruce and Thomas Randolph leading the Scottish army.

Although Robert did not participate in this raid, it is worth outlining its course because it set the pattern for many others to follow. It is

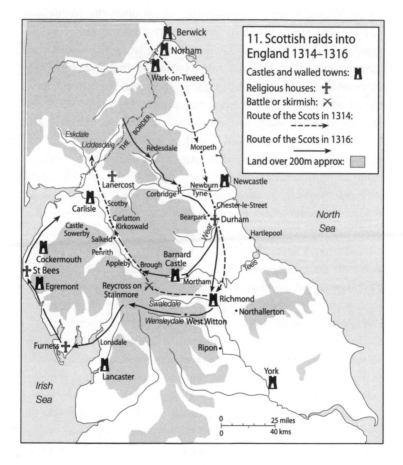

11. Scottish raids into
England 1314–1316

Castles and walled towns: ♜
Religious houses: ✝
Battle or skirmish: ✕
Route of the Scots in 1314: ⇢
Route of the Scots in 1316: →
Land over 200m approx:

Berwick
Norham
Wark-on-Tweed

Eskdale
Liddesdale
THE BORDER
Redesdale
Morpeth

Lanercost
Corbridge
Newburn
Tyne
Newcastle

Carlisle
Scotby
Chester-le-Street
Carlatton
Kirkoswald
Bearpark
Durham
Castle
Sowerby
Salkeld
Hartlepool
Penrith
Appleby
Brough
Barnard
Castle
Cockermouth
St Bees
Egremont
Mortham
Reycross on
Stainmore
Richmond
Swaledale
Northallerton
Wensleydale West Witton
Furness
Lonsdale
Ripon
Lancaster
York

North
Sea

Irish
Sea

0   25 miles
0   40 kms

particularly well attested by the English chronicles, which add that James Douglas and John Soules also led contingents. The Scottish infantry seems to have marched the length of Northumberland, where they stayed three days at Newburn on the banks of the Tyne, burning, wasting and perhaps trying to tempt out the Newcastle garrison. But the cavalry rode on, through Durham, which bought them off, over the Tees and into Yorkshire where, at Richmond, they turned westwards into Swaledale. At the Reycross on Stainmore they met with an ambush set by the Carlisle garrison, but the Scots fought off their assailants and entered the valley of the Eden. The Carlisle men were energetically led by Sir Andrew Harclay, who begins to feature prominently in the narrative from this point. The Scots burnt the towns of Brough, Appleby – where they disrupted the proceedings of the county court – and the castle of Kirkoswald. We can tell from the accounts of the estates of the honour of Penrith that they visited destruction upon its five manors: Penrith, Carlatton, Castle Soweby, Langwathby and Scotby. At Salkeld they destroyed the watermill. They used their stolen herds to trample the crops and then rode off into Liddesdale. The people of Copeland, terrified at what they saw happening to northern Cumberland, paid the Scots 600 marks (that is, £400) for a guarantee of safety from Christmas to Midsummer, then 24 June.

This, then, was the nature of the warfare that Robert unleashed upon the north of England. Infantry were involved only in border districts and places where the Scottish presence came close to permanent occupation. The long-distance raids were carried out by horsemen mounted on hackneys or ponies. These rode swiftly into England and swept down the East March, devastating villages and driving off cattle, taking hostages where payment could be expected, trampling standing crops and burning barns, mills, and homesteads. They were quite prepared to be bought off, and deals were struck with terrified inhabitants crowded into towers or churches, or onto castle parapets. Religious houses held a special attraction for the raiders: there they could find sacred vessels of precious metals, costly vestments, and other objects of high value besides the proceeds of estates, tithes and other collections from the laity. Sweeping westwards into Pennine dales, the raiders drove the stolen cattle before them, pausing only to wreak destruction upon the upland farmsteads as they crossed the Pennines. Finally, and having reached the West March, they turned northwards, bypassing the heavily fortified city of Carlisle, into Liddesdale, or crossing by the fords of the Solway Firth. Moray and Douglas regularly led these long-distance, U-shaped mounted raids through northern England. Raiding developed over time, with the Scots penetrating deeper and deeper into England and spending longer on each raid. This may have been due not only to their increasing audacity: they may have been forced to go ever deeper into England because there was practically nothing left where they had been previously. During Edward Bruce's invasion of Ireland, the raids became less frequent, for the Scots are known to have transferred lords and their troops from one theatre of war to another.

The raids were partly a natural consequence of victory over a hostile neighbour and partly an opportunity to reward and enrich loyal and successful lieutenants, but partly too they were an instrument of royal policy. Robert clearly hoped that such raids would force Edward II to negotiate with him and concede his right to the kingship of Scotland, but his hope was ill founded. Edward showed some concern over the devastation of his six northern counties, but his prime and overwhelming objective was the undermining and defeat of his cousin, Thomas of Lancaster, whom he hated with a passion. One fifth of Edward's kingdom was under tribute to Robert, yet his preoccupation with Lancaster was unrelenting. Once – and only once – Edward and Thomas managed to co-operate for long enough to launch an attack against Robert, but that effort, the siege of Berwick in 1319, collapsed amid a storm of recriminations and accusations of treachery on both sides, and their mutual antagonism redoubled. The failure of the raids to force the English to the conference table was one reason why Robert felt compelled to underwrite Edward Bruce's grand and ultimately disastrous strategy for the conquest of Ireland.

Following the battle and the raid of Edward Bruce and Moray, the first cessation of hostilities occurred in October 1314. On this occasion the English administration 'granted' a truce to the Scots on the intervention of King Philip of France. Negotiations with the English were able to commence at Durham on 20 October. They were to encompass both exchanges of prisoners taken in battle and discussions aimed at 'a perpetual peace'. But it is quite incredible that either side was genuinely interested in compromising on the central issues of kingship and sovereignty at this stage. Both still had high hopes of victory, and the futility of continuing the war had yet to be demonstrated. Moray was at Durham on 17 October 1314, presumably as Robert's chief negotiator. The details of the prisoner exchange were finalised, but the talks broke down soon afterwards, presumably as soon as they proceeded to the issues of kingship and sovereignty.

Robert had to apply further military pressure, not that it will have galled him to do so. The amnesty offered to irredentist Scots was due to expire, and at a parliament at Cambuskenneth Abbey near Stirling on 6 November 1314 proclamation was made that all who had died in opposition to King Robert or who had not yet come into his faith were duly disinherited for evermore. On the conclusion of this parliament Robert led another invasion of Northumberland. Chronicles contain no details of this expedition; indeed, with respect to the devastated and anarchic state of Northumberland, the chronicles at this point lapse into general lamentations and yield little detail. It seems likely, however, that this was the occasion of Robert's taking homage from the people of North Tynedale, and his grant of that region to Sir Philip de Mowbray, who had come into his peace on delivering to him Stirling Castle. Robert was in effect threatening to dismember the kingdom of England. This posturing appears to have had a salutary effect upon the English, for further negotiations took place, this time at Dumfries. By Christmas, they too had collapsed, neither side being prepared to give way on the substantive issue. Again Robert resorted to the threat of force, and early in 1315 Yorkshire was braced for imminent attack by the Scots.

In February and March intermittent violence on the Marches alternated with parleys. We know only that proposals concerning the kingship of Scotland were being discussed, but simultaneously both sides were preparing for a serious escalation of the conflict in Ireland and the west. Robert appears to have advertised his intention to intervene in Ireland. One well-informed chronicle notes that Edward wrote letters to the Irish proclaiming his objective of conquering not only Ireland but the isles. Presumably, that letter will have been similar to that which he wrote to the Welsh. Early in 1315 the English chancery learned that the Scots were expecting 'thirteen great cogs' loaded with arms and supplies from Flanders, probably intended to equip the expedition. A messenger of the Scottish king was arrested in Dublin that month. Pre-emptive action was organised and before 15 February 1315 John of Argyll's forces recaptured the Isle of Man for Edward II in anticipation of the Scottish invasion of Ireland. On 18 February John received orders to raise 10,000 men and 60 ships, manned at double strength, to be ready by 6 April for an attack on the west of Scotland. Furthermore, John appears to have made progress in suborning Robert's Gaelic subjects. He was given power in March to take into the king's peace 'Donald of the Isles', who must be Donald MacDonald of Islay, Godfrey, his brother, John Macnakild and Patrick Graham. Stable leadership rarely prevailed in the Gaelic kin groups. Just we saw Angus Óg in the service of the English king in 1310, we now see his rival for the MacDonald chieftainship playing the same game.

These developments in the west undermined any progress made in negotiations. Neither side was sufficiently interested in a settlement at this stage: in Scotland Edward Bruce was urging extension of the war to Ireland, while in England Lancaster's administration was simply playing for time until the summer, when it hoped to organise a fresh invasion of Scotland.

The invasion of Ireland was an enormous gamble, and the reasons why Robert sanctioned it are many and complex. One source suggests that Edward had received an invitation from an Irish chief 'with whom he had been educated in his youth'; however it is much more likely that the impetus for the invasion came from Scotland, rather than Ireland. Edward Bruce had dynastic ambitions of his own, as Barbour relates:

> Sir Edward, earl of Carrick,
> Who was stronger than a leopard,
> And had no desire to live in peace,
> Felt that Scotland was too small
> For him and his brother
> Therefore he formed a purpose
> That he would become king of Ireland.

Here Barbour is borne out by another chronicler, who describes Edward thus: 'very mettlesome and high-spirited, [he] would not dwell together with his brother in peace, unless he had half the kingdom for himself; and for this reason this war was stirred up in Ireland.' Duncan points out that the prisoner exchange lately agreed with the English allowed for the reunion of Robert and his queen, and if children were forthcoming Edward Bruce would lose his position as Scotland's heir presumptive and any hope of gaining a kingdom of his own.

Another factor, unrelated to Edward Bruce's ambition, was the threat from Scottish émigrés, led by John of Argyll and Dungal MacDowall. John's fleet was destined no doubt for the west of Scotland. He had orders to receive to the peace of Edward II, magnates and communities of the Western Isles. His recent capture of Man provided a central base from which he could dominate the Irish Sea and threaten western Scotland. Man was surely captured in order to forestall the expected Scottish invasion of Ireland, for most of the twenty-two Scots and others captured were distributed to Irish garrisons to serve as hostages. John and the émigrés posed a threat that could not be ignored, and Edward Bruce's invasion was at least partly intended to take the war to them, and deprive them of their last refuge.

Other, lesser benefits would flow from a successful invasion of Ireland. One of these would be the capture of Carrickfergus Castle. This massive strength was owned by the earl of Ulster and was ideally positioned to serve as a base for those attacking Argyll or western Scotland. Devastating Ireland would also deprive the depot of Carlisle of the source of half its provisions, and similarly starve John of Argyll's fleet at Man. Finally, Robert hoped that by capturing some prize of enormous strategic value he might force Edward II to concede his right to the kingship. He certainly appreciated the diplomatic leverage that the capture of Carlisle and Berwick would bring; and he may have seen Ireland in terms of such a prize.

Thus Robert was pushed into approving the western adventure by the ambitions of his brother, and simultaneously drawn into Ireland by the troublemaking activities of the MacDougall affinity and the prospect of a ragbag of lesser benefits. And so in spring 1315 he vastly extended the scope of his war by assenting to Edward's invasion of Ireland. At Ayr on 26 April 1315, a council met to settle the evidently related questions of the royal succession, and the co-ordinated campaigns in Ireland and on the western seaboard of Scotland. A royal tailzie – a formal deed, which set aside the normal course of the law – settled the royal succession on Robert's heirs male, or, failing that, on Edward Bruce and his heirs male, or, failing that, on Marjorie, Robert's daughter and her heirs male.

Directly after the council, in the month of May, Edward's formidable army embarked for Ireland. With him went Moray and several prominent knights, including Philip Mowbray, John Soules and John Stewart of Menteith. On arrival, Edward's force appears to have been welcomed by the Gaelic Irish of those parts of Ulster which are closest to Scotland but, as our knowledge of Edward's Irish campaigns is heavily dependent upon non-Gaelic sources, this dimension of the Irish adventure is largely hidden from us. Edward, however, lost no time in investing Carrickfergus Castle – just as his brother began to besiege Carlisle on the opposite shore. He may have staged an inauguration of himself as king of Ireland shortly afterwards, or this may have taken place in May of the following year. After a brief expedition into Leinster, where he burnt the Irish Sea port of Dundalk, he defeated an army led by the earl of Ulster on 1 September 1315 at Connor. This forced the earl to vacate Ulster and move to his other lordship, that of Connaught. Edward co-operated closely with a squadron of four or five ships led by the privateer Thomas Dun, using this naval support to ferry his men across the River Bann and to convey Moray back to Scotland. Dun carried out a spectacular raid on the harbour of Holyhead in Anglesey on 12 September, when he captured a ship laden with provisions. In England, Dun's reputation as 'a cruel pirate' and a 'perpetrator of depredations on the sea' was growing.

Much of the value of these Irish campaigns for Robert was that they were one part of a two-pronged strategy against the Scottish émigrés in Ulster and the MacDougall homeland in Argyll. In view of the MacSweeney expedition of 1310, the capture by the Scots of Northburgh Castle in County Donegal is surely significant as it may have threatened or blocked the passage of similar expeditions to Argyll. It is important to recognise the co-ordination in the campaigns of the two brothers. The same fleet that carried Edward's force to Ireland then proceeded against Argyll, where Robert was taking the homage of the western lords. At East Tarbert Robert established a new royal burgh, intended to augment his influence in the area. Interestingly, while Walter the Steward accompanied Robert on the Argyll campaign, no less than three members of his extended family were with Edward Bruce across the North Channel: John Stewart of Jedburgh and an Alan Stewart were there during the course of the Irish campaigns, and the magnate John Stewart of Menteith was also present in Ireland. The Stewart connection was then heavily involved in both aspects of this strategy.

It was on this campaign that Robert had his men drag his ships with sails unfurled across the isthmus between the two Tarberts, while he himself remained in the ship. The king was doing rather more than just taking a shortcut, as Barbour underlines:

> For they knew, by an old prophecy,
> That whoever should have ships go
> Between those seas with sails
> Would so win the Isles for himself
> That no-one could withstand him by force.

In the year 1098, two hundred years before, the king of Norway, Magnus Barelegs, had performed the very same symbolic action when he too had needed the men, galley-fleets and money of the western seaboard for an invasion of Ireland. Robert was demonstrating, as Magnus before him had done, that he claimed mastery of the Western Isles and that he would exercise the fullness of that lordship. His campaign dealt another terrible blow to MacDougall influence in Argyll, and it was a MacDonald, Alexander Óg, who died bearing the title king of Argyll in 1318. By contrast, Edward Bruce had no such spectacular success; he was forced to invest Carrickfergus Castle and it did not fall until September 1316.

Before proceeding to the attack on Carlisle – the counterpart of Edward's siege of Carrickfergus – Robert had further unfinished business of a personal nature to settle, this time with the people of Hartlepool in the bishopric of Durham. The anomalous position of the bishopric of Durham during these years has long intrigued scholars. Since 1312 it had been well within range of the Scottish raiders, but from that date it had consistently bought off the threat. Governed by its prince-bishop as a state-within-a-state, it possessed a unity and cohesion that the English county communities of Northumberland and, more especially, Cumberland lacked. Unsurprisingly, Robert treated the bishopric as his milch cow. It continued to pay extortionately for truces long after Northumberland and Cumberland had sunk into chaos, and in one agreement with the community of Durham the Scots reserved to themselves the right to ride through the bishopric on their way to raid Yorkshire. But in June 1315 payments seem to have lapsed, and on 29 June opportunity was taken to settle a grudge against tenants of a former Bruce estate: 'Sir Robert Bruce came into the bishopric of Durham with a great army and so secretly had he come that he found people sleeping soundly in their beds. He sent Sir James Douglas to the district of Hartlepool with many armed men while he himself remained at the vill of Chester le Street. Sir James despoiled the said town, and he led back as captives many burgesses and many women. Having collected much booty from the whole countryside they all returned to their own country.' Another source adds that the townspeople took to sea in ships to escape the Scots, and this gives another clue as to reasons for this action: Hartlepool had become a naval base for the enforcement of Edward II's maritime operations, and from its harbour the English would intercept Scottish, German and Flemish ships trading and preying on English shipping in the North Sea. Scotland's continental trade, which brought in cash income and weaponry, was vital to the prosecution of the war. But, in addition to this, Hartness – and Hartlepool – had formed a part of the Bruce ancestral lands, and Robert took personally the active involvement of former tenants of his family undermining his war. Hartlepool remained a target for subsequent Scottish raids in 1318 and 1322, and was specifically excluded from the purchased truces with the bishopric. As a result of this raid a new truce with Durham was organised, beginning on

1 July 1315 and to last for two years. For this the bishopric coughed up the huge sum of 1,600 marks (that is, £1,066).

Now, more than ever before, Robert needed money: not only was Edward Bruce's siege of Carrickfergus draining his treasury, but in the very month after the Hartlepool raid he himself commenced the siege of Carlisle. That two such daunting challenges were undertaken simultaneously is testimony to the Bruces' confidence at this time; all the more so when one considers that they were attempted in concert with increased pressure on Berwick. With hindsight we can see that victory at Bannockburn had tempted Robert to overstretch his resources; had the combined resources of these three sieges been applied separately to these projects, all might have succeeded. As it was, in three years Robert gained two of his three targets.

A vivid narrative of the siege of Carlisle, 22 July to 1 August, clearly written by an eyewitness, is contained in the English Lanercost chronicle. The account reveals that Robert strove to apply the sophisticated techniques he had witnessed at Edward I's siege of Stirling Castle, but with fewer resources, inadequate materials and in adverse weather conditions:

> On every day of the siege [the Scots] assaulted one of the three gates of the city, sometimes all three at once; but never without loss, because there were discharged upon them from the walls such dense volleys of darts and arrows, likewise stones, that they asked one another whether stones bred and multiplied within the walls. Now on the fifth day of the siege they set up a machine for casting stones next to the church of the Holy Trinity … but there were seven or eight similar machines within the city, besides other engines of war.

Defence of the city was energetically organised by Sir Andrew Harclay, a remarkably able Cumberland knight. The Scots resorted to many ingenious stratagems. They built a siege tower – called a 'belfry' – to push up against the walls and gain the advantage of height on the defenders, but some distance from the walls it stuck in earth saturated by the torrential rains of the worst summer in living memory. The Scots attempted to fill up the moat by pouring into it huge bundles of corn and hay, but the material was simply swallowed up and borne away by the swollen waters. They built drawbridges, but these proved too heavy and sank completely into the moat. One can almost hear the howls of derision from the defenders on the city walls as these successive expedients failed. Then, on 25 July, an all-out assault on the eastern walls was launched as a diversion while Douglas's commandos tried to scale the western wall. Douglas himself may have been wounded in this attempt. The next day Robert gave up. Perhaps he was simply exasperated, but he may also have heard two pieces of bad news: 'A false report meanwhile spread throughout England that our army in Ireland had scattered the Scots, that Edward Bruce was dead and that hardly one of the Scots remained alive. Hence Robert Bruce, both on account of these wild rumours and because he had heard that the earl of Pembroke had recently arrived with many men-at-arms, gave up the siege and set out towards Scotland.' Abandoning their war machines the Scots marched off, in such disarray that the defenders were able to capture two Scottish knights.

Edward Bruce was alive and kicking. Not only had he kept Carrickfergus under constant siege, but he had also decided to risk a winter campaign too. Towards the end of 1315, with winter coming on, he marched south from Ulster for a second time – quite remarkably given the weather conditions – ranging far into Leinster, the very heartland of the Anglo-Irish colony. But the English managed to retain the loyalty both of the Anglo-Irish and of many Gaelic lords. A high-ranking royal clerk named John de Hothum, who had long experience of Irish affairs, had arrived in Ireland in September 1315 to put backbone into Edward II's Irish government. By taking oaths and hostages, and by judicious distribution of pardons, grants and privileges, Hothum made an invaluable contribution to keeping Irish magnates onside. Edward put to flight Roger Mortimer at Kells in

December 1315, and at Ardscull near Skerries in January 1316 he worsted in battle an assembly of Anglo-Irish magnates led by the justiciar Edmund Butler. Dublin made ready for desperate defence, and in the city Brother Walter de Aqua was paid to direct operations from 9 December to 5 May, but Edward did not attack. It is a feature of the Bruces' armies that they were ill-prepared to take cities by storm. Nevertheless some of the Gaelic Irish clans of Leinster and Munster were inspired by his success to rise in revolt against the English. By February, however, lack of supplies forced Edward to retreat to Ulster, his men 'so weakened, both from hunger and exhaustion that many of them began to die'. Some time before September 1316 Robert himself seems to have crossed to Ulster, causing the Carrickfergus garrison at last to throw in the towel. One of the main objectives of the Irish expedition had therefore been accomplished. The three warlords, Robert, Edward and Moray, returned to Scotland to hammer out a basis for continuing the conquest of Ireland, and part of the agreement reached was that Moray should be granted the Isle of Man, which was still in English hands.

There followed a lull in the raiding of England. Scottish energies and resources may have been drained by Edward Bruce's campaign in Ireland. Negotiations with the English government were resumed, and it appears that a truce until Midsummer 1316 was agreed. For his part, Edward II committed the keeping of northern England to a succession of commanders with widespread powers and – on parchment at any rate – significant forces at their disposal. None of the English commanders made any significant attack on Scotland, and for a particularly powerful reason already referred to above. In the years 1315–18 summer after summer was ruined by incessant rain. Sword and fire having been visited on northern England by the Scots, it was the turn of famine to immiserate the lives of the northern English peasantry. The rain destroyed crops and food prices began to soar. In northern England the famine was partly the result of the devastation wrought by the Scots. It became impossible for commanders to muster troops where the tenantry were deserting estates and where there was no food to sustain armies. In 1316 the Lancaster administration struggled and failed to mount a campaign against Robert, their efforts rendered hopeless by shortage of supplies, dissension, desertion of tenantry and incessant rain, which made roads and river crossings impassable.

On the North Sea there was no truce. The advantage which the English had gained through the establishment of the St Omer wool staple in 1313 was lost in the early summer of 1315, when Robert, Count of Flanders, rose in revolt against Louis X, his French overlord. The French called upon Edward II to honour his commitments under the alliance, by expelling Flemish traders and sending ships to support the French against the Flemish. It was in Edward's interest to do neither. He needed all his ships to supply Berwick in the North Sea, and to defeat Edward Bruce and Thomas Dun in the Irish Sea. The English were still trying to enforce a blockade on Scotland, maintaining a fleet of twenty ships to keep the privateers at bay; this they now had to divide. The added distraction allowed King Robert to blockade Berwick by sea, as well as on land, and by the autumn of 1315 the garrison was desperately short of food. By October men were reportedly starving and the desertion of the garrison was said to be imminent. In November relief vessels were forced to jettison most of their cargo to escape the privateers. Then, around 6 January 1316, Robert and Douglas launched an amphibious attack on the town:

> In the week of the Epiphany, the King of Scotland came stealthily to Berwick one bright moonlit night with a strong force, and delivered an assault by land and by sea in boats, intending to enter the town by stealth on the waterside between Brighouse and the castle, where the wall was not yet built, but they were manfully repulsed by the guards and by those who had answered to the alarm, and a certain Scottish knight, Sir J de Landels was killed and Sir James Douglas escaped with difficulty in a small boat.

Then, in March 1316, the warden wrote in bitter terms to Edward II: 'Assuredly, sire, your people are dying of hunger and I have nothing but fine words for them ... And now lately many are leaving the town and those who stay die in anguish from starvation on the walls.'

By May it was impossible for the English to supply the town by sea; on 10 May the mayor of Berwick reported that two vessels had recently been captured trying to supply the town. Attacks on English shipping increased: John Crabbe now had the wholehearted support of Count Robert. Flemish crews had been expelled from England and deprived of legitimate employment, and had no option now but to join the privateers and prey on English vessels. Crabbe had captured two ships from Great Yarmouth in March 1316, and off the Isle of Thanet he seized an English wine ship returning from Gascony. What saved the situation for the English on the North Sea, and for Berwick, was the cessation of hostilities between France and Flanders late in 1316, which meant that Edward II could once more deploy the whole of his North Sea fleet to supply Berwick and suppress the Scots and Eastlanders, while Flemish crews could abandon privateering and turn once more to legitimate trade.

As soon as his truce with the English ended, Robert mercilessly unleashed his raiders once more on northern England. The first major raid on Yorkshire took place at Midsummer, 24 June 1316. Moray and Douglas probably led this raid; Robert remained in Scotland. They rode through Durham and crossed the Tees at Mortham. That settlement was subsequently abandoned as result of destruction by the Scots. Then they split into three groups: some continued up Teesdale, devastating the estates at Barnard Castle, and into the valley of the Eden where they burnt Penrith and Carlatton. Another approached Richmond and was bought off by the nobles, bargaining from the safety of the castle ramparts. They turned up Swaledale to Stainmore. The third group rode into Wensleydale, destroying the village of West Witton and, meeting up with their comrades on Stainmore, rode on into Kendal and Lonsdale, and across the sands to Furness. Their route home along the Cumberland coast is borne out by taxation records, which reveal a string of impoverished parishes as far as Cockermouth.

In January 1317 Robert crossed to Ireland. By this time his old nemesis, John of Argyll, had retired to London 'impotent in body and his lands in Scotland totally destroyed'. John lived only a year and a half afterwards, and died around the beginning of 1318 on a pilgrimage to Canterbury. Other Scottish émigrés remained in Ireland or around the Irish Sea – Duncan MacGoffrey, Dungall MacDowell and others – keeping alive the flame of resistance to the Bruces. Robert joined forces with Edward and Moray, setting off southwards to lay waste the heartlands of Leinster. They approached Dublin just as Edward had done the previous winter with every appearance of assaulting the city but, as before, they veered away from it when the citizens prepared for a stout defence. From hindsight and on the evidence we have, this looks like a wasted opportunity to destroy the English colony in Ireland and gain that vital bargaining-counter that could have brought an end to the war. One possible explanation for the Scots' failure to attack Dublin is that the city was well supplied with hostages. Besides men captured in the Isle of Man, Sir Alan Stewart was being held in Dublin Castle and, as we have seen, his relatives the Stewarts contributed significantly to most Irish campaigns.

The Scots continued southwards, destroying the countryside, while the army of Edmund Butler, the justiciar of Ireland, followed them at a distance, not daring to attack. Then Robert received an appeal for assistance from a faction of the O'Briens – Clann Briain Ruaid – and hared off to the west towards Limerick. When the Scots arrived in Thomond, they discovered that the faction they had come to help had been defeated by their rivals – Clann Taidc – and they found waiting for them these hostile O'Briens. The decision was taken to retreat; Robert might have received wind of the arrival of a fresh English army under Roger Mortimer at Youghal on 7 April.

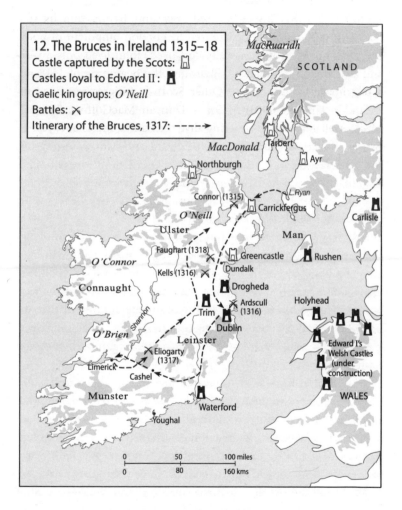

12. The Bruces in Ireland 1315–18
Castle captured by the Scots: 🏰
Castles loyal to Edward II : 🏰
Gaelic kin groups: *O'Neill*
Battles: ✗
Itinerary of the Bruces, 1317: ----→

MacRuaridh

SCOTLAND

MacDonald Tarbert

Ayr

Northburgh

Connor (1315) ✗ Carrickfergus

L.Ryan

O'Neill

Ulster

Man

Carlisle

Faughart (1318) ✗ Greencastle Rushen

Kells (1316) ✗ Dundalk

O'Connor Drogheda

Connaught Trim ✗ Ardscull (1316)

Holyhead

Shannon Dublin

O'Brien Leinster Edward I's Welsh Castles (under construction)

✗ Eliogarty (1317)

Limerick

Cashel

Munster Waterford WALES

Youghal

| 0 | 50 | 100 miles |

| 0 | 80 | 160 kms |

At this point in the narrative Barbour alludes to a curious incident. Robert halted the retreat of the army 'from Limerick' – we should say, rather, the banks of the Shannon, since the Scots did not enter that city – in order that a poor laundress suffering labour pains might give birth. Barbour includes the story to illustrate Robert's humanity; some commentators however have suggested that the laundress was bearing the king's child. The only action of the campaign occurred on 17 April, when a skirmish took place at Eliogarty in County Tipperary with Irish hobelars, and this was followed by a long hard march back to Ulster, during which the Scottish army a second time 'nearly perished with hunger and fatigue, and many were left there dead'. This costly and ultimately fruitless expedition is tantamount to a defeat. Just as the Scots avoided giving battle in England, the Anglo-Irish lords had avoided confrontation with the Scots and in this way saw off the King of Scots.

Following a good harvest and in a clement winter, campaigning would have been tough; in early 1317 it is incredible that the Bruces even attempted it. Wasting the Irish colony, though it deprived the English West March of provisions, can hardly have been justification in itself, and had Robert been serious about the capture of Dublin he would surely have brought or made a siege train, and used it. It is quite clear, however, that Robert had expected much more support from Anglo-Irish and Gaelic lords than was forthcoming. The O'Brien faction had clearly diverted the expedition for their own ends, and their manipulation of Robert recalls a similar attempt by an O'Connor faction to use Edward's expedition in 1315 against their local adversaries. By these two instances we are reminded that Gaelic was only a secondary cultural influence on the Bruces: they could 'talk the talk' of Gaelic lords, but might occasionally be shown up as naive Anglo-Normans, hopelessly bogged down in and sidetracked by the micro-politics of the *Gaidhealtachd*.

This diversion to the west of Ireland has never been satisfactorily explained. It seems unlikely that the Bruces would drop everything to go to the help of an Irish clan that they had probably never heard of. What drew them to the west and away from wasting the Anglo-Irish colony? One might speculate that they may have been co-operating somehow with MacDonald or MacRuaridh galloglass operating on their own behalf in the Irish *Gaidhealtachd*. In this same year, the Irish annals state that 150 MacRuaridh galloglass were slain in the kingdom of Breifne, which lies between Ulster and Connaught. That particular incident is too far north for it to be relevant to the march of the Bruces, but it shows that Scottish galloglass were present elsewhere in Ireland. That presence might have affected events in ways we cannot determine. That said, the brothers went to some lengths to promote their stance as leaders of a pan-Celtic alliance against England. Edward Bruce's propaganda was circulating in Wales at this time, and the Scottish royal chancery may have had a hand in composing the Remonstrance of the Irish Princes. In this letter to the pope, written in 1317 by Domnal O'Neill 'king of Ulster and by hereditary right true heir to the whole of Ireland', a list of oppressions and grievances committed by English kings and their ministers, and English settlers in Ireland is rehearsed, and O'Neill's hereditary right is transferred to Edward Bruce, 'illustrious earl of Carrick'.

It should be observed that Edward Bruce never claimed or was addressed as 'High King' of Ireland. In the annals and in Robert's deeds that refer to him, Edward is always described as 'King of Ireland', and the antique high kingship is never invoked. Robert's model of kingship, and Edward's, was the monarchy of Edward I of England.

Robert was back in Scotland at least by 14 June 1317, and probably well before that. On his return he commended William Sinclair, bishop of Dunkeld, who had seen off a seaborne invasion of Fife, calling him 'my own bishop'. Robert was in good time for an expected resumption of hostilities. The English chancery had issued orders for levies of troops and accumulation of foodstuffs in preparation for a campaign that summer. On 13 July Edward II wrote to his commanders in the north that from a fortnight after Midsummer – 8 July – the Scots had been mustering for an invasion and that he feared it was already in progress. But there was no chance of serious campaigning by either side in what passed for a summer in 1317. The harvest was disastrous and grain prices rocketed; the roads had become mires; and the peasantry, impoverished and displaced, were preyed upon by Scottish raiders and English garrisons alike. Such weather is likely to have been experienced in Scotland too, though, as explained earlier, the consequent agrarian crisis is unlikely to have been quite as harsh.

Unwelcome news had meanwhile been received from the Irish Sea in the summer of 1317. Thomas Dun, the privateer chief who had been the scourge of English shipping, had provoked the English government into taking resolute action. In May Edward II ordered two ships; one was a 140-man galley, and therefore much faster than other vessels on the Irish Sea, where ships were normally of 18, 22 and 26 oars, to hunt down the 'cruel pirate'. Already on the Irish Sea 'for the defence of Ireland and the king's land of Scotland' was a squadron led by John of Athy. On 2 July Athy encountered Dun's squadron and, after a fierce sea-battle in which 40 Scots are said to have been slain, the pirate chief was taken alive. A squire called Geoffrey Coigners was rewarded with a payment of £10 for this achievement. Before he was executed, Dun revealed, or was made to reveal, that Moray was preparing an attack on Man and also intended through treachery to capture Anglesey. This did not, however, prevent Moray's capture of the Isle of Man, which occurred around October 1317.

Unable to campaign in 1317, Robert turned to intrigue. A new pope had ascended the Throne of St Peter, John XXII, and he renewed the papacy's attempts to reconcile Edward II with Robert, whom he considered to be Edward's vassal. Two papal legates, both cardinals, had arrived in England to settle a variety of ecclesiastical disputes in the English Church, and also to impose a two-year truce on the Anglo-Scottish conflict at the behest of Edward II. This was to last from 1 May 1317 until 1319. Robert ignored the truce because in their letters the cardinals failed to acknowledge his kingship, and because he felt himself to be on the brink of capturing Berwick. He forbade publication in Scotland of the papal bull announcing the truce, and he had the cardinals' messengers assaulted and their letters torn up. The cardinals decided to visit him in person. In September 1317 they were on their way into Scotland to threaten Robert with renewed excommunication and to impose terms for a truce wholly unacceptable to him. Travelling with them was the bishop-elect of Durham, Louis de Beaumont, and protecting the whole party was his brother Sir Henry de Beaumont, a magnate and veteran commander of the Scottish wars.

As long as the papacy denied his royal title, Robert preferred to ignore its peace-making initiatives, but he could not afford to have these senior churchmen entering Scotland and undermining his royal dignity by denouncing him in front of his magnates. He avoided the unwelcome visit – it seems – by hiring a host of Northumbrian robber-knights, led by Gilbert de Middleton, to waylay the cardinals before they reached Durham. Consequently these princes of the Church were ambushed at Rushyford on 1 September 1317, their belongings – including the papal bulls so offensive to Robert – stolen, and, humiliated and seething with indignation, they were forced to continue to Durham on foot. At this sacrilege the outrage of English ecclesiastical and secular authorities was apoplectic. However, it was Middleton and his adherents who were roundly cursed, condemned and excommunicated; for Robert the whole affair had the great advantage of 'deniability', and enabled him to persist in his violation of the papal truce without an embarrassing showdown with the cardinals in Scotland. Several interests benefited from the robbery. The monks of Durham Priory had no love for their bishop-elect, Louis de Beaumont, whom they resented as he had been foisted upon them against their will. Similarly Gilbert de Middleton and other local knights, who habitually profited as middlemen organising the collection of Robert's tribute, feared the ascendancy of the warlike Beaumonts in the defence of the border, worrying that they would ruin their arrangements with the Scots. In the aftermath of the robbery Middleton and his associates, as content to be hung for a sheep as for a lamb, led the English Eastern March in a widespread revolt against royal misrule, lack of pay, lack of provisions, rapacious castle garrisons and the prospect of domination by the Beaumonts. In the Middleton Rebellion, as it is known, retainers of Thomas earl of Lancaster were prominent. Mysteriously, the earl himself had been on hand directly after the robbery to lead the unfortunate prelates to safety, almost as though Lancaster knew in advance of what was to happen. The robbery of the cardinals and the Middleton Rebellion is a murky episode, the full truth of which will never be known, but there is no mistaking the hand of the King of Scots, upon whose permission life in the English border counties outside castles and walled towns depended. The revolt, which even spread into Yorkshire, was crushed by castle garrisons and those anxious to do down their local rivals or curry favour with Edward II.

Capitalising on the confusion he had sown, towards the end of September Robert renewed his assault on Berwick. Edward II hastily dispatched reinforcements from York and a ship from Whitby with twenty-eight armed sailors on board. The siege lasted into the winter, and in December Robert was supervising siege engines between onslaughts, determined that 'he would have Berwick'. In the spring Robert resorted once more to guile, and on the night of 1/2 April 1318 a party of Scots led by Douglas scaled the walls of Berwick, at a place where the guard had been bribed. The town was taken at last. The garrison retreated to the castle and held out until 18 June, but the fall of the town of Berwick heralded a general collapse of English strongholds on the Eastern March. Wark on Tweed surrendered on 21 May, and Harbottle around that time 'because relief did not reach them on the appointed day' and Mitford was taken by guile soon afterwards.'

At the end of April or early in May Robert dispatched Moray and Douglas on a devastating raid on Yorkshire. The raid was a pointed defiance of the two-year truce which the pope had announced and sought to impose and, although there is no other evidence of collusion between Lancaster and the Scots at this date, it *may* have been intended to support a general Lancastrian revolt in England. Two groups of raiders left Scotland. On the Eastern March a first group passed through the bishopric of Durham, but stopped to devastate the area around Hartlepool in reprisal for the capture of a Scottish ship. Then they crossed into Yorkshire at Yarm. A second group appears to have entered England by the West March and rode up the Eden Valley and down Teesdale to Barnard Castle, devastating villages along the south bank of the river, until the two groups met and joined forces in laying waste the Vale of York. Taxation records enable us to trace the trail of devastation, and these are supplemented by chronicle accounts and chance survivals among administrative records. Richmond seems to have bought off the raiders a second time. Ripon was spared, in return for 1,000 marks, a sum negotiated with townsfolk crowded into the minster for safety. Fountains Abbey bought off the raiders, but a large part of the Scottish force stayed at the abbey, and many of the granges and outlying farms were destroyed. Northallertonshire was devastated by all accounts, and on Sunday 28 May the raiders destroyed the king's granary at Boroughbridge. The two groups converged on Knaresborough. They burnt 140 houses in the town, leaving only 20 standing, and they searched the Forest of Knaresborough for refugees who might be hiding there with their cattle. The arrival of Moray in Knaresborough may not have been by chance. The earl of Lancaster's rivalry with Edward II had developed into open war in some parts of England, and from October 1317 to the end of January Lancastrian rebels associated with the Middleton Rebellion had held Knaresborough Castle against the king. In January 1318 Moray was believed to have been approaching to aid the rebels,

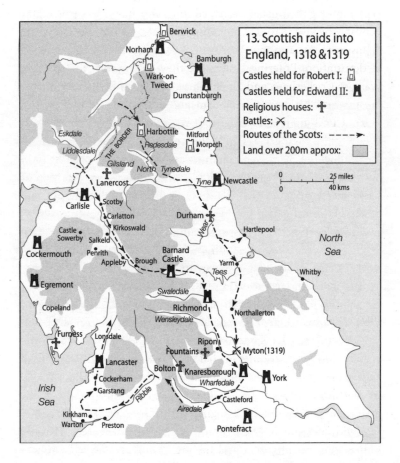

Berwick
Norham
Bamburgh
Wark-on-
Tweed
Dunstanburgh

THE BORDER
Harbottle
Redesdale
Mitford
Morpeth
Eskdale
Liddesdale
Gilsland
North Tynedale
Lanercost
Tyne Newcastle

Carlisle
Scotby
Carlatton
Kirkoswald
Durham
Hartlepool

*North
Sea*

Castle
Sowerby
Salkeld
Penrith
Appleby Brough
Barnard
Castle
Wear
Yarm
Tees
Whitby

Cockermouth

Egremont

Copeland
Swaledale
Richmond
Wensleydale
Northallerton

Furness
Lonsdale
Ripon
Fountains
Myton(1319)

*Irish
Sea*
Lancaster
Cockerham
Garstang
Bolton Knaresborough
Wharfedale
York

Ribble
Airedale
Castleford
Kirkham
Warton Preston
Pontefract

13. Scottish raids into England, 1318 &1319

Castles held for Robert I:
Castles held for Edward II:
Religious houses: ✝
Battles: ✗
Routes of the Scots: - - - - ➤
Land over 200m approx: ▨

0   25 miles
0   40 kms

and it may be that when he actually set out in May he expected to find the Lancastrians still holding out. Whether or not this was the case, Robert had nothing to lose by stirring the antagonism between Lancaster and his royal cousin.

Following their usual U-shaped itinerary, the raiders crossed the Pennines by several routes, including Airedale and Wharfedale, where tax assessments and the records of Bolton Priory reveal their wake of devastation. Entering Lancashire they destroyed it for six days; Warton, Cockerham and Garstang were said to be 'totally burnt'; Preston and Kirkham were 'burnt and destroyed'. Of their return journey nothing is known: since it was made through countryside already devastated, it does not figure in the records.

While these events were taking place in Britain we hear virtually nothing of what was happening in Ireland. After Robert left Ireland, Edward Bruce remained in Ulster for over a year, but in the autumn of 1318 he advanced to the borders of that province. An intriguing four-month gap in the sequence of Robert's dated acts leaves it just possible that the king took an army to Ireland at that time to assist Edward once again in his conquest of Ireland. There is no firm evidence in Irish sources of Robert's presence in that country, but that Robert was expected seems to be implied in the Annals of Clonmacnoise, where it states that 'fearing his brother Robert Bruce king of Scotland (that came to this kingdom for his assistance) would acquire and get the glory of that victory which he made himself believe he would get of the English which he was sure he was able to overthrow without the assistance of his said brother, he rashly gave them the assault.' At Faughart near Dundalk on 14 October 1318 Edward encountered three Anglo-Irish magnates: Edmund Butler, John Birmingham and the archbishop of Armagh, Roland Joyce. The best source for the battle, however, makes no mention of Robert, yet it claims that Edward had already been reinforced, and that he approached the town of Dundalk with 'a great army of Scots which had newly arrived'. Certainly Edward was accompanied by MacRuaridh and MacDonald chiefs; nevertheless his force was greatly outnumbered by the Anglo-Irish and his Gaelic Irish allies refused to commit themselves to a fight. The Lanercost chronicle provides the clearest description of the battle: 'They [Edward Bruce's army] were in three columns at such a distance from each other that the first was done before the second came up, and then the second before the third, with which Edward was marching, could render any aid. Thus the third column was routed, just as the two preceding ones had been. Edward fell at the same time and was beheaded after death; his body being divided into four quarters, which quarters were sent to the four chief towns of Ireland.' Barbour contends that the corpse of Gib Harper, who was wearing Edward's coat of arms – and who might have been Edward's herald – was mistaken for that of Edward himself, and that Gib's head was severed, placed in a box of salt, and sent to Edward II.

Robert, we may assume, was distraught at the loss of his last remaining brother. All of his four brothers had now been killed in vindication of his right; he will have grieved sorely. Had Edward's remains escaped the final indignities, it can have been of cold comfort to Robert, and he may have begun to wonder whether his regalian right was worth such slaughter. A nightmare of a war without end between Scotland and England now loomed, for the English might never concede defeat. From this stage in the struggle Robert abandoned any dreams of pan-Celtic leadership and the conquest of Ireland that he might still have entertained. Instead he redoubled his efforts to extract submission from the English and, if they would concede his title and Scottish sovereignty, began to offer remarkable concessions in hope of a lasting peace. Through a tiny window on Robert's personal grief it appears that he ascribed this disaster to the wrath of a long-dead Irish holy man: within a month of Edward's death he had provided for a lamp and a candle to burn perpetually at the altar of Blessed Malachy in the Cistercian abbey of Coupar Angus.

9

The struggle for peace with honour (1318–23)

A subtle but perceptible change occurred in the nature of Robert I's war against the English from the year 1318. That year witnessed the collapse of Scottish grand strategy with defeat in Ireland. However, it also witnessed the complete destruction of the Vale of York in the spectacular longdistance raid of 1318, the surrender of key Northumberland castles and the advent of an improved security for Scotland with the recapture of Berwick. The euphoria and unrealistic ambition that possessed the Bruces in the wake of Bannockburn was now curbed, yet there was no mistaking the reality of the Scottish military hegemony or the extent of English defeat. Robert only required to wrest admission of defeat from Edward II to enable a realistic settlement to terminate the incessant and destructive warfare. But Edward could not concede Robert's royal title or the fact of Scottish sovereignty. Moreover, the north of England, the part of England which was within Robert's range and which he could strike at regularly, did not rate highly in Edward II's priorities. Consequently, in this new phase of the struggle, Robert manifested a marked anxiety to capture a vital chess piece, a strategic prize or hostage, which he could trade for recognition of his kingship and peace.

On 13 April 1318 Edward II received the news that Berwick had fallen. One might imagine that the loss of Berwick would have wonderfully concentrated the minds of the English king and his magnates. The largest town in Scotland was recognised as the key to the security of estates on the Eastern March, a vital harbour in the battle against North Sea predators, and, indeed, a potent symbol of the English claim to Scotland. The folly of bickering in the face of such a powerful threat as Robert posed had been long apparent; now it was blindingly obvious that, if the English magnates did not combine to recapture Berwick, the war was lost. Already it was too late to organise a campaign for the 1318 season: terms for a peace between the king and his obstreperous cousin Lancaster were not hammered out until August 1318. At last, on the 7th of that month, they exchanged the kiss of peace.

Optimistically the chronicler of the *Vita Edwardi Secundi* begins at this point to list improvements in England's fortunes: the pope had now placed Scotland under an interdict; Edward Bruce had been defeated in Ireland; the food shortages of the last three years had been relieved by an abundant harvest in 1318; and now at last king and magnates were co-operating. He voices the pious hope that 'treachery, perjury and homicide, which brought Robert Bruce to the throne, will lead him at last to a desolate end'.

At the Easter 1319 parliament in York Edward II sought and was granted a subsidy to make war on the Scots, and the amassing of foodstuffs and the arraying of foot soldiers commenced. Envoys were sent to Robert claiming the kingdom of Scotland, but offering him personal safety in life and limb if he would desist. Robert replied that 'he did not not much care for the king of England's peace; the kingdom of Scotland was his and pertained to him both by hereditary right and by right of battle. He said that he was justified by these titles, and protested that he neither ought to nor would acknowledge any superior or earthly lord.' Early in September there assembled an army of perhaps 8,000 infantry. As to cavalry, the English king paid a formidable 1,400 horse to campaign, including the earl of Pembroke and contingents sent by Richmond and Arundel; in addition to this the great magnate Lancaster contributed his own contingent. The accounts also feature 1,000 light horse or hobelars, the majority of which were led by Andrew Harclay, the defender of Carlisle. The English advanced on Scotland. At first they brought no siege engines, and perhaps their original intention was to seek battle, but when they reached Berwick they settled in front of the town and began to invest it. Siege engines were summoned from York, Northampton and Bamburgh. Robert was not in the town but at Arbroath. The English, however, believed him to have sworn an oath to relieve Berwick before a certain time, and thus looked forward to bringing him to battle.

The brief but fierce siege of Berwick from 8 to 18 September 1319 is another of the great set pieces of the war, and Barbour clearly relishes the telling of it. He says that the tents and pavilions of the English magnates made a town bigger than Berwick itself, and then the English ships also arrived, filling the harbour to the utter amazement of the defenders. Each English lord was assigned a section of the wall to attack, and after six days of preparation, during which the attackers isolated the town by digging a ditch on its landward side as Edward I had done in 1296, the English unleashed their assault. They rushed the walls bearing ladders, which the Scots strove to topple backwards. The Scots had not had the opportunity to improve on Berwick's defences, and the town walls were in some places perilously low.

> In great peril they defended their town,
> For, to be perfectly frank,
> The walls of the town were then
> So low that a man with a spear
> [on the ground] could hit another above in the face.'

Inside the town the commander, Walter the Steward, and his followers rode around the circuit of the walls, helping wherever the defenders were hardest pressed. The English made full use of their naval support, and tried to position a tall ship against the wall on the seaward side so that it could drop a drawbridge onto the wall. Using barges rowed by oarsmen to tow the ship, they endeavoured to keep her against the wall, while the defenders fended off the ship with spears and long poles, attacking crew and oarsmen with missiles. The tide began to ebb, however, and the ship soon ran aground. When she was high and dry, the defenders sallied out, attacking the ship and setting fire to it, killing or putting to flight the crew, before bolting back into the town on the approach of another ship.

The attackers resumed their efforts by building scaffolds to tower over the walls. They also constructed a 'sow', a large and very robust wheeled shelter, designed to shield sappers from missiles and rocks thrown from above while they undermined the town walls. It probably incorporated a great battering ram. The defenders had captured an experienced engineer, whom they forced to work for them, and they deferred to his advice on how to deal with the sow. This engineer, whom Barbour identifies as John Crabbe the privateer, constructed a wheeled crane to lower flaming bales of pitch, tar, flax and timber onto the roof of the sow. On 13 September the English launched a general assault. Again they tried to scale the walls with ladders; again the Scots shoved back the ladders and sent them crashing to the ground. Then the English began to manoeuvre their sow into position under the walls. The engineer attacked it, not with the crane, but with a 'mangonel' or catapult, launching huge boulders. With an eye to keeping his audience hooked, Barbour describes how the first attempt overshot the sow by a long distance, and the second fell short, but the third struck the sow directly and broke its main beam, causing the sappers within to scramble out and flee for their lives, and the Scots to laugh gleefully:

> The men ran out pretty fast
> And those on the wall shouted
> That their sow had farrowed there!

The English then renewed the attack on the seaward side, sending high-castled ships against the wall in an effort to gain a height advantage over the defenders. Boats full of armed men were hoisted high up the masts to bring them level with the parapets, but one boat suffered a direct hit from the catapult, smashing the boat, and tumbling the men into the water.

While Edward II and Lancaster were attacking Berwick, Robert, to distract them, had dispatched Moray and Douglas into England at the head of a large raiding party. They crossed the border on the Western March and rode down Tynedale. From there they ravaged Northumberland and the bishopric of Durham. They had been in Yorkshire from as early as 3 September, but the English army had refused to fall for such an obvious ploy and had continued its approach to Berwick, beginning to invest and besiege it. However, the daring of the Scots at this time knew no bounds, and Moray and Douglas appear to have hatched a plot to win for Robert that vital edge, the elite hostage that he could trade for recognition of his kingship. A story is recounted in independent narratives that the raid of 1319 included a plot to kidnap the queen of England from her household quarters in York. As one chronicler remarks, 'if the Queen at that time had been captured, I believe that Scotland would have bought peace for herself'. It appears that the Scots approached York stealthily, assisted by an English spy, Edmund Darel – one of Lancaster's men – and established a secret lair not far from the city, near Myton-on-Swale. In the city, however, another of their accomplices revealed the plot to Archbishop Melton and the citizens, and offered to lead them to where the Scottish raiders lay in wait.

Edward II had ordered the whole of the Yorkshire militia to Berwick for the siege, and the city of York lay defenceless. Queen Isabella was sent to safety in Nottingham, and Melton assembled a makeshift army of citizens, peasants from nearby villages, clergy and chancery clerks – including the chancellor himself, John de Hothum. This rabble he led out on 12 September to confront the veterans of

Moray and Douglas, and it met with disaster. The Scots set fire to haystacks to create a smokescreen, and, emerging out of this, they set upon the inexperienced English clerics, citizens and peasantry. Great slaughter ensued; many were drowned trying to flee across the River Swale, and many royal servants were taken prisoner. Because of the large numbers of English clergy involved, the whole episode was dubbed the Chapter of Myton. Thereafter the Scots caused widespread destruction in Airedale, Wharfedale and in Lancashire too, before escaping homewards by the West March.

Tension ran high in the English camp at Berwick as news from Yorkshire was awaited. On 10 September most of the large contingent of almost a thousand archers and 350 hobelars led by the Cumberland knight Andrew Harclay ceased to be at the king's wages; clearly they had departed, either to try to cut off Moray's retreat by the Western March or to defend estates. News of the Chapter of Myton reached the English camp at Berwick on 14 September, and instantly the English fell out among themselves over how to react. Northern lords led by Lancaster wanted to leave and defend their estates. Edward II and the southerners were for pressing on with the siege regardless. Accusations of treachery began to fly, 'For it was commonly said that the earl had received £40,000 from Robert Bruce to lend secret aid to him and his men, and that at the siege while everyone was attacking the wall, none of the earl's retinue assaulted it, and that the town of Berwick would have surrendered if the earl's caution had not fought against this, and that James Douglas on his way back to Scotland passed through the earl's lines, and that the earl went through the midst of the Scots.'

Amid bitter recriminations Edward's army began to disintergrate and he was forced to call off the siege. Thus the raid of 1319 had precisely the effect that Robert intended: the English had been diverted from the capture of Berwick and returned home on 17 September 1319 more divided than ever. Edward II blamed Lancaster, of course; he also blamed John Crabbe, the privateer chief and engineer, and the count of Flanders for his refusal to prohibit trade with Scotland. He complained bitterly to the count that Crabbe had been prominent in the town's defence and that ships which had sailed from Zwyn had borne arms to Scotland, enabling the Scots to defeat his siege of Berwick. To this, the count replied on 14 November 1319 that John Crabbe was wanted for murder and would be punished on the wheel if caught. He protested that he had already prohibited the shipping of military aid to the Scots. Of the convoy to Scotland the count said he knew nothing; he believed that ships had gone to Scotland and Ireland only to trade.

There followed an interesting sequel to the siege of Berwick. On 1 November 1319 'when the crop had been stored in barns' Moray and Douglas crossed the West March into Gilsland and laid all waste, as far south as Brough on Stainmore. There are indications that the Western March had been recovering from earlier devastations, and this recovery had been reflected in the size of the force Andrew Harclay had brought to Berwick. To judge from the chronicle account, this destruction was of a particularly intensive nature, more concentrated even than the burnings visited upon the Vale of York, and designed to inflict famine and dislocation upon the West March for years to come. Moray and Douglas returned to Gilsland by way of Westmorland after ten or twelve days and devastated 'Cumberland', before retiring to Scotland with a great spoil of cattle and prisoners. Clearly the threat posed by Andrew Harclay had been recognised and acted upon.

Before Douglas and Moray had returned home from this demonstration of Scottish power, the trusted clerk and court favourite Robert Baldock was on his way to Berwick with a new invitation for King Robert to negotiate. The talks took place in Newcastle in December, and the English negotiating team comprised three magnates who had the full confidence of the English king: Pembroke, Bartholomew Badlesmere and Hugh Despenser the younger, who was Baldock's patron and a powerful court favourite, soon to monopolise all access to Edward II. Also present, as chancellor of England and bishop of Ely, was the able John de Hothum, he who had contributed so much to saving Ireland from conquest. The Scottish team was undistinguished, but Robert and his court moved to Berwick, within proximity of the negotiations. Terms for a truce were agreed. Remarkably for one who held the upper hand, Robert made most concessions, the chief of which involved castles. He handed back the castle of Harbottle, the gateway to Redesdale, to Edward II's envoys – as private persons – on condition that if no final peace were agreed by Michaelmas 1321 it would be destroyed or handed back to him. He undertook to build no new castles in border sheriffdoms. In addition, English ships, men or property wrecked on Scottish coasts would be returned, and disputes between England and Scotland would be settled by representatives from both sides. These concessions, and indeed the two-year truce itself, were incentives that Robert had to provide to persuade the English even to talk about the substantive issues of sovereignty and kingship. At Christmas it was settled that there should be a two-year truce to run from 29 December 1319, during which it was hoped that a final peace could be agreed.

To increase his leverage at the coming peace conference, and also because Robert and four bishops were cited to appear before the papal curia at Avignon, the decision was taken to send a carefully chosen delegation, armed with a comprehensive statement of the Scottish case, to John XXII in 1320. This document was the Declaration of Arbroath, an impassioned statement of Scottish rights and of Robert's title to the throne. The declaration is discussed in the subsequent chapter. In the spring of 1320 Robert sent Edward II a letter inviting negotiations. Its formality and the lofty terms of its introduction suggest that it was probably intended to be presented to the pope as evidence of English intransigence. It is unconditional in its desire to achieve a peace:

> Since while agreeable peace prevails, the minds of the faithful are
> at rest, the Christian way of life is furthered, and all the affairs of

holy mother church and of all kingdoms are everywhere carried
on more prosperously, we in our humility have judged it right to
entreat of your highness most earnestly that, having before your
eyes the righteousness you owe to God and to the people, you desist
from persecuting us and disturbing the people of our realm, so that
there may be an end of slaughter and shedding of Christian blood.
*Everything that we ourselves and our people, by their bodily service
and their contributions of wealth can do we are now, and shall be
prepared to do sincerely and honourably for the sake of good peace.*

In the event nothing much was done in the first year of truce: both
kings were preoccupied, Robert with the Soules conspiracy and
the Black Parliament – discussed in the next chapter – Edward
with journeying to France to do homage to Philip V of France, and
magnate politics. Early in 1321 Robert granted safe conducts for fifty
English envoys to come to Berwick. Still, the English envoys were in
no hurry to reach a settlement; while they were anxious for the respite
of truce to continue, their royal master refused to countenance any
concession on his claim to the sovereignty of Scotland. During March
and April 1321 earnest negotiations took place at last in the castles of
Bamburgh and Berwick. Present were representatives of Philip V and
of Pope John, who had now received and replied to the Declaration of
Arbroath. But since neither Edward II nor Robert would compromise
on the vital issue of sovereignty, these talks were still doomed to fail.
Peace would not be achieved until the English admitted Robert's royal
title and Scottish sovereignty. Unable to extract such an admission
from Edward's representatives, the Scots changed their tactics and
proposed a long truce. Twenty-six years was the term they suggested.
Such a proposal would have sensibly shelved the intractable problem,
allowing time for the Bruce dynasty to establish itself. But Edward II
would not compromise, nor could he be seen to do so.

Both parties were to blame when the conference, predictably,
broke up without settlement, and the expiry of the two-year truce

now loomed on the horizon. Confident that the failure of the conference had proven his point, Robert sent his account of the Scottish case to the curia. Edward had bought time to recover from a succession of humiliating defeats, confront the barons of the Welsh March, and he now planned to invade Scotland. At once Robert and his lieutenants began to stir up domestic trouble for him, by entering into secret talks with his hated cousin, the earl of Lancaster. The political temperature in England had risen sharply when the king's favourites, the two Hugh Despensers, father and son, provoked to violence the lords of the Welsh March, including Lancaster's main ally, the earl of Hereford. Moray and Douglas began to correspond with Lancaster, who in these letters is referred to by the code-name King Arthur. Robert can scarcely have seen Lancaster as one who might be able to deliver a settlement, but the Scots may have secured a promise of inaction on the part of the earl should war between the kingdoms be resumed.

The truce expired on 1 January 1322 and the Scots wasted no time in once again visiting death and destruction upon the north of England. In the last fortnight of January, Moray, Douglas and the Steward launched a particularly severe raid against the bishopric of Durham, intended to coincide with a revolt staged by Lancaster, Hereford and other disaffected English magnates. An anonymous letter now known to be written by Lancaster to an unnamed addressee – clearly a Scottish lord – describes the assembly of his forces and asks him to name a meeting place, and to grant permission for thirty horsemen 'to come safely to your parts'. King Robert sealed the required safe conduct, though whether it was issued or used is unknown. On his way to Durham, Moray issued a further letter of protection to an emissary of Lancaster, who was on his way to Scotland to beg for help. According to a document later found on the corpse of the earl of Hereford, the three leaders of this Scottish invasion were to join Lancaster and Hereford in making war on their enemies in England, Wales and Ireland.

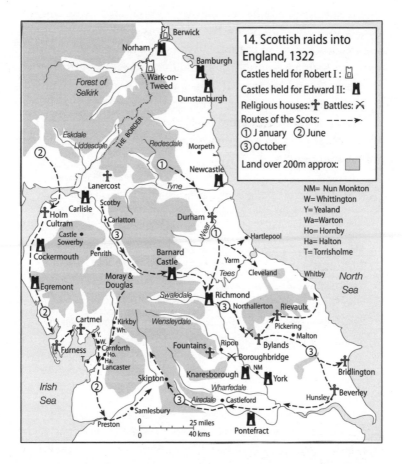

14. Scottish raids into England, 1322

Castles held for Robert I : 🏰
Castles held for Edward II: 🏰
Religious houses: ✝ Battles: ✗
Routes of the Scots: - - - →
① January ② June
③ October
Land over 200m approx:

NM= Nun Monkton
W= Whittington
Y= Yealand
Wa=Warton
Ho= Hornby
Ha= Halton
T= Torrisholme

The Scots, however, continued to work to their own agenda. The accommodating prior of Durham, Geoffrey de Burdon, had just been deposed by the warlike bishop, Louis de Beaumont. Possibly as a result of this the community of Durham ceased to pay tribute due to the Scots, and Robert decided upon a severe punishment. Moray took up position on the Tees, poised to intervene in the uncertain situation to the south. Walter the Steward led a raiding party to Richmondshire, which could be relied upon to pay up if menaced, and he exacted a heavy fine from the inhabitants in return for sparing them from destruction. Douglas ravaged Cleveland and the area around Hartlepool, a favourite target of the Scots. They spent a whole fortnight in Durham, pillaging and robbing thoroughly:

> That same year [1322] around the Purification of the Blessed Virgin [2 February] the Scots entered the bishopric; and the whole of the eastern plain was destroyed. They burnt barns full of grain and then they made as though to cross the Tees into Richmondshire; but at night they returned secretly to the east. Men and women who had returned by boat from Cleveland suspected nothing, and reckoned that the Scots had crossed the Tees. They took them in their beds. And having perpetrated many evil deeds, they returned to their own country. So great a famine followed that devastation in the bishopric that a quarter of wheat might often fetch 40s. that summer, if it could be had at all.

So comprehensive was the devastation of 1322 that in a contemporary document the episode is referred to simply as 'the burning of the bishopric'. Financial records survive for the estates of Durham Priory, revealing that a 'sudden and catastrophic' loss occurred at this time. The flock of the priory was successfully evacuated to Cleveland for the duration of the raid; nevertheless the stockman reported that he had lost forty sheep as a result of the 'abominable depredations of the Scots and other robbers'. At the end of the month this punitive raid came to an end.

Robert, however, kept up the pressure on the border districts throughout the spring, threatening invasions on east and west marches. Andrew Harclay pleaded with the king of England for assistance. A chronicler well informed about events at court characterised Edward II's response to him as follows: 'You may know for certain, Andrew, that if Robert Bruce threatens me from behind, and my own men who have committed such enormities against me should appear in front, I would attack the traitors and leave Robert Bruce alone. Small wonder if the Scots, who are in no way bound to me, invade my kingdom, while those who are bound to me by fealty and homage rise against me, plunder my men and set fire to my towns.' But the smouldering resentment in England against royal misrule erupted into civil war when the allies of Lancaster and Hereford besieged the royal castle of Tickhill. Edward II and the Despensers marched north and confronted them at Burton on Trent on 10 March, causing the earls to retire to Pontefract. There the decision was taken to retreat to Lancaster's Northumberland castle of Dunstanburgh and there await the support of the Scots. But Andrew Harclay, having received orders to raise a force on the West March, moved swiftly south and across the Pennines to intercept them. He met the earls in battle at Boroughbridge on 16 March, drawing up pikemen as a schiltrom 'in the Scottish fashion'. In the battle that followed Hereford was killed and Lancaster surrendered, to be executed a few days later.

For his service to Edward II Andrew Harclay was created earl of Carlisle, and there is no doubt that, for his part, the King of Scots recognised in Harclay a formidable opponent. English preparations for an invasion of Scotland, to commence on 1 August, went on regardless. Robert decided to pre-empt the attack by repeating his efforts in 1319 to impoverish and weaken the Western March, and hopefully neutralise the threat posed by Harclay. Robert himself took the field. At the age of forty-eight he was already an old man by medieval standards, yet he saddled up and led an army into England, proving himself to be a strenuous knight yet:

> The king [Edward II] mustered an army in order to approach Scotland about the feast of St Peter in Chains [1 August]; hearing of which Robert de Brus invaded England with an army by way of Carlisle in the week before the nativity of St John the Baptist [that is, around 17 June], and burnt the bishop's manor at Rose, and Allerdale, and plundered the monastery at Holm Cultram, notwithstanding that his father's body was buried there; and thence proceeded to lay waste and plunder Copeland, and so on, beyond the sands of Duddon to Furness.

The path of destruction described by the chronicler is borne out by administrative records; we know, for example, that two watermills pertaining to Egremont castle were burnt around Midsummer's day. The abbot of Furness went to meet Robert and paid a ransom to save that district from destruction. Robert stayed at the abbey, but the chronicler relates that, despite this, the Scots set fire to various places and robbed them. He pressed on further into England, beyond the sands of Leven to Cartmel, and burnt the lands of Cartmel Priory, robbing the monks and driving off their cattle. He crossed the sands at the mouth of the River Kent, visiting destruction upon Yealand, Warton and Carnforth to arrive at Lancaster. There the Scots burnt the town, sparing only the Benedictine and Dominican religious houses, no doubt at a price. At Lancaster Robert's force was joined by another, led by Moray and Douglas. They had arrived by way of Kendal, Whittington, Hornby Castle and Quernmore Forest. Perhaps this second party had met with some resistance, for two Scots had been taken prisoner at Hornby Moor on 2 July. Tenements at Torrisholme, now a part of Morcambe, were destroyed. The combined force stayed at Lancaster for four days and nights and there was extensive damage, robbery and trampling of crops. The castle was burnt, and the townsfolk subsequently petitioned the English king for the right to take timber to rebuild the town. Still the raiders rode on, driving before them large numbers of refugees. They entered Amounderness; at Preston a rent roll of 1324 bears evidence of their visitation. Only the house of the Friars Minor was spared, and again the townsfolk had subsequently to petition Edward II for timber to rebuild. The whole village of Skerton was destroyed and corn trampled down. Some of the Scots raided fifteen miles to the south of Preston; the manor of Samlesbury was pillaged.

No details are available of Robert's return journey, except in the register of the bishop of Carlisle, where it is recorded that the Scots stayed about Carlisle doing destruction for eight days, doubtless to tempt Harclay and the garrison into battle. The main chronicle source however adds that the Scots 're-entered Scotland on the vigil of St James the Apostle [24 July] so that they spent three weeks and three days in England on that occasion.' It goes on to say that the Scots who rode beyond Preston were some eighty miles within England; in fact it describes a ride of about a hundred and forty miles into England. For the Scots the western raid of 1322 was a considerable achievement, which not only diminished the menace which Harclay represented, but accumulated funds for the expected defensive campaign in Scotland and raised to new heights the morale of the Scots and their confidence and pride in their king. It is possible too that the Scots were searching for a very specific target in the upland forests of Lancashire, namely the enormous herds of cattle pertaining to the earldom of Lancaster which are known to have grazed there in summer months. If the earl of Lancaster's collusion with the Scots had safeguarded them from raiding in 1319, his recent execution meant that they might now be driven off. It is impossible to say, however, whether the Scots gained this enormous booty.

The raid on Lancashire would not prevent the English invasion of Scotland, preparations for which were now far advanced. Edward II had now wiped out virtually all domestic opposition, and was free to demand military service of unprecedented severity from his subjects. The royalist parliament of York in May 1322 nullified the Ordinances of 1311 and went on to grant extravagant taxation to Edward to facilitate his attack on Scotland, including a grant of one foot soldier from every village to serve for 40 days. This was on top of writs of array for 37,800 men, coming from almost every county in England, 10,000 from Wales and 7,000 from Ireland. Furthermore, 11,000 men were to be stationed at the Western March. Only a percentage of this service materialised; nevertheless Edward II entered Scotland with the largest English army yet deployed: almost 20,000 infantry and 1,200 hobelars were paid by the royal wardrobe. He insisted upon increased requirements for armour, and favoured heavily armoured foot spearmen. His army was, however, deficient in cavalry, the result of his having recently eliminated so many English magnates upon whom the royal host depended for unpaid service. There were about 300 knights – including earls, bannerets and barons – and about 950 men-at-arms. A massive purveyancing operation swung into action to feed such a force. An Italian merchant, Manentius Francisci, supplied 2,614 quarters of wheat to the Newcastle depot. Edward was dependent upon ships, however, to transport supplies to the army in Scotland, and this was to prove a fatal weakness.

About 10 August 1322 Edward II's huge army left Newcastle upon Tyne and marched up the Tweed, bypassing Berwick. They entered Scotland by way of Melrose Abbey and Lauderdale, making for Edinburgh. Barbour recounts that Robert withdrew across the Forth. He had prepared for invasion by evacuating all the livestock from Lothian; we may assume that he also removed or destroyed supplies of grain and other sustenance. It was in effect a 'scorched earth' reaction to invasion.

> He lay quietly with his army
> At Culross, for he meant to try

> To cause his foes to lose strength
> By starvation and by long marches,
> Then when he had weakened their strength
> He would engage in a fight with them.

On 18 August Edward II was at Crichton, and next day he moved to Musselburgh, on the coast. He was at Leith, where there was a good harbour, on 20 August, and some provisions from his fleet must have arrived the next day, for he was able to issue stores to his troops. The army meanwhile amused itself by sacking Holyrood Abbey. But the fleet bearing the bulk of the provisions did not arrive, and two explanations are advanced to account for this. A draft letter of the king to his bishops indicates that fear of Flemish privateers prevented the fleet from reaching Leith: 'The Flemings had come to the aid of our enemies, the Scots, and they put to sea in ships just as our fleet was nearing Scotland. They took ships with goods on them so that none dared to come to us.' Not only had the fleet been menaced by privateers, but storms had destroyed fourteen of the supply ships. With the vast army already starving, Edward had no choice but to retreat to Musselburgh on 22 August and from there across Ancrum Moor on 30 August, returning to England on 2 September. On their retreat the English sacked the monasteries of Melrose and Dryburgh. A Scottish chronicler describes with horror how monks were killed, and various impieties committed by the English troops.

Robert himself led the retaliation, accompanying Moray and Douglas for yet another long-range raid into England. He mustered troops from the Western Isles, Argyll and north and south of the Forth, and on 30 September 1322 he crossed the Solway Firth at Bowness, and 'ravaged the district around Carlisle for five days'. Andrew Harclay, who might have proved a very able opponent, had just dismissed the force of 500 hobelars he had maintained at Carlisle during Edward's invasion. While Robert wasted the vicinity of Carlisle, his raiders, led no doubt by Moray and Douglas, swept on purposefully down the valley of the Eden, raiding the villages of Castle Sowerby, Scotby and Carlatton on the way. Shortly afterwards Robert followed them. A well-informed chronicle claims that from the first Robert was seeking to encounter and capture Edward II himself. The seizure of a crucial hostage would have been a very apposite reaction to the English invasion, for only such a prize would prevent future English invasions and force the English to concede Robert's kingship.

English perceptions of Scottish movements are interesting. Edward II became aware that Robert had entered the West March on 2 October, and he summoned ten magnates, including Harclay, to attend him at 'Blakehoumoor', an unidentified location on the North Yorkshire Moors. Harclay, however, had just retired into Lancashire to raise an army. Writs were hastily issued to sheriffs, keepers and castellans on 2 and 5 October in a frantic effort to raise troops from local militias. By 5 October Archbishop Melton at Nun Monkton had heard already that the Scots were in Yorkshire and near Richmond. The next we hear is that Edward II, on 13 October at Rievaulx Abbey, understood them to be at Northallerton, and began to panic. He was extremely angry that Harclay had not yet shown up. We know from another source that Moray was on that day only 15 miles away, at Malton, and already almost in a position to cut off the English king's retreat. The English magnates assembled on a hilltop position near Rievaulx and Old Byland that has been identified by Barrow as Roulston Scar, to bar the progress of the Scots and to give their king time to escape. Battle was joined, and for a time the English magnates succeeded in holding off the Scots, but Robert used the Isles-men to scale the rocky cliff to the rear, and the English position was turned. Meanwhile, Edward II 'chicken-hearted and luckless in war', fled to Bridlington and to York, leaving loot worth a fortune. The haul from the Battle of Byland was vast. Byland and Rievaulx Abbeys were sacked. Among the prisoners was the haughty earl of Richmond, John of Brittany, who had been Guardian in Scotland in 1305 and again in 1307. Robert and he clearly had unfinished business, and an angry row developed:

> When he saw John Brittany
> He showed him great indignation
> For John was accustomed to speak haughtily
> And too maliciously at home
> The king ordered that John be taken quickly away
> And see that he was closely imprisoned,
> Saying that if he had not been such a wretch
> He would have bought his disgraceful words dearly
> And John miserably begged him for mercy.

The unfinished business might well have been the earl's possession of the Bruce family possessions of Hart and Hartlepool, which Edward II had granted to Richmond in 1322. Richmond was held in captivity for two years, after which his ransom was set at a crippling 14,000 marks (that is, £9,333), perhaps twice the annual income of a rich magnate. Henry de Sully, butler of France, was captured by Robert, and three French knights were taken prisoner by Douglas. The knights were redeemed and released by Robert, with an eye to the French king's favour, to return to France without ransom.

Robert did not resist the urge to flaunt his mastery of northern England and his humiliation of the English king. Moray was sent to occupy the Vale of Pickering, where a ransom was extracted from the men of the vale. Subsequent reductions in parish tax assessments suggest that the damage inflicted by the raiders was widespread, extending even to coastal parishes. Robert took temporary possession of the East Riding, an area that had hitherto escaped raiding, and set up his standard at Hunsley. The religious houses of Bridlington and Beverley sent emissaries to Robert at that place to offer co-operation and money, hoping in return to be spared destruction. On the approach of the Scots, the canons of Bridlington evacuated their valuables, relics and muniments to their church of Goxhill across the Humber. Nine Scots and eighteen horses arrived at Bridlington to take up billet at the monastery. The nearby villages of Rudston and Kilham were burnt and despoiled, their cattle being driven off. Finally, about 22 October, Robert led his raiders back towards Scotland. Destruction in Airedale, at Skipton in Craven and at Barnard Castle, detailed in administrative accounts, reveals the routes home taken by the raiders.

Though Robert failed to capture Edward II on this great raid of 1322, it was an awe-inspiring demonstration of Scottish power. The personal prestige of the English monarch was at an all-time low. He had now twice been humiliated in battle. He had shown himself incapable of providing protection even for vassals living far south of the border regions of his kingdom. Yet even this was insufficient to persuade Edward II to make peace, and in February 1323 he was issuing orders for a fresh campaign against Scotland.

While Edward II's insistence upon fighting a war he could not win was making genuine peace negotiation impossible, there were magnates of northern England so utterly exasperated with their king that they were prepared to take matters into their own hands. At Lochmaben on 3 January 1323 Robert met with Andrew Harclay, the victor of Boroughbridge and recently elevated earl of Carlisle, and they hammered out proposals for a peace treaty. Harclay's motives were mixed. He is known to have been grasping and acquisitive, and his star – so recently in the ascendant – had plummeted from royal favour on his failure to save Edward II from humiliation at Byland; clearly Edward II suspected him of awaiting the outcome of the battle, in expectation of an English defeat. Nevertheless, Harclay was surely representative of those northerners whose lands had been devastated and lives blighted by the ruinous continuation of the war against Scotland. The details of the proposed settlement were as follows: Robert was to have his kingdom 'free and quit, for himself and his heirs'; each kingdom was to be distinct and separate, each governed by its own laws and customs; twelve arbiters, six from each country, were to form a committee to settle differences that might arise between the kingdoms. If Edward II could be persuaded to accept these terms within a year, Robert undertook to pay England at a rate of 4,000 marks per year for ten years, to found and generously endow a monastery in Scotland to pray for the souls of those killed in the war, and to assent to a marriage between his heir and the English royal family. Finally, neither king would be forced to accept back into his kingdom or restore forfeited lands to anyone who had fought against him.

The most striking aspect of the Bruce-Harclay treaty is the generous terms for peace offered by the victorious side. This is proof positive that Robert longed for an equitable and lasting cessation of violence and that – saving his royal dignity and Scotland's independence – he was prepared to make enormous sacrifices to achieve it. There is further evidence from Barbour that the loss of life engendered in pursuit of his right troubled the king on his deathbed. Yet Robert also had a less altruistic reason to pursue peace at this time. Robert, Count of Flanders, had died in September 1322, leaving a child as his successor. The regents who governed Flanders thereafter were less inclined to turn a blind eye to co-operation between Scottish and Flemish privateers on the North Sea, and Scotland had, in effect, lost an important ally that had bought her wool and brought her vital imports of foodstuffs and weaponry.

As might be expected, news of a possible settlement was hugely popular in the north of England, and Lanercost reports that 'the poor folk, the middling sorts and the farmers in the northern parts were not a little delighted that the King of Scotland should freely possess his own kingdom on such terms that they themselves might live in peace.' Harclay was quite incapable of delivering Edward II's assent to any such agreement, and before he had even broached the subject with his royal master, local rivals, jealous of his success, lost no time in relaying accounts of his secret negotiations with Robert to the government. Harclay had received a commission to treat with the Scots for a final peace in the failed negotiations of February 1322, but he had no sanction whatever for committing his king to such terms, and consequently he had violated his allegiance and his homage. On 25 February 1323 Harclay was arrested in Carlisle Castle by his local rivals, and he was tried and hanged, drawn and quartered shortly afterwards.

Yet, even as he prepared for a campaign in 1323, it dawned on Edward II that he could no longer persevere in yet another costly, futile expedition. He had just executed the one magnate competent to defend the north. Robert sought the assistance of Henry de Sully, whom he had recently captured at Byland, to convey a message to Edward II while he travelled through England en route for France. In person, Robert asked the French magnate to transmit an offer of a truce until 22 May. Returning to France by way of the English court in March 1323, Sully bore Robert's letters and his oral comments to Edward II. Sully sent Robert a draft version of the letter which would shortly be forthcoming from Edward II and which was addressed not to Robert as king, but to 'the people of Scotland who are at war with him'. Barrow sees in the text of Robert's reply to Sully a sense of humour, but it can also be read as an explosion of outraged dignity:

> We desired and desire always to negotiate with the king of England aforesaid in the form of a final peace between him and ourselves, saving always to us and to our heirs our kingdom free and quit and also the condition of our allies ...
>
> Sir on this matter we have received letters of yours and transcripts of [Edward II]'s saying that he has granted *to the people of Scotland* who are at war with him a truce; and this manner of speaking is very strange to us, for in other truces which have been made between him and us, we have been named as the principal as he has been on the other, though he would not style us king ...

> … there is no more reference made to us than to the meanest
> of our realm. And do not wonder therefore that we have not agreed
> to this truce, but if it had appeared in the proper manner we should
> willingly have accepted it …

In fact the finished version of Edward II's letter *does* address Robert as principal. Robert was in deadly earnest about his claim to the throne and his insistence on royal dignity.

Nevertheless, by the beginning of May teams of negotiators met once again, this time at Newcastle. The English were represented by Pembroke and the current royal favourite Hugh Despenser the younger among others; the Scottish envoys were led by Moray. By a pragmatic compromise each side acknowledged that a final peace could not be reached in current circumstances, but undertook to shelve the conflict for the time being, and to hope that a solution would somehow emerge in the future. Fundamental issues were left unsolved: neither Robert's royal title nor Scottish sovereignty was acknowledged by the English. Instead, it was agreed that there should be a truce from 12 June, and that it should last for thirteen years. No new castles were to be built in the English or Scottish marches. The goods of Scottish ships driven aground on the English coast would be restored. Edward would not stand in the way of Robert's approaches to the papacy to have sentence of excommunication lifted. On 30 May 1323 the agreement was reached, and it was subsequently sealed at Bishopsthorpe near York on 12 June 1323.

As it was, the English nobles could barely stomach the compromise. At the Bishopsthorpe council, ominous rumblings of discontent were heard from those who had lost titles and estates. Henry Beaumont, who, having fought for many years in Scotland and married Alice Comyn, considered that he held a title to the earldom of Buchan, refused to give the king counsel when asked, had to be ordered out, and on his way out remarked contemptuously to Edward II that he preferred to be absent. Magnates who harboured such grievances became known as 'the Disinherited', and over time they were to become a force powerful enough to destabilise the truce.

It stands to the enormous credit of Robert Bruce that he did not insist on full recognition of his rights but agreed to such a 'fudge'. Now, since the execution of Harclay, he would have found it easier than ever to inflict further misery and starvation upon the population of northern England, devastate more territory, extract more silver, enrich his followers and enhance his reputation still further. It is unlikely that Robert realised fully the growing unpopularity of Edward II's regime at this stage, or foresaw any danger of its collapse and replacement by a more belligerent regime. But he would have been deeply troubled by the loss of support from Flemish privateers who had acted as his navy in the North Sea; his fears were realised when, on 18 April 1323, all Scots were ordered to leave Flanders. He was certainly looking over his shoulder at Balliol opposition within Scotland. Crucially, Robert was still without an heir, and expectation of one must have been diminishing with time. Consequently he keenly felt the need for stability and peace to assist in establishment of a dynasty. Finally, to judge from his offer in the Bruce–Harclay agreement of a monastery to pray for the souls of those killed in the war, he was moved by Christian humanitarian considerations to postpone extraction of the recognition he demanded in order to spare the present generation the evils of another war. Thus he allowed Edward II this face-saving formula, trusting that the future would bring about conditions for a final settlement. Forty-nine years old, war-weary and plainly most anxious for a peace, Robert would have expected the truce to last at least for the remainder of his own lifetime. He would have been surprised to learn that his fighting days were not yet over.

10

Robert, King of Scots

The governance of Scotland

Defence of the realm was a fundamental duty of all medieval kings, and Robert still had much to do to secure Scotland from attack. Yet defence was only one facet of medieval kingship, though perhaps the most important. Above all, a king was expected to shower his faithful followers with favours, privileges, gifts and silver. Robert's expenditure on war was heavy, and the economic burden probably fell heaviest on his poorer subjects, but the rewards of successful war were copious. Raiding the relatively rich counties of northern England and dispossession of his Scottish opponents enabled Robert to reward his nobility generously, to create at least the impression of a golden age, fondly remembered for generations.

The cessation of hostilities that lasted from 1323–26 affords a break in the narrative, and an opportunity to assess aspects of Robert's kingship unrelated to warfare. A king in early fourteenth-century Europe was expected to look every inch a king; to behave regally in word, gesture and deed; to brook no equal; and to dominate the political and social landscape. One who failed to live up to expectations – as Edward II of England did – could find himself in serious trouble. Among his other roles, the king was expected to: maintain the laws and customs; provide for the royal succession; safeguard the interests of the Church (without however accepting dictation from churchmen); protect his own position against treachery; manage his nobility through royal patronage; maintain a record-making bureaucracy; and sustain relations with other kingdoms and communities.

Legislation was a crucial function of the medieval monarch, and the tendency at this time was increasingly for laws to be promulgated in parliament, which implied the fullest possible assent of the community of the realm. No votes were taken in medieval parliaments; rather these assemblies were used by the monarch to gather consent or legitimacy for his rule, for spreading responsibility for decisions, and especially for spreading financial responsibilities. Penman has identified 19 parliaments held by Robert and lists some 15 other assemblies which might have been parliaments. On three occasions – 1312, 1326 and 1328 – Robert invited burgesses from each royal burgh to attend to represent business and urban interests. Since the burghs generated considerable wealth their involvement was crucial when the king required a grant of taxation. In July 1326, at the parliament of Cambuskenneth, Robert was granted for life one tenth of all rents and 'ferms' (profits or contracts) throughout Scotland and, in the summons to the following parliament at Edinburgh in February 1328, burgesses were obliged to bring with them the seals of their communities so that their assent would be binding. At that parliament the burgesses were also to give authority for the collection of the first instalment of the £20,000 'contribution for peace' in accordance with the Treaty of Edinburgh–Northampton. After 1326, burgh representation at parliament became the norm in Scotland.

Robert was anxious not to be seen as an innovator, and the laws he introduced were for the most part re-enactments of the laws of previous kings. At the Scone parliament of December 1318 a series of twenty-seven laws – the Laws of Good King Robert – were promulgated, many of them repetitions of laws supposedly passed by King William the Lion in the twelfth century. They begin with a declaration that the freedoms of Holy Church were to be respected, and include: an 'assize of arms', which laid down what weapons and armour were to be produced at the muster by men of varying degrees of wealth; an adjustment of property law to take account of the extensive changes in property ownership brought about by forfeitures of war; and injunctions that magnates should keep the king's peace. Other laws relate to everyday rural life: one regulates the mesh of fish traps so that fry might escape; another restates the old law regarding the salmon close season; a third lays down firm measures to prevent the spread of sheep murrain – infected beasts to be slaughtered within eight days on pain of a £10 fine. This last measure was apparently a response – somewhat belated – to the epidemic of sheep disease which accompanied the famine years 1315–17.

Provision for the succession was a fundamental duty of the king, and this was difficult for Robert because war had taken such a heavy toll on his blood relatives. The return to Scotland of Queen Elisabeth in 1315 after an absence of eight years, as part of the prisoner-exchange following the battle of Bannockburn, renewed Robert's chances of an heir – and, as we have seen, deprived Edward Bruce of the prospect of a throne, motivating him to invade Ireland. At that point, the royal succession had been settled by a royal 'tailzie' or entail, which set aside the normal course of the law. Robert's son, were he to have one, would succeed, but, in the event of his having no son, the claim of his daughter Marjorie, his child by his first marriage, would be – with her permission – set aside, and Edward Bruce would inherit the kingdom. Such was the premium placed on having a soldier on the throne, able to protect the kingdom. On the death of Edward Bruce in Ireland in 1318, the royal succession was settled once again by tailzie at the Scone parliament: in the event of Robert's dying without male heir, the throne would pass to Robert Stewart, the child of the marriage between Walter the Steward and Marjorie.

Elisabeth de Burgh had previously borne Robert two girls: Matilda, who first married a simple squire, but was then wedded to Hugh, earl of Ross; and Margaret, who married William, earl of Sutherland. Robert has had as many as six illegitimate children ascribed to him. None of these could succeed to the throne, though the elder, named Robert, was knighted on the eve of Bannockburn and seems to have been especially trusted and able. At last, on 5 March 1324 male twins were born to Robert. The first born was probably John, who died an infant in 1326. It is surprising that he was not given the name Robert, the established name for Bruce heirs for generations. Penman suggests that the child was named for St John the Baptist, on whose feast day the great battle of Bannockburn had been won. In the event, the second-born twin inherited. He was called David probably after the wise and saintly King David (1124–53). In the event, David II died childless and Robert Stewart succeeded him, initiating the Stewart dynasty. On David's second birthday in 1326 the nobles congregated at Cambuskenneth to perform homage and fealty, and there it was settled, once again by royal tailzie, that Robert Stewart would inherit only if David Bruce died without heir. It was always envisaged that, in the event of Robert's dying before David should come of age, Moray should become Guardian of the kingdom for the duration of the royal minority. This came to pass in 1328, when the five-year-old David succeeded to the throne.

Religion being such a dominant aspect of medieval life, every king had to manage ecclesiastical affairs carefully. As stated already, the Scottish Church was remarkable for its group solidarity and the closeness of its ties with Rome. Yet in spite of papal disapproval and application of the strongest religious sanctions, Robert was able to rely upon the bishops of Glasgow and St Andrews, Abbot Bernard of Arbroath and other leaders of clerical opinion to maintain the Church as a mainstay of the Bruce monarchy. The Declaration of the Clergy published at the St Andrews parliament of 1309 was successively reissued by the Church to emphasize its support for the regime. A general council of the Church was held at Dundee, in the church of the Friars Minor in February 1310 and, on the release of the aged bishop Robert Wishart after Bannockburn, all the bishops of Scotland appended their seals to the declaration showing the solidarity of the Scottish episcopate with the monarch. In return for clerical support, Robert was a munificent patron. His patronage of the Franciscans – the Greyfriars – was partly perhaps in penitence for the sacrilegious murder of Comyn in 1306. He granted the Greyfriars of Dumfries, in whose church the murder had been committed, an annual rent of 40 marks, and 20 marks to each of the other houses. He compensated the Cistercians of Deer Abbey for damage probably caused during the herschip of Buchan. In the presence of seven bishops and fifteen abbots, Robert attended the dedication of the newly completed St Andrews Cathedral on 5 July 1318, making over to the canons of the cathedral the parish church of Fordoun, which was in his gift. The Cistercian house at Melrose however benefited most from Robert's generosity. For the rebuilding of that house – possibly after war damage – in 1325, he granted it a class of royal revenues from Roxburghshire until it should have £2,000. Then, early in 1326 he made a remarkable grant to the monks of Melrose, providing daily to each monk an expensive luxury, a dish of rice in almond or pea-water 'to be called the king's dish'. If any monk refused it, it was to be given to the poor. Out of incomes set aside for this purpose, the monks were to clothe and feed fifteen paupers annually.

Robert was first excommunicated in 1306 as a murderer and rebel against the authority of Edward I, and that made normal relations with the papacy impossible. By 1308, this had been cancelled. However, Pope John XXII, newly elected in August 1316, accepted the English view that the Scottish War of Independence was nothing more than rebellion and he called on the Scots to desist: 'their contumacy a cause of peril to Christian souls and the cause of the spilling of much Christian blood, while only the infidel who trampled on the Holy Land could find in it cause for rejoicing.' Dispatching the cardinals

Gaucelin and Luke to Scotland in 1317 as we have seen, the pope attempted to impose a two-year truce between 'our dear son in Christ, Edward, the illustrious king of England' and 'our beloved son that noble man Robert de Brus, *calling himself* king of Scotland'. At first two envoys were sent by the cardinals, bearing letters announcing the coronation of John XXII and others relating to the truce between the kingdoms which the papacy was attempting to impose. On entering Scotland the envoys were interviewed in August 1317 at Roxburgh Castle by James Douglas and Alexander Seton, the steward of the royal household. They were then escorted by a royal clerk to Melrose where Robert told them 'not without indignation and wrath' that he would not accept bulls or letters that did not address him as king, and that he had no intention of allowing publication of the letters which addressed him only as 'Governor of Scotland'. Robert pointed out that there were in Scotland several Robert Bruces who, in common with other nobles, were governors of the kingdom of Scotland and, while he opened and read papal letters bearing address to the Scots in general, he refused to open sealed papal letters that were not addressed to him specifically as king. In their report the envoys cited a letter written by the barons of Scotland to the cardinals stating that, even if the Scottish king were willing to forgo the royal title, his council and barons would overrule him. This did not reflect political reality; Robert was merely using this convenient fiction to spread responsibility for refusal to co-operate with the papacy from his own shoulders onto the community of the realm. He apparently hired Northumbrian bandits to ambush the cardinals and prevent their entry into Scotland as they approached the border on 1 September 1317, as described in a previous chapter. Later in the year Robert sent the cardinals a letter composed by his barons that spelt out that their king had no power to waive his rights in this matter. 'Without the royal address, there could be no discussion.'

Unable to deliver their letters into Scotland, the cardinals complained that Robert had 'stopped his ears after the manner of a deaf adder, lest he might hear the words of the wise father who exhorted him'. Two friars who entered Scotland bearing the letters had them snatched and torn to pieces, and the friars themselves were set upon and robbed. These at least were allowed to go unharmed; the next messenger, Adam, guardian of the Franciscan house at Berwick, was not so lucky. In trepidation he set out to find the King of Scots on 16 December. He did not have far to go: Robert was in the woods at Old Cambus, preparing siege engines for an assault on Berwick. Seton, the royal steward, denied Adam access to the king but demanded the letters from him, saying that he would deliver them to Robert. Before handing them over to Seton, Adam bravely proceeded to proclaim the truce there and then, while a crowd gathered to shout him down. As expected, Robert refused to accept the letters from Seton's hand because they did not address him as king, and Seton returned them to Adam, telling him to clear out of Scotland. Seton, however, denied him a safe conduct, and on his way back Adam was roughed up by four men and robbed of the letters, his clothes and everything he possessed. Robert went on to capture Berwick and raid England in pointed defiance of the papal truce. By this he provoked the renewed papal excommunication of 29 May 1318, of himself by name and of his supporters, and the imposition of an interdict on their lands, excluding the faithful from participation in certain services and rituals. So far as we can tell, the sentence was ignored in Scotland. The king and his bishops will have blocked any such proclamation.

The cardinals gave up trying to deliver the papal sentence, and decided that publishing the letter everywhere else in Britain and Ireland would have to do. Accordingly, by letter posted upon the church doors throughout England on 19 August 1318, Robert Bruce and his supporters were given ten days to desist, or face immediate excommunication. This new sentence extended not only to Bruce's supporters but to all who so much as provided them with supplies. All obligations or debts to the Scots were to be regarded as null and void. The cardinals withdrew to France fulminating that Bruce had 'hardened his heart in an idolatrous manner, not without suspicion of heretical depravity.'

On 8 January 1320, the pope cited Robert and the four bishops of St Andrews, Dunkeld, Aberdeen and Moray to appear before him in person or by proxy on 1 May, and he furnished safe conducts to enable them to do so. Robert and the bishops ignored the summons but, following a royal council at Newbattle in March 1320, decided upon a written reply to the barrage of papal sanctions. The response to John XXII is a masterpiece of patriotic rhetoric, which expresses lucidly the passion of small nations everywhere for freedom and justice and recognition. In the Declaration of Arbroath some see only Robert's response to the accusing papal bulls, others the origins of Scottish constitutionalism, while others still view it as an expression of medieval nationalism.

This famous letter of the barons of Scotland to Pope John XXII, dispatched to the papal curia after 6 April 1320 and delivered at Avignon between 17 June and 29 July by three handpicked envoys, has many antecedents. The earliest and most obvious model is the letter of the English barons to Boniface VIII of 1301, rejecting papal interference on behalf of the Scots. Though it bore the seals of seven earls and sixty-four barons, it had been framed by royal clerks. The Declaration too, though it purported to be the spontaneous response of the community of the realm, was clearly organised and written by Robert's chancery. A second document that furnished much of the reasoning in the Declaration was the *Processus* of Baldred Bisset, also written in 1301: it contained a comprehensive list of arguments for rejection of Edward I's claims. A third antecedent, the Remonstrance of the Irish Princes was sent to the papal court by Donal O'Neill in 1317, and complained bitterly and at length of English injustices in that country and embraced Edward Bruce as king of Ireland. However, the immediate forerunner of the Declaration appears to have been the letter, now lost, written from the Scottish barons to the cardinals in 1317. The text of the declaration was thus the culmination of a long thought process, to which there had been many contributors.

The form and sentiments of the Declaration had then been developed over twenty years, and it was composed with great care, probably under the supervision of Robert's chancellor, Abbot Bernard of Arbroath. Certain of its phrases are drawn from the classical authors Sallust and Cicero; other internal evidence points to familiarity with the Old Testament books of the Maccabees; it also draws freely upon canon law arguments. Since it was drafted by royal clerks, the Declaration reflects the Bruce regime's view of itself, rather than the objective view of the barons. It is scarcely surprising then to find in the document a panegyric on Robert's achievements, and stress on the debt Scotland owed to Robert:

> But from these countless evils we have been set free, by the help of him who though he afflicts yet heals and restores, by our most valiant prince, king and lord, the lord Robert, who, that his people and his heritage might be delivered out of the hands of enemies, bore cheerfully toil and fatigue, hunger and danger, like another Maccabeus or Joshua. Divine providence, the succession to his right according to our laws and customs which we shall maintain to the death, and the due consent and assent of us all have made him our prince and king. We are bound to him for the maintaining of our freedom both by his rights and merits, as to him by whom salvation has been wrought unto our people, and by him, come what may, we mean to stand.

When a fair copy of the document had been made, the matrices of the magnates' private seals were collected in order that seals could be attached at once and without the document having to be brought all over the country to their various residences. The fiction that the document expressed the views of the barons was played upon to great effect; however, it is thought that the government's rounding up of magnates' personal seals generated resentment and may have contributed to support for the conspiracy of that year. The following clause – the 'constitutional clause' – expressed the idea that the king's hands were tied by the unanimous and resolute opposition of his magnates to any dilution of his demands: 'Yet if [Robert] should give up what he has begun, seeking to make us or our kingdom subject to the king of England or to the English, we would strive at once to drive him out as our enemy and a subverter of his own right and ours, and we would make some other man who was able to defend us our king; for as long as a hundred of us remain alive, we will never on any conditions be subjected to the lordship of the English.'

The theme that the King of Scots' power could, under certain circumstances, be limited had been first anticipated in King John's response to Edward I's accusations at the Westminster parliament of 1293, and then echoed in the barons' letter to the cardinals of 1317. This idea is unlikely to have had any foundation in law or custom; it represents a convenient fiction adopted by Scottish kings when unwilling to adopt a particular course of action, a rhetorical flourish, rather than evidence of any proto-constitutional arrangement or actual limitation of royal power. The language of the Declaration builds slowly to a memorable climax: 'For we fight not for glory, nor riches, nor honours, but for freedom alone, which no good man gives up except with his life.' There has been much discussion as to how this 'freedom' is intended to be understood: the personal freedom, of men from an overweening lord – in contrast with serfdom? Or group freedom, of a people from subjection? If the latter, then there is substance to the claim that the Declaration expresses nationalist sentiment. Yet Robert never claimed to be fighting for the Scottish nation. He displayed an understanding of 'the nation' that is difficult to reconcile with nationalism as we understand it. In his letter to 'all the kings of Ireland, to the prelates and clergy and the inhabitants of Ireland' he seems to have conceived of 'our nation' as embracing not just the people of Scotland but the peoples of Ireland as well. His idea of the nation was therefore archaic, far removed from modern nationalism as we have known it from the French Revolution onwards.

The Declaration is the greatest monument to Robert Bruce: it is his mission statement, his justification for waging war. Its values – justice, acknowledgement of independence and respect for ethnic difference – apply across history; and it raises perennial questions: what is freedom? What is the nation? What is sovereignty? And what justifies resistance to government? The Declaration may not be the fount of Scottish constitutionalism, it may not have inspired the American Declaration of Independence, but its timeless qualities save Robert from denigration as 'just another warlord'. Robert conceived of himself as fighting for right, and engaged in a just but uneven struggle worthy of the attention and recognition of the known world. In the face of Robert's trenchant opposition, the medieval papacy, less impressed by the Declaration of Arbroath than painfully aware of its own weakness in the face of intractable monarchies, knew when to seek accommodation, and by the end of the reign (1329) had lifted all the excommunications and the interdict, restoring Scotland fully to its position in medieval Christendom, even to the extent of granting the rites of coronation and unction to its kings.

The Declaration of Arbroath was intended to present a picture of a baronage united in its demand for recognition of Bruce's kingship. It is ironic that, virtually coincident with the sending of this document, there emerges into the partial light a conspiracy against that kingship, known as the Soules Conspiracy. History has been so thoroughly rewritten by Robert's admirers that scant record survives of opposition to the Bruce monarchy. Yet we know from English sources that such opposition – for example the continued MacDougall and MacSweeney activity in Argyll and Knapdale – was significant and often sponsored by the English government. Legitimacy was a very strong claim to kingship, and it is not surprising that support for the Balliol claim persisted. In

1320, a glimpse is afforded of the strength of legitimist opposition to Robert, and a sense of the potential for instability which existed in the realm of the hero-king.

Until recently the collection by force of lords' private seals for appending to the Declaration of Arbroath was considered to be a principal cause of the conspiracy. Michael Penman however has traced its origins back to 1318, and identified other causes: a weakness in the Bruce regime after defeat in Ireland and application of renewed papal sanctions, namely Robert's excommunication and the interdict laid on the whole country; the efforts of Edward II to effect regime change in Scotland through his sponsorship of Edward Balliol as an alternative candidate for kingship; failure of the Bruce land settlement in the south-west to place a single strong lord in control of the chieftains of Galloway and the former Balliol retainers; and exclusion from royal patronage of Balliol and Comyn retainers who had defected to Robert's side and expected to be rewarded with titles, lands and grants.

Chronicles are fairly consistent as to who was involved in the plot: the magnate William Soules; Agnes, widow of earl Malise of Strathearn; the prominent knights Sir David Brechin and Sir Roger Mowbray; and the minor knights Sir Gilbert Malherbe and Sir John Logy. To this list Barbour adds Richard Broune, a squire. There are many puzzling features to the conspiracy. Barbour claims that it was revealed to the authorities by 'a certain lady' – usually taken to mean the countess of Strathearn – whereas another source states that it was Murdoch Menteith who informed the regime. Barbour also relates, improbably, that the conspirators intended to install William Soules as king. Conspiracy in favour of Balliol and Comyn interests is however vastly more likely. It is remarkable how many of the malcontents had Comyn wives or mothers. Countess Agnes of Strathearn was a daughter of Alexander Comyn earl of Buchan; so too were the mothers of William Soules and David Brechin, and the wives of Gilbert d'Umfraville earl of Angus and Patrick earl of March and Dunbar – all of whom were, to a greater or lesser degree, involved in the plot. Although Soules's father had been a Competitor for the Scottish throne in 1286, the Soules interest had never been canvassed as a serious alternative to the Bruce monarchy. Furthermore, had William Soules been the focus for revolt, he would most certainly have suffered execution when found guilty, whereas he was merely imprisoned for life. Most likely the conspiracy aimed to replace Robert with Edward Balliol, the son of King John, who subsequently, in 1324, was invited to England and whose claim to the Scottish throne was accorded full recognition by the English king.

In the spring of 1320 the arrests were made. Soules was captured in Berwick, where he had been assembling his followers, suggesting that execution of the plot was imminent. Penman does not rule out the possibility of an open confrontation by the rebels, a battle or indeed a short campaign, culminating in the surrender of Soules's 360 liveried followers in Berwick in 1320. In August, at the Black Parliament at Scone, a show trial was held, the leading conspirators – the countess, Soules and Menteith – admitting their guilt. Menteith, the informer, was acquitted; Soules and the countess were both sentenced to life imprisonment. Brechin, Malherbe, Logy and Broune were all sentenced to be dragged by horses and beheaded. Roger Mowbray had died before the trial commenced, but his corpse was carried into court on a litter and made to stand trial – a fact omitted by Barbour. The reason for this macabre proceeding was that forfeiture of lands could only be pronounced over the body of the convict, and thus the presence of the corpse enabled Robert to claim Mowbray's lands. Robert spared the corpse mutilation, and permitted burial, yet this anxiety to seize the dead man's estates reveals a petty or grasping side to his character. Patrick Graham and four others were acquitted in the trial; Alexander Mowbray, also reported to be involved in the plot, fled to England to avoid trial. Suppression of the conspiracy may have cost Robert dearly in terms of public affection. Barbour shows great affection for 'good Sir Davy of Brechin' and sadness at his execution;

he has Sir Ingram Umfraville leave Scotland, disgusted and grieving for Brechin. Umfraville is more likely to have fled Scotland in fear of his life, since members of his family were involved in the conspiracy. These may be reflections of noble revulsion against the executions. That Robert weathered the storm must be down to the handling of the crisis, and to his accumulation of sufficient support to withstand attacks from Balliol legitimists.

One of the main factors that permitted Robert such control of his nobility was the fact that during his long war to establish himself as king he had destroyed virtually all the private fortifications in Scotland, denying the aristocracy the luxury of remaining uncommitted to his cause, and placing them at his mercy. All the authorities agree upon the conservatism of Robert I with respect to his anxiety to preserve the titles and property rights of the Scottish nobility. Few of the great aristocratic lineages had supported the Bruce claim from 1306, the principal exceptions being Malcolm earl of Lennox and Alan earl of Menteith. To a large extent the story of the reign is how Scotland's great families became reconciled to the Bruce monarchy. Some he won over to his side by persuasion, others he compelled by threats and intimidation. William earl of Ross he had at first to intimidate in 1308, though from then Ross remained a faithful ally. Malise earl of Strathearn was compelled early to do homage. Malise then defected to the English and defended Perth against Robert in 1312 and, though he was allowed to live in peace, he appears to have been divested of his lands and title and his son installed as earl in his stead. David earl of Atholl defected to Robert's side in 1312; Duncan earl of Fife in 1315. Since Duncan had left his wife in English custody, a special tailzie had to be devised on this occasion to ensure that there would always be an earl of Fife; it was, after all, the earl of Fife who by custom led the monarch to the throne on the occasion of enthronement.

Robert did not generally raise up pretenders to earldoms where the earl sided against him. We have seen how, at the parliament of

Dundee in October 1313, Robert issued an ultimatum that, after one year, any opposition nobles who had not come to his peace could not expect to inherit in Scotland. A year later it was duly proclaimed at the parliament of Cambuskenneth in November 1314 that Scots who 'had not come into his peace and faith, although often called and lawfully awaited, be disinherited forever of their lands and holdings and all their other estate within the kingdom of Scotland, and be held as enemies of the king and kingdom, deprived of all vindication of heritable right or any other right hereafter for themselves or their heirs for ever.' Robert had refused to disinherit Mar, March, Angus or Atholl when these earls chose to stay loyal to Edward II. During thirty years of warfare, Robert in only two cases was driven to disinherit earls: Atholl deserted Robert on the very eve of Bannockburn, and as a consequence he could hardly do otherwise than disinherit him in November 1314. The title of the Umfraville earls of Angus, who fought consistently against Robert, was not interfered with until the very end of the reign when Robert granted it to Sir John Stewart of Bunkle.

Just as there was no wholesale intrusion of men of lower status into the ancient earldoms, so there was a minimum of interference in their structure. Robert dismembered one earldom and created one other. He had already destroyed the lands of the earldom of Buchan with fire and sword when the Comyn earls failed in the male line, with the death without children in 1308 of John Comyn, Constable of Scotland. There were two co-heiresses, John's nieces: one, Margaret, wife of Sir John Ross, came into half the estate but since her sister Alice was outside the king's peace – she was the wife of the king's enemy Henry Beaumont – Robert took advantage of the situation to dismember an earldom which was a focus of bitter opposition. He parcelled off its lands and appurtenances to his faithful followers: Sir Robert Keith, Sir Gilbert Hay, Archibald Douglas and others. The earldom which Robert created was that of Moray in 1312, for his nephew and chief lieutenant Thomas

Randolph. It comprised various lands held by the crown, including Badenoch and parts of Lochaber, which had been held by the murdered John Comyn. Robert is to be faulted for diminishing the estate of the crown, yet, given that the king was expected to reward his faithful followers, this is scarcely to be wondered at. The earldom was created, after all, for his own closest companion and his chief commander, a man to whom he owed a very great debt. Accordingly Randolph received many generous titles: the lordship of Nithsdale from about 1306, the earldom of Moray from 1312, the old Bruce lordship of Annandale from the same time, and the lordship of Man in 1316, a reward for promised service in Ireland. The Isle of Man was subsequently regranted to him in 1324, in terms that were spectacularly complete in their alienation of royal rights. Even pleas of the crown and administration of royal justice on Man were made over to him. In terms of the largesse he received from the crown, Moray eclipsed even Edward Bruce: Edward's earldom of Carrick, granted in 1313, carried no comparable privileges. Moray's pre-eminent position among the nobles of Scotland was undoubtedly an important factor in motivating Edward to seek a kingdom of his own in Ireland.

Forfeitures of war provided Robert with enormous reserves of patronage with which to reward faithful followers and tempt recalcitrant nobles to come to his peace. Seizures of the property of such powerful magnates as John Balliol, John Comyn of Badenoch, and, as we have seen, John Comyn, earl of Buchan, gave the king vast estates, privileges, titles and rights to dispose of. A 'dangerous mess' of claims and counter-claims existed – especially in the south-west of Scotland – in the wake of two decades of warfare. The chief flaw in Robert's post-war land settlement was his failure to appoint a single controlling interest in this deeply troubled region, over the former Balliol lands in Galloway and Wigtownshire. John Balliol's lordship of Galloway was granted first to Edward Bruce and, following Edward's death in 1318, the king granted the chief castle of that lordship,

Buittle, to James Douglas. Douglas also received Balliol's property of Lauder. Robert Boyd received Kilmarnock and Robert Stewart, the king's grandson, gained former Balliol lands in Cunningham. In the far west of Scotland, Robert I's expulsion of the MacDougalls allowed him to reward John of Menteith – to whom Robert gave the MacSweeney territory of Knapdale – and the relatives of Sir Neil Campbell. Arthur Campbell received Dunstaffnage Castle and Lorn, and Duncan Campbell was given Loudon and Stevenston in Ayrshire. But Robert's main allies in the west were the MacDonalds, led by Angus Óg from 1318. Robert probably accorded him many grants and privileges but there are no charters to the MacDonalds extant. There exist only 17th-century indices of undated grants. Angus was probably confirmed in his possession of Islay and the traditional MacDonald lands in Kintyre, and he was rewarded with the former Comyn lordship of Lochaber, Morvern and Ardnamurchan, along with Duror and Glencoe. Former MacDougall lands of Mull and Tiree were granted to Alexander of Islay. Perhaps the MacDonalds received many more territories that we know nothing of, but perhaps not, for Robert seems to have been conscious of the danger of raising up over-mighty subjects in the west. Many lands that might have been granted to the MacDonalds went to others, and Robert himself retained Dunaverty Castle in his own hands, and built another castle at Tarbert, increasing royal power and diminishing that of the Gaelic lordships. Nevertheless, MacDonald support for Robert provided the foundation of their eventual accession to power, for the 'lordship of the Isles' emerged within a few years of Robert's death.

The Stewarts, the Campbells, and the earls of Ross benefitted from the downfall of the MacDougalls. The third of the great Gaelic kinship groups, the MacRuaridhs of Garmoran, however, did not. This is perhaps surprising in view of Robert's early dependence upon Christina MacRuaridh, the Lady of the Isles. Christina, the legitimate heir, remained alive into the 1320s, but left the business of the lordship to her half-brothers. Gillespie MacLachlan represented

the MacRuaridhs at the parliament of 1309; and perhaps it was
Ruaridh MacRuaridh who fell alongside Edward Bruce at the battle
of Faughart in Ireland in 1318, and whom the Irish annals call
'King of the Outer Isles'. The chieftainship passed then to Raghnall,
Ruaridh's son, but at the parliament of 1325 Raghnall was declared
forfeit. It seems he had rebelled on facing disinheritance by a deed
of Christina's which passed many of the MacRuaridh territories to
Arthur Campbell. Robert himself embarked upon a military passage
to Tarbert in the early summer of that year, and this suggests that he
was actively enforcing the forfeiture and Christina's charter. In the
exchequer rolls of 1327, it can be seen that Robert retained hostages
from the MacRuaridhs.

Along with Moray and the MacDonalds, there were others
particularly favoured. The family of the hereditary steward of Scotland
was repeatedly and lavishly rewarded. Walter the Steward received in
1315 the hand in marriage of Marjorie, then Robert's only child. He
also received the barony of Bathgate and most of the Comyn barony
of Dalswinton. His son and his relatives, the Stewarts of Bunkle, also
benefited from royal largesse. James Douglas too was granted many
forfeitures: Buittle, Lauderdale, Cockburn, Bedrule and others. Besides
rewarding his leading commanders, Robert also remunerated those
who had shown faith in him at an early stage: the small group of early
supporters who embraced his cause in 1306 and those who shared his
outlaw existence in Galloway and Carrick in 1307–8. They included
Neil Campbell and Alexander Fraser, each of whom was rewarded
with marriage to a sister of the king. Sir Robert Keith, the marischal;
Sir Gilbert Hay, the hereditary constable of Scotland; and Sir Robert
Boyd all received special marks of royal favour.

On the back of a hugely successful foreign war, Robert I did
not perhaps need to be a consummate manager of royal patronage.
Nevertheless there was nothing random or unpredictable about
the distribution of favours, titles and privileges, and those who
supported the regime were rewarded, often handsomely, and at

the long-term expense of the crown. The England of Edward II furnishes a stark contrast, where access to the cornucopia of royal favour was controlled by a narrow clique of greedy royal favourites, and where a growing sense of insecurity characterised relations between magnates and crown.

It is remarkable how the royal bureaucracy, shattered by defeat in 1296, was revived, first by the Guardians, and then by King Robert. The whole of the existing royal archive – the rolls upon which copies of outgoing letters were made – appears to have been carried off by Edward I. But Robert will have been able to call upon some of Alexander III's chancery personnel to compensate for this, among them Abbot Bernard. Bernard served Robert as chancellor from 1310 or 1311 to 1328. For the last year of the reign, Walter Twynham took over the office. Chancellor and chamberlain co-operated closely and, because of the small size of both bureaucracies, there appears to have been great flexibility in their operation. A register of deeds was kept on rolls of parchment and, though all but one of the original rolls were lost with the foundering of a ship in 1660, much of the information they contained has now been recovered from other sources. Robert's charters have been painstakingly collected from scattered sources and edited by Professor Duncan, forgeries discovered and discarded. Like the chancery, the chamber, the royal financial apparatus, must have been fully restored and functioning according to usage of Alexander III's time by about 1309, when the Bruce court was possessed of sufficient gravitas and cash to conduct relations with the king of France, to entertain three English earls, and to stage-manage a general council of the Scottish Kirk. The exchequer roll of 1326–27 shows that restoration of the chamber was conservative, as we might expect. Nevertheless, the resuscitation of the apparatus of the Alexandrine bureaucracy was a tremendous feat, and the single accomplishment that underpinned most of Robert's other achievements.

Regulating the economy was of course far beyond the competence of any medieval monarch, yet the activities of kings had profound economic repercussions. Robert's achievement of keeping the English largely out of the country will not have protected Scotland from the ill effects of the movement of friendly armies, often every bit as harmful as foreign invasion. During the 1310s Scotland was bound to have been affected by the same meteorological disasters as the rest of Europe: she will not have escaped the famine and may have been particularly badly affected by diseases of sheep in 1315–17 and of cattle from 1318 to 1322. In these difficult circumstances spoils of successful foreign war will have helped secure Robert on his throne, but it is impossible to say whether the influx of loot and the ransoms extorted from the north of England eased the plight of the poor in any respect, or whether there was in any sense a general enrichment of Scotland. A rise in the prices of food and everyday commodities might indicate an influx of bullion into the country, but there is insufficient data on the behaviour of prices at this stage. A great deal of cash must also have left the country, much of it for the pockets of Irish kings and magnates to purchase their alliance. Much too was spent on imports of foodstuffs and war materials – the cargoes of the thirteen great cogs of 1315 will have come at a heavy cost.

Kings were, however, expected to 'live off their own', to provide for the royal household out of royal estates and customary incomes, and only exceptionally to burden their subjects with demands for taxation. Financial records of the king's income exist only for the very end of the reign however: the half of the exchequer year 1327 and the whole of 1328 and 1329. This represents a partial snapshot of royal finances; what is lacking is a film showing their development, and it is impossible to know whether Robert's incomes were increasing or decreasing. Export duties on wool and hides were a major source of revenue, the king's 'great custom' brought in £1,851 in 1328. One third of this came from Berwick, and the ports of Edinburgh, Aberdeen and Dundee contributed successively smaller amounts. Towns produced lesser incomes too, but rather than collect these through royal officials in large towns, Robert farmed out the profits of the burgh to the citizens. In 1319 he allowed the profits of the burgh of Aberdeen to be held 'in fee-farm' by the citizens, and, in return for an annual payment of £213, all revenues due to the king were waived. Tolls on produce entering and leaving the burgh, fees and levies were henceforth collected by the citizens and used for communal projects. Larger towns too were granted fee-farm charters: in 1320 royal profits of Berwick were sold in this way by the crown for 500 marks (£333); in 1329 those of Edinburgh were commuted for £34. Little can safely be inferred from the differing rates of commutation; much will have depended upon royal whim, and we are uncertain as to whether these agreements were but a part of wider bargains struck between crown and burghs. This was good for the burghs, which suffered less from royal interference and enjoyed more self-government, but not so good for the monarchy which had settled for an annual fixed sum. Profits of the twenty-six royal burghs came to £1,133 in 1328. Robert created a new burgh at Tarbert, the narrow isthmus between Kintyre and Knapdale, which appears to have been an economic success while his reign lasted. There he also built a large castle, costing in excess of £450 at East Loch Tarbert, and had a track cut for the haulage of galleys to West Loch Tarbert, where he built a smaller fortification. Clearly Robert hoped to underpin a strategic consolidation of royal power in the west by the establishment of a prosperous urban community.

Medieval monarchs had, finally, to manage relations with other kingdoms and communities. Since they dominate the history of the reign, relations with England herself are not considered in this brief survey. Robert reopened relations with Norway in 1312 by the Treaty of Inverness at a time when the mustering of galley fleets for war in the Irish Sea became of crucial importance. One wonders whether he received direct assistance from the Norwegian territories of Shetland and Orkney for his assaults on the Isle of Man and Ulster; however that may be, harmonious relations with Norway will have served him well when he needed to assemble the galleys of the Hebrides. France was, of course, potentially Scotland's most powerful ally, and in 1309 and 1326 Robert pursued, as best he could, the already time-honoured tradition of the 'auld alliance', cultivating France when England threatened. France, however, was but rarely available to Robert as an ally. The early fourteenth century was characterised by co-operation between France and England against their smaller northern neighbours, Flanders and Scotland. In the Declaration of Arbroath 'the Scottish nobles' remind the pope bitterly that the larger kingdoms co-operated to crush smaller countries: 'Then rouse the Christian Princes who for false reasons pretend that they cannot go the Holy Land because of wars they have with their neighbours. The other reason that prevents them is that in warring on their smaller neighbours they anticipate a readier return and weaker resistance.'

However, Robert was remarkably fortunate in the 1310s that the count of Flanders at this time was sufficiently independent of France to tolerate the co-operation of Scottish, Flemish and German privateers in robbing English wool ships. This indeed was Robert's most notable 'foreign policy' enterprise: co-operation not with powerful princes but with smaller communities and 'irregulars' in the North Sea that allowed lifelines – access to foreign markets for Scottish produce and imports of food and materiel – making possible the maintenance of Scotland's independence in spite of English blockade. It is not going too far to say that, without the Flemings, Robert would not have succeeded in winning Scotland's independence, and when in 1323 French interests came to control Flanders, Robert wisely made a truce with England. Robert may have seen his relations with Ireland in the same light: an alliance of smaller communities – the Gaelic kinship groups – and 'irregulars' – disaffected Anglo-Norman lords – against the major players – the lordship of Ireland, and the Anglo-Irish lords. In the west, however, the vital commercial axis was lacking. Ireland provided supplies, and perhaps some war materials, but not in the same quantities as

Flanders, and certainly nothing that justified the enormous Scottish commitment represented by the invasion of Edward Bruce and the involvement of Moray and Robert himself in 1317. The Irish Sea and North Sea theatres differed in that the former returns were meagre and the outlay vast. What is surprising is that Robert did not abandon his western aspirations in 1318, but returned to them in 1327 and again in 1328, as is related in the following chapter.

Robert's 'art of kingship' had its limitations. The Bruce court was never at any stage a centre of great art or culture so far as we can tell; there was neither an Edwardian overhaul of legislation, nor an Angevin development of administration such as occurred in the reigns of great English kings. Many of Robert's grants of extensive privileges to nobles and religious houses reduced royal government, impoverished it and ultimately tended towards weakening the monarchy. Some medieval kings, such as Edward I, are remembered as great builders; Robert, by contrast, was a great destroyer of castles, and, besides Tarbert, built few that we know of. The Soules Conspiracy and the Black Parliament cast the reign in a slightly sinister light. Victory over the invader did not expunge earlier loyalties, and Robert lived with a usurper's insecurity and suspicion. Recovery of the kingdom; repulse of English invasions in 1311, 1314 and 1322; the raiding of England; and the attempted conquest of Ireland must all have enormously disrupted every aspect of life in Scotland. Nevertheless, against this turbulent background, Robert's governmental achievements are impressive: revival of local government through bolstering the power of magnates and baronage; restoring the machinery of justice through sheriffs and justiciars; renewal of foreign relations with France and Norway; and winning round the papacy from a position of complete alienation to a position where it was prepared to grant not only relief from excommunication and interdict, but right of full coronation to Scottish kings. In addition to these, Robert succeeded in achieving – albeit for a short time – that key to Scotland's security and prosperity, peace with England.

11

Endgame with England, and death (1323–29)

We have seen the enormous difficulty that Robert I experienced in trying to convert his string of impressive military victories into diplomatic and political triumph. In 1323, with the thirteen-year truce of Bishopsthorpe, it seems that Robert gave up for the present the idea of forcing the English king to concede defeat and yield recognition of his sovereign right in Scotland. Yet after twenty-seven years of war, the truce could hardly usher in a new era of geniality in Anglo-Scottish relations. Contacts between the kingdoms continued to be frosty at best, and occasionally violent. At sea, English mariners continued to harass and attack the Scots en route to Flanders, and Scots and Flemings who put in at English ports were ill treated and might be killed. An appalling massacre occurred when a Flemish vessel, the *Pelarym* was seized by English sailors, bearing a cargo worth £2,000. Scots on board, including pilgrims, women and children were killed. In 1324 Edward II wrote to Edward Balliol, who was to many Scots the legitimate heir to the Scottish throne, inviting him to come to England with the obvious intention of undermining the Bruce regime. Balliol did not take up the invitation until 1331; however, this move was clearly inspired by the birth of a male heir to Robert. Both sides continued to lobby the papal court, and in 1323 a mission led by Moray succeeded in having the Pope address Robert for the first time as King of Scots. Contrary to the truce,

Edward II wrote to the pope on 24 September 1325 urging him not to revoke the excommunication of Robert Bruce, and wrote again to thank him when the pope had done his bidding. In retaliation, the Scots made border forays in violation of the truce and mounted a nocturnal attack on Carlisle Castle in the spring of 1325.

Though humiliated by Scotland and increasingly threatened by France, Edward II of England was, in domestic terms, at the height of his power in the 1320s. He had cowed opposition from the barons of the Welsh March; he had used Harclay to see off the Lancastrian threat in 1322; and the following year he had dispatched Harclay himself for treasonable negotiations with the Scots. Wealth flooded into the English royal coffers from confiscated lands and, opposition vanquished, unpopular exchequer reforms were forced upon the country to further increase the tax yield. A narrow coterie of favourites controlled all access to the king and to royal patronage. The two Hugh Despensers, father and son, Robert Baldock and Edmund fitz Alan, earl of Arundel between them monopolised royal patronage and terrorised all opposition. The regime was deeply unpopular and oppressive, and its failure to defeat Scotland added to the opprobrium in which it was held.

Edward II was no more adept at managing relations with France than he was with Scottish affairs. Relations between England and France deteriorated markedly in 1324 as a result of the accession to the French throne of aggressive Charles IV in 1322, a dispute over the judicial rights to the town of Saint-Sardos and the demand that the English king perform homage for his French fief of Gascony. Seeing his chance, Robert began pressing more aggressively for a final peace, and issued a stern warning. A chronicler paraphrases Robert's words: 'Many of my men have agreed to these truces with difficulty. Whence I fear that if peace is refused I may be unable to keep my word, for I cannot alone restrain the fury of a raging throng.' Negotiations took place at York in November 1324, but according to this account Robert's demands by this time included a claim to perambulation of the marches, return of the former Bruce barony of Writtle in Essex and return of the Stone of Destiny. He also proposed a royal marriage between a daughter of his and Edward II's young son Edward – later Edward III – to seal a perpetual peace. Edward II, however, refused to countenance these proposals:

> For how, without prejudice to our Crown, can we surrender the right we have in Scotland, which from the coming of the Britons to the coming of the Saxons and down to our own time is known always to have been subject to our ancestors? … They cannot claim any right in the March, of which they never had possession … Robert Bruce claims the inheritance which my father once took from him for manifest crime … We should make little difficulty about returning the stone, if their other demands were not beyond all reason … The marriage which Robert offers we do not agree to at present, since we think that, as offered, it is unsuitable for us … Their demands are too damaging to us, they shall return home unsatisfied.

On rejection of his draft treaty Robert nevertheless agreed, showing immense forbearance, that the truce should continue to be observed. But when the War of Saint-Sardos broke out between England and France in 1324, Robert seized the opportunity to ratchet up pressure on the English and he negotiated a treaty of mutual assistance with France, threatening England with war on two fronts. The pact is known as the Treaty of Corbeil, sealed on 26 April 1326 and ratified by the Stirling parliament of July. By it each kingdom undertook to give military aid to the other in the event of either going to war with England. It included clauses forbidding either kingdom to make a separate peace with England.

Relations with England had become strained to a point where a renewal of the war had become almost inevitable. But a revolution in England intervened before war materialised. The leader of the English marcher barons, Roger Mortimer of Wigmore, had been imprisoned by Edward II in the Tower of London, but in August 1323, his gaolers having been drugged with a sleeping potion, he escaped to France. Queen Isabella, who had brokered peace with France following the War of Saint-Sardos, used the opportunity of a diplomatic mission to France to escape the English court for that of her brother, Charles IV. Before her disaffection became overt Edward sent his heir – the future Edward III – to France to perform homage for his French fiefs in his stead. He feared, with every justification, that if he himself left England his favourites would be overthrown. At the French court, Isabella and Mortimer commenced an open liaison and refused to return the young Edward to England. In France, and later in Hainhault, a county in modern Belgium, a growing band of English émigrés coalesced and plotted the downfall of Edward II. Isabella adopted widow's weeds as though her husband had died, refusing to return until traitors to the king and realm had been removed from Edward's company and punished. Henry Beaumont, whose claim to Scottish estates had been swept aside by the truce of Bishopsthorpe, joined her; so too did Edmund of Woodstock, the king's half-brother and earl of Kent. In September 1326 Mortimer and Isabella invaded England with a small force spearheaded by 700 men-at-arms led by Jehan de Hainault. Among those in England who flocked to Isabella's side were others of the Disinherited, Thomas Wake and Henry Percy who, like Beaumont, felt that Edward's peace with Scotland had cheated them of estates and titles. The tyrannous regime of Edward II collapsed almost without a whimper. The London mob rioted and murdered several prominent courtiers and in November Edward II himself was pursued by Mortimer and others, as a chronicle relates, into Wales:

> lest they should embark there and sail across to Ireland, there to collect an army and oppress the English as they had done before. Also the aforesaid lords feared that if the king could reach Ireland he might collect an army there and cross over into Scotland, and by

the help of the Scots and the Irish together he might attack England. For already, alarmed at the coming to England of the French and some English with the Queen, the king had been so ill-advised as to write to the Scots, freely giving up to them the land and realm of Scotland, to be held independently of any King of England, and (which was far worse) bestowed upon them with Scotland and a great part of the northern lands of England lying next to them, on condition that they should assist him against the queen, her son and their confederates.

There is no evidence that Edward II made any such offer to Robert, but Edward sought safety in the west. He was accompanied by Donald, heir to the earldom of Mar, who was a possible contact with Robert. Captured in 1306 when he was only four years of age, Donald had refused to be repatriated in accordance with the exchange of prisoners that followed the Battle of Bannockburn. He was a close confidant of the English king and was then associated with the futile efforts of Hugh Despenser the elder to resist Queen Isabella's invasion of England. Edward II was soon captured and imprisoned by the queen's supporters, and in January 1327 there occurred in England a strange and, for the Middle Ages, rare event, the deposition of a living monarch. A deputation of churchmen and nobles renounced homage on behalf of the kingdom, and in a brief ceremony Edward II was tried and deposed, with the loss of Scotland cited as one of many reasons for his inadequacy. His heir was crowned Edward III on 1 February 1327.

As might be expected, the former king became a focus for restoration plots and escape attempts. The King of Scots may have preferred the ancien regime of his old adversary, with whom he had a treaty, to the unpredictable and illegal regime of Isabella and Mortimer and its Disinherited supporters. On the very night of Edward III's coronation, the Scots attempted to capture by surprise the critically important border castle of Norham. Following the triumph of Isabella and Mortimer, Donald fled to Scotland. Robert received him back with cordiality, and Donald was invested with his earldom. However, he did not abandon the cause of Edward II. One chronicle describes Mar as 'hoping to rescue [Edward II] from captivity and restore him to his kingdom, as formerly, with the help of the Scots and of certain adherents the deposed king still had in England'. Mar sent agents to the Welsh Marches to stir up trouble for the new English regime, and he may have made headway in persuading Robert to support his plans to restore Edward II.

Isabella and Mortimer had every intention of making war on Scotland when they were ready. But in March 1327, to ward off further Scottish attacks, they appointed envoys to treat for a final peace in York and confirmed the truce of Bishopsthorpe. At the same time however 'precautionary' measures were put in place. A muster was planned for Newcastle on 18 May, to restrain possible Scottish aggression, and fleets were prepared on both North and Irish Seas. Isabella appealed for help to Jehan de Hainault, who had provided mercenaries for their invasion of England the previous autumn, and towards the end of May the Hainaulters returned to England. Among them was Jehan le Bel of Liège, who kept a record of his experiences in his narrative, *Les Vrayes Chroniques*. Just as Scottish envoys arrived in York to treat of the peace, further writs of array were issued to muster an English army. The negotiations, intended only to buy time for the English to prepare for war, soon broke down. On their departure the Scottish envoys nailed to the door of St Peter's church in Stangate the following curious satirical comment on English dress and customs:

> Long beard heartless
> Painted hoods witless
> Gay coats graceless
> Make England thriftless.

Patience at an end, Moray, Douglas and Mar struck deep into England in the middle of June. Moving unpredictably and with great speed the Scottish veteran raiders burnt and plundered various locations in the bishopric of Durham.

On 15 July the English host arrived at Durham. Le Bel gives a graphic account of the Weardale campaign of 1327, a madcap chase after the raiders through bogs and forests, barren hillsides and swollen rivers that lasted three weeks. In these reminiscences he recounts his disorientation as a foreigner, the fighting between the English infantry and his compatriots the Hainhaulters, the discomforts of life in the field and disappointments at the failure, time and again, to bring the Scots to battle. When le Bel and his comrades finally encountered the Scots on 30 July, the raiders were ensconced in a position of extraordinary natural strength in Stanhope Park, from which they could not be tempted to move or give battle. They had droves of stolen cattle to live off and could not be starved into surrender, while le Bel and his comrades starved and shivered in the rain. Before finally giving the English the slip on the night of 6/7 August, Douglas mounted a daring foray into the English camp, during which he cut the guy ropes of the royal tent. It is tempting to see in this incident a further attempt by the Scots to capture a royal prisoner and force the English to concede Robert's sovereignty. Moray and Douglas turned back, driving a great booty of cattle into Scotland, and on their way home met the earls of March and Angus leading a fresh force of raiders into England to ensure that the enemy was given no respite.

Robert had not been idle during this time. In the spring of 1327, now aged 53, he intervened again in Ireland. He may have done so on the urging of Mar but he also had other reasons for acting. The earl of Ulster, Richard de Burgh, had died on 29 July 1326 and for eight months, while the chaos of invasion and revolution paralysed the administrations of England and Ireland, the earldom had been lordless and without governance. There exists a report addressed to the mother of the heir of Ulster, Elizabeth de Clare de Burgh. As a result of Edward Bruce's invasion and continued Scottish intervention, the comital

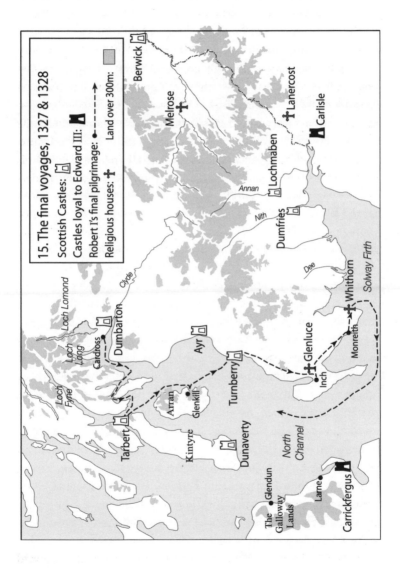

15. The final voyages, 1327 & 1328

Scottish Castles: 🏰

Castles loyal to Edward III: ◼

Robert I's final pilgrimage: •---►

Religious houses: ✝

Land over 300m:

Berwick

Melrose ✝

Lanercost ✝

Carlisle ◼

Lochmaben 🏰

Annan

Nith

Dumfries 🏰

Dee

Whithorn ✝

Solway Firth

Loch Lomond

Clyde

Loch Long

Loch Fyne

Cardross •

Dumbarton 🏰

Glenluce ✝

Monreith •

Ayr 🏰

Inch •

Tarbert 🏰

Arran

Glenkill •

Turnberry 🏰

Kintyre

Dunaverty 🏰

North Channel

The Glendun Galloway Lands •

Larne •

Carrickfergus ◼

lands had deteriorated greatly and lay burnt and devoid of tenants. The report stated that unless the heir, the young William de Burgh, arrived soon to claim his earldom the men of Ulster might 'choose another lord in order that they might have maintenance'. The Irish administration, which was still loyal to Edward II, was anxious to ascertain how the chief men of Ulster would act. At a date unspecified, it dispatched the senior chancery clerk Roger Outlaw, Prior of Kilmainham, to Ulster 'to treat with the men of Ulster and to scrutinise their hearts on resistance to the Scots, enemies and rebels of the said Lord King, and on curbing their malice if it should happen that they land there'. Robert King of Scotland, the dead earl's son-in-law, was an obvious choice of alternative lordship, and he arrived in strength near Larne around Easter, 12 April 1327. Quite what his intentions were we do not know, but any king of Scotland would have been sensitive to a power vacuum in Ulster and keen to see a friendly earl installed.

Speculating a little, Robert's presence in Ulster may have been indicative of a wider ambition to restore Edward II to power in England. As yet there had been no revolution in Ireland corresponding to that which had occurred in England. John D'Arcy, who had been Edward II's justiciar, remained in office and as early as February 1327 he had sent a Franciscan friar as a special messenger to Scotland 'to further certain confidential business touching the Lord King'. What confidential business might have been on the table at this tumultuous time? Darcy will have asked Robert his intentions. He may have joined Mar in soliciting Robert's help to depose the illegal and unsavoury regime in England and restore Edward II. It is not only the English chronicles that expressed the fear that Scots, Irish and Welsh were combining to effect a restoration of the ancien regime in England. The report to Elizabeth de Clare stated that Robert had arrived to secure Irish co-operation for the landing of an army in Wales which was to attack England. However, by the time the report was written, Robert had fallen gravely ill.

There has been much speculation as to the nature of this illness. Elisabeth de Clare's informant seems confident that Robert was dying: 'Robert Bruce is so feeble and so failed that he will not last that long with God's help, because he cannot move anything except his tongue.' Robert was paralysed, possibly by a stroke. Yet his condition left him able to speak, and thus pursue his aims by diplomacy and war if necessary. Robert stayed in Ulster for four whole months. Perhaps he was too ill to be moved, or perhaps there was a purpose behind his continued presence. Probably he had too much respect for property rights to consider intruding himself as earl. Nevertheless he seems to have effectively taken the earldom into his own hands during the period of the heir's minority, 1326–28, as though he – and not the king of England – were overlord, awaiting payment of a relief from the heir. The knights and minor lords of Ulster decided not to resist him and it is even possible that he stayed initially with the connivance of John Darcy. However, John Darcy was forced to flee Ireland when the government of Isabella and Mortimer imposed Thomas fitz John, earl of Kildare, as the new justiciar on 12 May 1327. The next day the reign of Edward III was proclaimed belatedly and for the first time in Ireland. Robert had then to sound out a second set of Irish officials.

In the meantime, on 12 July at Glendun on the Antrim coast, Robert made an agreement with the steward of Ulster, Henry de Mandeville. The location may be significant: Robert's presence in lands which were granted in the twelfth century to his great-grandfather, Duncan of Carrick, may indicate that he was striving to revive that claim. Robert may not then have coveted the earldom of Ulster itself, but was rather pursuing the old claim to the Galloway lands, long since absorbed by that earldom. That would be in character. We have seen him attempt to revive Bruce family claims to Writtle in Essex and to Hartness in Durham. By the agreement he granted a truce to the people of the earldom of Ulster for one year in return for 100 measures of wheat and 100 of barley, half at Martinmas – 11 November – and half at Whitsun – 22 May 1328. Robert's allies among the Gaelic Irish of Ulster were also to be included in the truce, which may have been particularly galling for Mandeville to accept, for Robert had bound him to do so, on pain of forfeiture. During the summer of 1327 there was all over Ireland a marked rise in the level of violence between the Gaelic lords and the Anglo-Irish colony. We surmise that Robert's intervention in Ulster was intended to menace the new Irish government, and perhaps his very presence was enough to cause Gaelic Irish revolts.

A chronicle entry, apparently misdated to 1328, relates that Robert 'sent to the jusiciar of Ireland and to the council that they should come to Greencastle [the earldom's southernmost castle] to draw up a peace between Scotland and Ireland, and because the said Justiciar and Council did not come as he wished he returned to his native land after the feast of the Assumption of the Blessed Virgin Mary [15 August]'. This is borne out by an inquisition into the episode taken in 1331 by the Irish government, and by payments of 100 shillings to Robert Cruys and John Jordan 'for going to Ulster to expedite certain matters touching the business of the king and his land of Ireland'. Furthermore John Jordan was paid a small reward for 'good and praiseworthy action'. This praiseworthy action was probably breaking the news to the King of Scots that the new Irish government would stand by the regime of Isabella and Mortimer, and not be bullied into alliance with Scotland. On receiving this response Robert gave up trying to detach the Irish government from the English, and with it probably all thought of restoring Edward II to the English throne. He returned to Scotland just a day or two earlier than stated in the Irish chronicle, for he was at Melrose on 14 August. Moray and Douglas had just returned from giving the English host the runaround in Weardale, and March and Angus were keeping the English occupied.

Elisabeth de Clare's informant may have exaggerated the extent of the king's infirmity, for soon after his return to Scotland he mounted horse and rode on a last campaign into England. It was a critical time. His heir was but a three-year-old child, so he must have been extremely anxious to wrest final and lasting recognition of his sovereignty from the English before his own death. He had tested and given up on the possibility of effecting a restoration of Edward II to the English throne: the only course left to him was to bring such military pressure to bear on the north of England that Isabella and Mortimer would have no choice but to concede his right. Any air of desperation that accompanied Robert's last great campaign has been written out of history by Robert's propagandists, and there is, if anything, a light-hearted feel to the Scottish narratives, full of admiration at Robert's magnificence and daring. It takes an effort to remember that neither in Weardale nor in Northumberland were the Scots toying with the English: both campaigns were in deadly earnest, for Robert probably knew his days were numbered. He set his sights on the great border castles of Northumberland, the loss of any one of which might bring the English government to the negotiating table. Accordingly he raised a great army and divided it into three: one part to besiege Norham, one Alnwick, and one to range freely across Northumberland, devastating, taking hostages and money, and weakening the Eastern March in every conceivable manner. Barbour recounts that the king left the detailed prosecution of the sieges to others, and took his leisure hunting in the parks of border lords and granting away their lands to his own followers:

> The king left his men before those castles
> As I explained
> And held his way with the third host
> From park to park for his recreation
> Hunting as though it were all his own.
> To those who were with him there
> He gave the lands of Northumberland
> That lay there nearest to Scotland
> In fee and in heritage
> And they paid the fee for sealing.

If fees were paid for the sealing of these deeds, Robert's granting away of Northumberland estates was regarded as no empty gesture. In the past he had made speculative grants of land in the English borders to encourage grantees to take possession, but, in the context of sieges and tribute taking, this looks like a determined effort to annex Northumberland permanently, and was intended to be understood as such.

Moray and Douglas besieged Alnwick castle, held by Henry Percy, for a fortnight, hostilities being interspersed with occasional jousts with the enemy. Then they gave up that siege and attacked Warkworth instead, allowing Percy to sally out on a raid into Teviotdale. They prevented Percy from returning to Alnwick however, and forced him to retire to the safety of Newcastle. Finally they retired to assist with the siege of Norham, where the Flemish engineer and privateer chief John Crabbe had built siege engines to hasten its collapse. Witnessing the devastation of Northumberland, other county communities of northern England hastened to purchase immunity from attack. The bishopric of Durham, Carlisle, Westmorland and even Cleveland and Richmond in Yorkshire, all paid up readily. In the accounts of Durham Cathedral Priory there is evidence of a levy on each manor and another on each church living to meet the ransom demand for a truce until 22 May 1328.

The English government had the impression that Robert was reviving the Scottish king's ancient claim to Northumberland, and feared a general collapse of resistance and ultimately the area's annexation. They summoned a parliament to Lincoln for 15 September, and subsequently stated that Bruce had threatened to subjugate the people of England and to destroy them; that he had built and garrisoned peels and fortalices in Northumberland; and that he had granted away English lands by charter. In the mid 1310s Robert had also built peels in English territory and granted lands in Northumberland to his followers by charter, but it appears to have been the combination of these with the threats to England's crucial

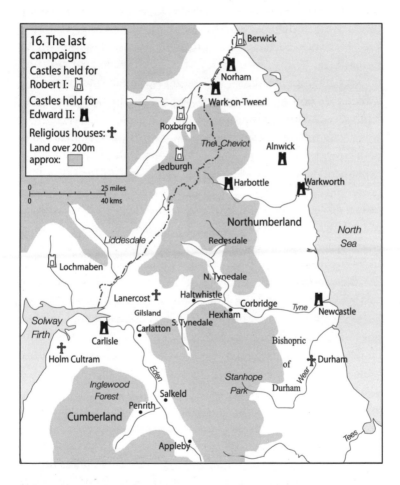

16. The last campaigns

Castles held for Robert I: 🏰

Castles held for Edward II: 🏰

Religious houses: ✝

Land over 200m approx: ▨

| 0 | | 25 miles |
| 0 | | 40 kms |

Berwick

Norham

Wark-on-Tweed

Roxburgh

The Cheviot

Alnwick

Jedburgh

Harbottle

Warkworth

Liddesdale

Northumberland

North Sea

Redesdale

Lochmaben

N. Tynedale

Lanercost

Haltwhistle

Corbridge

Tyne

Newcastle

Gilsland

Hexham

S. Tynedale

Solway Firth

Carlatton

Carlisle

Bishopric

Holm Cultram

of

Durham

Inglewood Forest

Stanhope Park

Wear

Eden

Salkeld

Durham

Penrith

Cumberland

Appleby

Tees

frontier castles that was so deeply disturbing. The unstable rule of Isabella and Mortimer could not afford further military catastrophe, and their government was panicked into fresh peace negotiations. Plots and attempts to release Edward II had continued to plague their regime of dubious legality. On the night of 21/22 September 1327 Mortimer's henchmen are thought to have disposed of the former king. To this day it is not certain how the old king died; and theories of his survival after 1327 are still advanced by scholars. Such rumours do not concern us, for Robert appears to have given up all hope of resuscitating Edward II's regime.

For the first time both English and Scottish governments were both truly desperate to achieve a peace. On 9 October the English appointed Henry Percy and William Denholme to treat of a final peace, and on 18 October Robert set out six terms which to us seem extraordinarily reasonable: he insisted, of course, upon recognition of his kingship and upon holding the kingdom of Scotland free of any obligation; he offered his infant son David in marriage to Edward III's sister, Joan 'of the Tower' as a means of making the settlement last; there was to be no restoration of the Disinherited, those English and Scottish lords who had lost estates and titles in Scotland; each kingdom was to assist the other against its enemies – though this was not to apply to Robert's recently negotiated Treaty of Corbeil with France; the English were to assist in the removal of papal sanctions against Scotland; and finally, and most striking of all, Robert offered £20,000 to be paid within three years of confirmation of the peace. We have seen from the Bruce–Harclay treaty of 1323 that Robert had for some years been prepared to pay handsomely to secure a peace, a strange position for the victor of a long and bitter struggle. It was not specified exactly what the payment was for; it was neither compensation for Robert's tribute taking in England, nor was it compensation for loss of the king of England's rights in Scotland. It is not described as reparation for the exaction of ransoms or the immense damage which Scottish raids had inflicted: Durham alone claimed to have paid £20,000 to the Scots over the years. It is simply described as 'contribution for peace'. Robert may have seen payment as a device to give the English a greater stake in the peace; perhaps he knew that paying off of the Hainhaulters and the costs of campaigning had left the English government flat broke – the Weardale campaign had cost £70,000.

Isabella and Mortimer rapidly responded that these terms could serve as a basis for negotiation. The English parliament of February 1328 at York considered the terms, and sent two bishops to discuss certain articles with the Scots. On 1 March Edward III formally agreed that the 'magnificent prince, Lord Robert by the grace of God the illustrious King of Scots' should hold Scotland free from any subjection or demand, 'separate in all things from the kingdom of England, assured forever of its territorial integrity, to remain forever quit and free of any subjection, servitude, claim or demand'. It is significant too that the English had to travel to Edinburgh to sue to conclude the treaty. Two bishops and three nobles were nominated to journey to Edinburgh, any two of whom were empowered to swear on the king's soul that he would abide by the articles. They arrived around 10 March, and Robert summoned a parliament for the occasion. On 17 March 1328 the agreement was formally concluded in the king's chamber at Holyrood, where Robert again lay ill. It was indeed 'the substance of everything for which Bruce had fought'. Final negotiations added refinements to the terms. Robert conceded only one of his six points: a general prohibition of the claims of the Disinherited was not written into the treaty, and he first permitted Henry Percy the right to sue in Scottish courts for lands granted his father by Edward I, and then made him an outright grant of those lands. In exchange for this recognition of the rights of the most important Disinherited lord, it may have been intended that Scotland should receive back the relics looted by Edward I in 1296. The Stone of Destiny was ordered to be removed to Scotland, but the Londoners and the Abbot of Westminster prevented its removal.

It is possible, however, that at this time the Scots regained the Cross of St Margaret, the Black Rood; at any rate they had possession of it in 1346 – when they lost it again to the English at the Battle of Neville's Cross. All documents implying the subjugation of Scotland were to be surrendered and a record made of their delivery. Great importance was attached by Robert to the marriage between David and Joan, as though he considered this to be a means of ensuring that the settlement would last. As dower, Joan would receive lands worth £2,000 in annual rent in Scotland. The King of Scots was not to aid the enemies of the king of England in Ireland; nor was the king of England to aid the enemies of the King of Scots in Man or other Scottish isles. The rights of the Church in both realms were to be safeguarded, which seems to have implied that lands forfeited from religious houses were to be restored. The ancient Laws of the Marches between the kingdoms were to be kept, and any disputes referred to the councils of the two kings. Finally, the English parliament was to ratify the peace before Ascension Day – 12 May 1328; it was actually ratified by the parliament of Northampton on 4 May. It is a sign of Isabella and Mortimer's great weakness at this point that the Treaty of Edinburgh was one of very few foreign treaties made by an English medieval government to be submitted to parliament for ratification.

Robert conveyed to David the earldom of Carrick, in order that his son should be dignified with a comital title for the occasion of his marriage. But, clearly as a mark of his personal disapproval, Edward III gave no dowry with Joan. On 17 July 1328 the royal marriage between David, aged 4, and Joan, aged 7, took place at Berwick, but although Isabella, now queen mother, was present, Edward III conspicuously absented himself from the ceremony. Explaining Robert's absence from the nuptials of David and Joan, Barbour states:

> For an illness afflicted him so badly
> That in no way could he be there.

> His disease arose from catching a chill
> Through his cold lying
> When he was in his great tribulations
> That serious illness came upon him.

His 'cold lying' seems to refer to Robert's sleeping rough in the heather while a fugitive and guerrilla chief. But the absence of the English king, intended as a snub, may have required Robert's reciprocal absence.

However, the question of what Robert was suffering from in Antrim in 1327 and possibly again at Berwick in 1328 remains unsettled. It may have been a symptom of a final, lingering illness. English chronicles, including the generally reliable *Lanercost*, assert that he had contracted leprosy. Considered a vile and loathsome disease, leprosy was regarded as a 'disease of the soul', and often interpreted as divine punishment for lechery. These reports in English chronicles may be false, but cannot altogether be discounted. Scottish chronicles, by the same token, cannot be expected to own up to their king's contracting leprosy, as it would detract from the vision of regality that they sought to portray. The medieval diagnosis of leprosy might in any case have extended to virtually any serious skin disorder. Recently an authority on the osteological appearance of leprosy claimed to have detected features associated with facies leprosa, the facial characteristics of leprosy, in the plaster of Paris cast that survives of Robert's skull made in 1820, though he added that, without examination of the skull itself, he could not be certain. The fact that there is no record of Robert's segregation from human contact does not necessarily have a bearing on the question. Baldwin IV, the twelfth-century leper king of Jerusalem, was not segregated in any way during his reign. More significant, perhaps, are the facts that no contemporary source, not even those most hostile to Robert's regime, levels at him the accusation that he had contracted leprosy. Other medical authorities assert that the cast bears evidence of sporadic syphilis. Professor Kaufman considers that the cast bears characteristics consistent with either leprosy or syphilis. However, the jury is still out on the issue of leprosy. A Canadian professor, Andrew Nelson, has examined the cast and categorically ruled out the possibility of leprosy. However, all the authorities have been working from casts of the skull, and there is now doubt as to whether it was the skull of Robert Bruce. A third suggestion is that Bruce had contracted Raynaud's disease – which can be contracted from lying in the damp – and that its symptoms might, in the Middle Ages, have been confused with those of leprosy. There survives a finger bone, looted from the exhumation of 1819, analysis of which may yield further evidence of maladies from which Robert suffered.

The illnesses of 1327 – the first real enough, the second probably a 'diplomatic' illness – did not prevent Robert from attending to matters he considered important. William de Burgh, the young and recently knighted heir to the earldom of Ulster, had attended the Berwick nuptials and sought assistance from both Isabella and Robert in gaining control of his patrimony. The English government begrudgingly issued the necessary warrant for transferring custody of Carrickfergus Castle into William's hands in November 1328, and assented to Robert's taking personal charge of the young earl's installation. This is an indication both of Robert's residual power in Ulster and of his anxiety to ensure that the strategically important castle should remain in the care of a client earl. Together with Murdoch, earl of Menteith, Robert set sail for Ulster, escorting William to Carrickfergus and making him a present of stockfish to help him provision the castle. Here again, as quid pro quo, Robert may have been seeking restoration from the new earl of Ulster of the 'Galloway lands' in Antrim, to which he might have laid claim. He dated a letter at Larne Lough on 13 August 1328, and probably returned to Scotland soon afterwards.

During his last years, 1327 to 1329, Robert's favourite residence was his manor house at Cardross, a retreat which he had planned and built for himself. His queen, Elisabeth de Burgh, predeceased him in November 1327. She had died at Cullen, where she may have been on pilgrimage, and her entrails were buried there in the Lady Chapel. One surmises that, given the antagonism between Robert and his father-in-law, Elizabeth's reported remarks at Robert's inauguration, and the existence of illegitimate children, their marriage had never been a close union. Robert arranged that a chaplain at Cullen was paid £4 annually for celebrating masses for her soul. This was modest provision for the soul of a queen; Robert had set aside £20 per annum for the souls of Alexander III and John, earl of Atholl. Nevertheless Robert shows attachment to Elisabeth in that her body was borne to Dunfermline Abbey for burial: he clearly wanted his spouse at his side in death.

Having endured the loss of his four brothers, Robert seems always to have valued male companionship more dearly than female. The closest of all his companions was Moray, often with him in these last months and sharing his activities. The king had a new chamber built at Cardross – with glasswork in the windows and a painted interior – a garden, and a shed for his falcons, and he maintained a considerable hunting establishment. He lived well, threw feasts and dispensed gifts and charity. He kept a pet lion, as the young and riotous Edward of Caernarfon had done twenty years before. He and Moray took special interest in the king's 'great ship', making repairs and ordering sails, pitch, iron and other materials. On one occasion Robert had it hauled from the seashore into the river beside the house for maintenance.

The king's health continued to deteriorate. Payments to apothecaries show that various medicines were purchased. The king's chief physician was Gille Pàdraig Beaton, who was from a Gaelic family of learned hereditary physicians, and he must have been often in attendance at Cardross. Another learned doctor who was present, the Italian Maino de Maineri, later showed concern over the king's diet. Eels and lampreys are listed among the provisions purchased for Cardross and, from observing Robert's symptoms, de Maineri later reflected:

I am certain that this fish should not be eaten because I have seen it during the time I was with the king of Scots, Robert Bruce, who risked many dangers by eating eels, which are by nature like lampreys. It is true that these eels were caught in muddy and corrupt waters.

Robert's last journey appears to have been a pilgrimage; this was possibly in search of a miraculous cure, though equally, as pilgrimages often provided excuse for wandering, it may have been merely a pretext for an outing on his great ship. With Moray he set off from Cardross for Tarbert, thence to Arran where he celebrated Christmas 1328 at the hall of Glenkill near Lamlash, and thence he sailed to the mainland to visit his son and his bride, mere children, now installed at Turnberry, the head of the earldom of Carrick and once his own main residence. He journeyed overland to Inch, south of Stranraer: houses were built there and supplies brought to that place, as though the king's condition had deteriorated while he was being carried across the isthmus. At the end of March he was staying at Glenluce Abbey and at Monreith, from which St Ninian's cave was visited. Early in April he arrived at the shrine of St Ninian at Whithorn. He returned by sea to Cardross, where he was placed upon his deathbed, Moray no doubt by his side. Barbour relates – and he is borne out by other sources – that Robert summoned the lords of the kingdom to his bedside for a final council, at which he made copious gifts to religious houses and repented of his failure to fulfil a vow to undertake a crusade. He dispensed silver to religious foundations of various orders, so that they might pray for his soul. Into the mouth of the dying king Barbour puts a speech which includes an almost modern repentance for 'war crimes':

> I thank God for giving me
> Time in this life to repent,
> For because of me and my war-making

> There has been much spilling of blood
> In which many innocent men were slain;
> Therefore I accept this sickness and pain
> As reward for my transgressions.

Whether these sentiments were actually expressed by the dying king is uncertain; it is unconventional for a medieval king to express guilt about 'collateral damage' inflicted on innocents in pursuit of his right, and for this reason it might indeed represent an actual deathbed utterance. Robert's final wish, however, reflects conventional piety expressed in a novel fashion, quite possibly intended to perpetuate his memory: after his death his heart was to be removed from his body and borne by a noble knight, one honest, wise and brave, against God's enemies – probably intended from the first to be James Douglas.

Robert died on 7 June 1329 having lived a life extraordinarily rich and varied. He died utterly fulfilled, in that the goal of his lifetime's struggle – untrammelled recognition of the Bruce right to the throne – had been realised, and confident that he was leaving the kingdom of Scotland safely in the hands of his most trusted lieutenant, Moray, until such times as his infant son could hold the reins of state. However great his final agony, he could not have asked for greater comforts. Six days after his death, to complete his triumph still further, papal bulls were issued granting the privileges of coronation and unction at the enthronement of future Kings of Scots.

The obsequies of Robert I were as befitted a great king. The body was embalmed. Separate burial of heart and body had been forbidden by a papal bull of 1299, but the custom was attractive in that more than one religious community could be involved in intercession for the soul. It had been carried out at the funerals of Louis IX of France, Richard I and Henry III of England, Eleanor of Castile – Edward I's queen – and, as we have seen, in the case of Robert's own queen. Accordingly the breastbone of Robert's corpse was sawn to allow extraction of the heart, which Douglas placed in a silver casket to be worn around his neck. The body was taken from Cardross, through Dunipace and Cambuskenneth to Dunfermline, the mausoleum of the Scottish kings. Barbour claims that:

> when his people knew that he had died
> Sorrow spread from home to home.
> You could see men tear their hair,
> And frequently knights weeping copiously,
> Striking their fists together and tearing their clothes like madmen,
> Mourning his seemly generosity,
> His wisdom, strength and his honesty
> But above all the warm companionship
> Which, in his courtesy, he often shared with them.

We cannot tell whether the gilded hearse was followed by crowds of mourners; nor does there survive any more reliable indication of genuine widespread grief. There will have been some relief and anticipation from the anti-Bruce elements that Robert had suppressed, yet we can scarcely doubt that the funeral was an occasion for an outpouring of affection such as Barbour describes, for a king who had ended foreign occupation, led successful and lucrative foreign war, distributed largesse abundantly and triumphed magnificently and repeatedly.

An enormous weight of wax – 478 stone, or just over 3,000 kg – was purchased, presumably for the making of funerary candles; copious lengths of fine linen and black cloth were procured for mourning clothes: black 'budge' for knights, other varieties for officers of the household and their followers. Robes were bought, and furs for knights. A marble tomb, which Robert had commissioned years previously to be made in Paris, was brought by way of Bruges to Dunfermline. Gold leaf was acquired in England for its decoration, and an iron railing placed around the grave. A chapel of timber was erected over the grave on the day of the funeral, and Robert was interred in what was then the very centre of Dunfermline Abbey, beneath the high altar, and beside his queen. Though the church around it is greatly altered, the place is now marked by a magnificent Victorian brass.

The faithful Douglas had been selected – probably preselected – to fulfil Robert's crusading vow. In a coda to his epic poem Barbour relates how Douglas set off from Berwick for Spain to do battle with the Moors. It was an act of piety, but for both Bruce and Douglas it was also self-promotion, a 'farewell European tour'. No one had ever gone on crusade in quite this fashion, and the excursion was intended to cultivate the legends of Robert Bruce and the Black Douglas. No expense was spared to deck out Douglas with a splendid entourage. He passed through England, and in September 1329 Edward III's chancery equipped him with letters of protection and commendation to King Alfonso XI of Castile. His ship anchored in the busy port of Sluis in the southern Netherlands for twelve days, but Douglas did not disembark. Rather, guests were invited on board to bid farewell to a legend, and Douglas entertained them 'as though he were king of Scotland'. Douglas's fame went before him and he was received in Spain with honour, above all from the English knights. In broad terms Barbour's version of events in Spain is borne out by le Bel and by a Spanish source. Douglas was clearly preparing to exit this life, and had no intention of returning safely from Spain. He was killed in a skirmish on 25 August 1330 at Tebas de Ardales, the day before the main engagement there, along with Sir William Sinclair, and Robert and Walter Logan. Tradition has it, from lines interpolated into the Barbour text, that, seeing his position to be hopeless, Douglas tossed the casket bearing the king's heart into the thick of the fight, and charged the enemy with the words:

> Now pass thou forth before,
> As thou was wont in field to be,
> And I shall follow or else die.

Recovered from the field, Douglas's body was boiled in order to remove flesh from bones – another not uncommon funerary practice – and then his bones, together with the heart of Robert Bruce, were borne back to Scotland by Sir William Keith of Galston. Douglas was buried in his parish church, St Bride's Kirk at Douglas, where in 1307 he had ambushed the enemy garrison, and, in accordance with the king's earlier wish, the heart of Robert Bruce was interred at Melrose Abbey.

12

The image, the legend and the long shadow of Robert Bruce

The life of Robert Bruce was not the unqualified success which propagandists for his dynasty have represented. In particular, Barbour, Fordun and Bower exaggerate the degree to which Scotland united behind Robert. The strength of anti-Bruce feeling in Scotland is revealed by the dogged resistance of John of Argyll, by the treason trials of the Black Parliament that reveal enduring pro-Balliol sympathies and by the sudden collapse of the Bruce powerbase within a few years of Robert's death. Undoubtedly too, Robert Bruce had been fortunate. He appears to have acknowledged readily that the incompetence of Edward I's successor enabled him to recover the kingdom of Scotland. Also readily apparent is Robert's good fortune in the powerlessness of English government that occurred in the decade after Bannockburn, caused partly by strife between the English king and his barons, and partly by the natural catastrophes of famine and disease of animals.

It is not surprising that Robert failed to achieve sainthood, that ultimate accolade of popular medieval kings, from either Church or people. Sainthood was associated with cases when the body did not, for one reason or another, decay, but Robert's body – whether leprous or not – was already manifestly in decay long before his death. 'Canonisation by popular demand', or 'political canonisation', was accorded to certain popular lords in the Middle Ages, and contemporary examples of this occurred in England. After his execution in 1322 Earl Thomas of Lancaster was widely recognised as a martyr and saint, and pilgrimages were made to the site of his grave. Edward of Caernarfon, Robert's contemporary and old adversary, had a lively 'afterlife'. Stories about how Edward II escaped murder in 1327 and wandered far and wide until as late as 1338 were sufficiently convincing and numerous to cause the magnificent tomb in Gloucester Cathedral to be opened in October 1855 to establish the existence of a coffin, and to have sown doubt in the minds of some modern historians as to whether Edward was murdered as reported. The purpose of invented afterlives and popular canonisation was to salvage sullied reputations and lacklustre careers to the embarrassment of political authorities. But to his supporters Robert's reputation among Scots was unsullied – despite the murder and sacrilege of 1306 – and to contemporaries his career lacked no lustre. Canonisation and 'afterlife' were unnecessary and inappropriate.

The truly great are never allowed to rest in peace. During the Protestant Reformation, Dunfermline Abbey was attacked by Calvinist reformers and the marble tomb with gold-leaf decoration was smashed, probably for no other reason than it represented a graven image, forbidden by Old Testament stricture. But centuries later, in 1817, magistrates of the burgh of Dunfermline decided to build a new church on the site of the abbey, and the land had to be cleared to allow rebuilding. Robert Bruce's tomb was one of many discovered – others included those of St Margaret and Malcolm Canmore. Such was the fascination of contemporaries with the Middle Ages that, after the new church had been built around it, Robert's remains were exhumed in November 1819, measured, and left above ground for five days to allow for thorough examination.

There was at the time no doubt that the remains belonged to Robert Bruce: the breastbone had been sawn to allow for the removal of the heart. A plaster of Paris cast of the skull was made, during which two or three teeth may have come out. Examination yielded considerable evidence of injury to the head. The official report read, 'There is a kind of mark on the right side of the sagittal suture, most probably the consequence of a severe injury, and of subsequent exfoliation.' It is also of interest that a considerable portion of the left zygomatic arch, on the side of the skull, is missing from the cast. According to Pearson, who wrote in 1924, 'The cast lacks the left zygomatic ridge, whether broken off in the skull or more recently from the cast is not clear ... detailed analysis of the cast strongly suggests that this deficiency was present when the cast was made, and the two ends of the arch appear to show evidence of healing ...' In life, then, the subject had sustained a severe blow on the top of his skull, and another on the left side of the head, exactly as we might expect of a warrior king. He will have been badly scarred, and it may be that such scarring gave rise to the notion entertained by his detractors that he had contracted leprosy.

Phrenology was a pseudo-science much in vogue in the nineteenth century, and the skull was subjected to examination by phrenologists who claimed to read character traits from the shape of the head. Phrenological observations were published, and though couched in 'scientific' terms it is clear that they were heavily dependent upon written accounts for their assessment of Bruce's personality. A curious story exists that, during this time, a local dignitary entered the church at night and removed a toe, together with a piece of the shroud and fragments from the coffin. Although these items are preserved in the Hunterian Museum in Glasgow, it has been impossible for the museum authorities to verify that particular piece of antique flesh as Robert's toe: it is too decayed for DNA tests or carbon-dating. A finger was also retained by a souvenir hunter, as referred to in the previous chapter. Other reputed bone fragments are held at St Conan's Kirk at Lochawe, and also in the museum of Dunfermline Abbey. When the scientists – and the souvenir hunters – had completed their work, the body was returned to the lead coffin. Molten pitch was poured into the coffin, a measure intended to preserve the skeleton, and then a number of articles were placed in it, among them a copy of the 1714 edition of *The Bruce*, one of Kerr's *History of Scotland* and seven gold and nine silver coins. The tomb was then rebuilt and resealed, and a superb Victorian brass now marks the place of burial.

Of course, deductions about wounds the king received in life from the cast of the skull are only valid if the remains exhumed in 1819 are indeed the corporal remains of Robert Bruce. His most recent biographer, Penman, puts the cat among the pigeons by suggesting that they may not have been. He points out that heart burial was not uncommon among the aristocracy of the time, so the remains exhumed with breastbone sawn to enable removal of the heart could have belonged to any medieval aristocrat. He also suggests that Robert commissioned a canopied box-tomb with effigy, better suited to elsewhere in the abbey church; and that the location of the grave opened was more suited to the king who raised Dunfermline to abbatial status, namely King David I.

Further exhumations took place in the twentieth century. A conical lead container, ten inches in height and believed to hold Bruce's heart, was discovered beneath the floor of the Chapter House at Melrose Abbey in March 1921. It was confirmed that a heart was enclosed, and the container was reburied. The same container was found a second time in 1996 and investigated using fibre optic cable. This revealed an inner casket, also of lead. Since however there was no doubt it contained the much-decayed heart of Robert Bruce, nothing was to be gained by penetrating it and the container was reburied intact in 1998. On that occasion the secretary of state for Scotland unveiled a plaque on the floor over the place where the heart is buried. The inscription on the stone is taken from Barbour, and reads 'A noble hart may have no ease, gif freedom failye.' The plaque bears a simple carving of a heart entwined with the St Andrew's Cross.

Fascination with the subject's corporal remains is only one of a number of yardsticks by which the significance of an historical figure may be assessed. Another test of 'greatness' is how long after death the individual's achievements last. A third is his contribution made to the host society. A fourth indication of significance might be the degree of interest taken in the subject since his death. There are yet others still: what place the subject holds in the popular pantheon of heroes, and whether the subject has any relevance for contemporaries.

In so far as Robert helped to preserve a distinct and vibrant Scottish identity, his contribution survives the test of time; however, his particular achievement, the political settlement of 1328, was doomed to last less than four years. Aware that no scrap of parchment was any real guarantee for his son's throne, Robert had built into his settlement such safeguards as were available to him: installation of his most trusted and able lieutenant, Moray, as regent; marriage between the royal families of England and Scotland, designed to lock the kingdoms together in harmony; and payment of a very large sum of money to England spread out over the three years following. These terms however were not nearly sufficient to reconcile the English to the treaty they dubbed the Shameful Peace. English chronicles uniformly denounce the Treaty of Edinburgh–Northampton as a sell-out. Realising the depth of its unpopularity, the English regime did not even publish its terms, and the secrecy surrounding the agreement served only to attract further vilification. Young Edward III, however, being under-age, was absolved from the opprobrium: 'accursed be the time that this parliament was ordained at Northampton, for there through false counsel the king was there falsely disinherited; and yet he was within age'. That king had made no secret of his displeasure at the settlement, and when the time came Edward III used this pretext to avoid honouring the agreement.

On 19 October 1330 Edward III carried out a daring *coup d'état*, overthrowing the government which his mother and her lover had carried on in his name. Mortimer he executed; Isabella he sent into honourable confinement; and so at the age of eighteen he grasped the reins of power. Waiting in the wings were the Disinherited, led by Henry Beaumont and Thomas Wake, who felt themselves cheated by the peace of titles, lands and incomes in Scotland. Beaumont's claim to the earldom of Buchan was through his wife, Alice Comyn; Wake claimed the barony of Kirkandrews and the border lordship of Liddesdale through his great-grandmother, Joan d'Estuteville. Among the other Disinherited lords were Gilbert de Umfraville, whom Robert had disinherited of the earldom of Atholl and half the lands of John Comyn, whom Robert had killed at Dumfries. The other half of those lands was claimed by Richard Talbot, who had married the other co-heiress. Edward III now lent unofficial English royal support to the demands of the two most powerful of the aggrieved lords. The Scots paid no attention to his advocacy of the Disinherited cause; they might have been wiser to buy off Beaumont and Wake, the two most dangerous, as Robert had virtually promised them restoration in any case. On Midsummer's Day the last instalment of the promised £20,000 was paid, and Scotland lost the security that the promise of payment had afforded. Beaumont began to organise the Disinherited lords for an expedition to Scotland to realise their claims by force, and in an astute move he brought over to England Edward Balliol, the son of King John, to lead the expedition. The invaders would then be able to tap into legitimist sentiment that was still strong in Scotland. Edward Balliol secretly did homage to Edward III for the kingdom of Scotland, and Edward III lent Balliol and the Disinherited his tacit co-operation.

In view of the growing threat posed by the Disinherited, Moray, Guardian of Scotland, brought forward the date of the coronation of Robert's son as David II, and on 24 November 1331 the seven-year-old David was crowned and anointed in a parliament at Scone. He was the first King of Scots to be accorded the full rites of royal inauguration; for decades Scots had been lobbying the papacy for the rights to coronation of their kings, and the solemnities and festivities on this occasion may be considered as the last triumph of Robert Bruce. Yet Scotland had been profoundly weakened by the deaths of many of her leading magnates. King Robert's death had been followed by that of James Douglas, Walter the Steward, the former chancellor Bernard of Arbroath and bishops David of Moray and William Lamberton of St Andrews. This string of catastrophes concluded with the death of the guardian, Moray himself, at Musselburgh on 20 July 1332, while organising the defences of southern Scotland against the anticipated onslaught. It is alleged that he was poisoned at the command of Beaumont, though the evidence for that is unconvincing.

Hearing the news of Moray's demise, the Disinherited were quick to set sail, and they landed at Kinghorn on 6 August with 500 men-at-arms and 1,000 foot. Invasion by sea was a master stroke: it was intended to allow Edward III deniability in the event of a debacle, it kept the Scots guessing as to where they would land, and finally it deprived the Scots of the opportunity to retreat behind scorched earth. The invaders vanquished the first force that met them, and thus gained a foothold. The enormous army which then confronted them was poorly led and disorganised. The leaders squabbled: Donald of Mar, recently elected Guardian in place of Moray, fell out with Sir Robert Bruce, the late king's illegitimate son, on the day of confrontation with the invaders. The battle at Dupplin Moor on 11 August should have been won easily by the Brucean army, but the host showed lack of discipline and its commanders completely mismanaged the encounter. Defeat of so many by so few was widely interpreted as a mark of divine favour, and when the Disinherited captured Perth, Scottish nobles began to defect to Balliol's side. The coalition of noble interests that Robert had welded together by force of personality and by fear now strained and cracked: incredibly, Duncan, earl of Fife, led Balliol to the throne at Scone on 24 September 1332, and Bishop William Sinclair of Dunkeld – whom King Robert had fulsomely praised as 'his own bishop' – crowned Balliol King of Scots at Scone.

Thus the stage was set for a renewal of that Scottish civil war which Robert I had all but won at Bannockburn.

The reawakening of the Bruce–Balliol civil war, fuelled by Edward III's support, and the unravelling of Robert's plan for dynastic union on an equal basis between the kingdoms were catastrophes for England and Scotland alike. Though Balliol was driven out of Scotland before the year 1332 ended, he returned, this time with England's declared backing. An army headed by English magnates captured Berwick and won a signal victory at Halidon Hill on 19 July 1333, and Balliol was re-installed in Scotland. But Edward III soon lost interest in Scotland, as from 1336 Scotland became a sideshow in England's Hundred Years War against France. King David's fortunes ebbed and flowed: from 1334 to 1341 he was exiled in France; in 1346 he had recovered sufficiently to raid Northumberland and Durham; then, having been captured at the Battle of Neville's Cross, was from 1346 to 1357 a prisoner in English jails. Edward Balliol enjoyed a similar ebb and flow of fortune; but eventually, having lost his last foothold in Scotland in 1356, he resigned to Edward III his claim to the kingship. This claim to Scotland Edward and his successors pursued during respites from the French war. Scotland and England became locked into a futile cycle of violence, in which each kingdom could inflict great harm on the other, but neither could win decisive victory. The Scots raided the English border counties periodically, devastating the countryside and wasting the labour of centuries; the English marched expeditions to Edinburgh virtually whenever they wished, forcing the Scots into temporary retreat north of the Forth. The Anglo–Scottish border, a precisely defined and mutually agreed line that in 1296 crossed the countryside from one landmark to the next, blurred, expanded in width, and became a broad tract of bandit country, where clans of raiders rode at will, and where the writ of neither king ran.

Robert – no more responsible than Edward I or his son for unleashing war – can scarcely be blamed for the well-nigh perpetual hostility between England and Scotland in the Middle Ages. Before his death he had done everything in his power to promote lasting peace between the kingdoms. It is true that he had ordered and participated in the impoverishment of northern England, yet by doing so he demonstrated to Scottish kings who came after him how Scotland might withstand its hostile neighbour. Good King Robert was traditionally said to have bequeathed to the Scots the example of how she might best defend herself. The popular belief that Robert's innovations in tactics and strategy assisted later generations of Scots to resist foreign occupation is reflected in the verse known as 'Good King Robert's Testament'. Penned by an unknown author in the mid fourteenth century, it represents the folk memory of Robert's response to the invasions of 1319 and 1322:

> On foot should be all Scottish war
> Let hill and marsh their foes debar
> And woods as walls prove such an arm
> That enemies do them no harm.
> In hidden spots keep every store
> And burn the plainlands them before
> So, when they find the land lie waste
> Needs must they pass away in haste
> Harried by cunning raids at night
> And threatening sounds from every height.
> Then, as they leave, with great array
> Smite with the sword and chase away.
> This is the counsel and intent
> Of Good King Robert's Testament.

These strictures amount to common sense for a small nation faced with a mighty enemy, but there is justice in the claim that Robert pioneered the methodology of resistance and shattered chivalric taboos against guerrilla warfare.

Paradoxically perhaps, Scots of the later Middle Ages also claimed that Robert was a paragon of chivalric virtue. The myth of himself was perhaps Robert's main legacy to the kingdom of Scotland; as we have seen, he represented himself as the most gallant of knights, a crusader, 'another Maccabeus or Joshua' who had saved his people from servitude. In his own lifetime Robert had become a legend of chivalric valour. Jehan le Bel, the Hainaulter mercenary who in 1350–58 wrote of his own experiences in the Weardale campaign of 1327, recounted some of the stories of Robert's career that were current. This passage from le Bel implies that Robert himself contributed to the legend: 'One time, it is said, and found in a story told by the said King Robert, that the good King Edward had him chased through these great forests for the space of three or four days, by dogs and leash hounds to blood and train them, but he could never find him, nor, whatever the miseries he endured, would he obey this good King Edward.'

Robert himself actively contributed to his myth, and his legend grew and grew. The chronicler Jehan le Bel explicitly refers to a story made by the said King Robert as a source for his account of Robert's being chased by tracker dogs in the moors of south-west Scotland. So Thomas Gray, anthor of *Scalacronica*, and Bower both refer to what seems to have been an official or approved history of Robert's life. Robert represented his own career in glowing terms as is evidenced by the Declaration of Arbroath. But an altogether separate aristocratic dynasty founded its fortunes on the Bruce legend: the Black Douglases incorporated 'the Bludy Hart' into their heraldic arms, and made the most of the kudos afforded them by the participation of Good Sir James in King Robert's heroic achievements.

The Bruce legend was most famously expounded in Barbour's *The Bruce*, composed around 1375, but was also popularised by Fordun, written after 1363, then in the fifteenth century by Walter Bower. Barbour describes Giles d'Argentine as the third-best knight of his day; later, in his narration of the battle of Byland in 1322, he indicates that Sir Ralph Cobham was esteemed the best knight in all England, but that from that day forth his companion at Bylands, Sir Thomas Ughtred, was esteemed above Sir Ralph. Who then was the pick of the chivalric crop? An anecdote is retailed by Bower, that at the court of Edward II the question of who was the greatest knight in Christendom was put to a herald, who 'said openly before everybody that the most peerless and gallant, the most daring and mightiest in warlike deeds, was that invincible prince King Robert Bruce; and this he openly supported and made good by many arguments, and he offered to defend his opinion with his body. Hence he incurred the great displeasure of the English; but he earned the respect and good word of the strangers who loved the truth.'

Long after the Middle Ages, the memory of Robert Bruce remained a powerful symbol of patriotism and political independence. There is a sense in which Robert shaped the Scottish identity: his career determined that Scottish identity would henceforth to a large extent be defined in, and associated with, opposition to England. He revived the Scottish monarchy, which the Edwardian settlement of 1305 had placed in abeyance and which Edward I might well have abolished. That is why, again and again, from his death until the present, the memory of the self-declared hero-king has been pressed into service to inspire Scotland to cherish her independence and separate identity. From the early nineteenth century, public meetings have been held annually on the site of the battle of Bannockburn to celebrate the victory of 1314. It is surely the most frequently re-enacted battle of the Middle Ages. Magnificent statues have been erected in Robert's memory. In the early twenty-first century Robert's memory, and his mission statement, the Declaration of Arbroath, were freely availed of by Scottish nationalists and figured prominently in the devolution and independence referendum debates. Throughout the centuries to the present day Barbour's *The Bruce* has enjoyed continuing and widespread popularity; the stirring rhetoric of the Declaration of

Arbroath has been recited wherever threats to the Scottish identity have been perceived.

Yet in some ways it is surprising that Robert has not achieved warmer recognition from subsequent generations of Scots. In Scotland his memory is revered, rather than cherished. His career was one of several factors which ensured that Scotland's 'national question', the issue of whether her identity was to be merged with that of her southern neighbour, was settled early – much earlier than similar disputes between European nationalities and, indeed, well before modern nationalism itself was born in the French Revolution. Robert's part in the early settlement of Scottish identity effectively meant that his own reputation, glorious in the Middle Ages while there was an external threat, would grow stale when that threat receded. Consequently, when in 1603 the throne of England passed to the King of Scots and the crowns were united in the person of James VI and I, Scotland no longer had need of a mythic hero-king, or an ideology of resistance. The images of Robert, Bannockburn and the Declaration rapidly became hackneyed, stock epithets, recalling past glories which often contrasted ruefully with present adversity. When, in 1707, union of the two kingdoms and parliaments was debated, the duke of Hamilton tried to stir Scottish peers into resisting the Union by asking, 'Are none of the descendants here of those worthy patriots who defended the liberty of their country against all invaders, who assisted the Great King Robert Bruce to restore the constitution and revenge the falsehood of England and the usurpation of Balliol?' George Lockhart of Carnwath remarked that Hamilton 'outdid himself in his patheticall remonstrance'. The pre-Victorian and Victorian learnèd elites, fascinated by all things Gothic, showed considerable interest in the figure of Robert Bruce following the exhumation of 1819, but their conception of him appears to have lingered overlong with us, and now his image appears often as stuffy, moribund and of merely antiquarian interest. In many minds Bruce, Bannockburn and the Declaration of Arbroath belong, as it were, to the outmoded history of 'dates, kings and battles' rather than to the trendier histories of ideas, perspectives and social relations. Furthermore, Robert's reputation has been one of the casualties of the division of history into narrow national perspectives. Fresh approaches to history have recognised his place in the history of northern England, Ireland, the 'Irish Sea Province', the *Gaidhealtachd*, the British Isles, the 'North Sea community' and indeed Europe.

Robert rarely stands on his own: he is habitually mentioned in the same breath as Sir William Wallace and often appears somewhat in Wallace's shadow. This situation dates from the early nineteenth century, when the martial virtues shown jointly by Wallace and Bruce were extolled as anticipating the contemporary exploits of the British army in empire-building. The selfless, patriotic and uncomplicatedly martial figure of Wallace was more easily absorbed into the ideology of Britain and the Empire than that of the wily soldier-politician who had himself made king. From 1800 to 1858 over sixty works on the life of Wallace were published, and statues to Wallace sprang up at Dryburgh, Falkirk, Ayr and Craigie in Ayrshire, before the Wallace monument at Stirling was constructed. There was not the same interest in Bruce. In the 1859 design for an Edinburgh monument to the Wars of Independence, the figure of Bruce was included as representing Perseverance, while that of Wallace was presented as the epitome of Patriotism. It is interesting to note, in this and similar designs, that mid nineteenth-century tendency to commemorate the Wars of Independence, not because they secured Scottish independence from England, but because they ultimately enabled Scotland to enter on an equal basis into peaceful and prosperous union with England five hundred years later! The career of Robert Bruce was difficult to accommodate within such an historical overview.

Robert Bruce's reputation generally suffers from comparison with Wallace. On many levels comparison with Wallace is invalid. We know only a little of Wallace, his background, properties, activities and motives. In fact, we know only the bare highlights of his career; whereas we know a great deal about Bruce, his shortcomings and errors as well as his brilliance. Wallace is thus a simpler character to portray, while understanding Bruce requires a more sophisticated appraisal. Portrayal of Wallace as a proletarian hero, a democratic dynamo who eclipsed the vacillating and timid Scottish nobles of his day is not founded in fact. The son of a squire and thus a member of the *gentil* classes, Wallace had certainly no more regard for the opinions and welfare of the Scottish people than had Bruce. The popular appeal of Wallace lies in his perceived simplicity: his single-minded devotion to his liege King John and his martyr's death for what he believed. As far as we know, Wallace had no dynastic or personal interest in the war; no claim to the throne to consider; no lands in England that might be forfeited, and no tenants whose welfare had to be taken into account. Robert Bruce by contrast came with all these complications. Thus it is easy to portray Wallace as an attractive, unselfish idealist who suffered a martyr's death, while Bruce is vulnerable to caricature as a shifting politician, a pragmatist who compromised and delivered, but who looked after his own interests above all.

Such a contrast between Wallace and Bruce may suit twentieth-century taste in narrative and cinema, but there is no historical basis for it. The truth is that in siding now with Edward I, now with the Comyns as his family interest required, Robert Bruce was behaving in the same way as most of his peers and contemporaries. Probably, as Professor Duncan has neatly expressed it, contemporaries thought none the worse of him for it. The contrast between Wallace and Bruce is therefore superficial. Conversely, Bruce did not 'succeed where Wallace failed'. Rather, Bruce built upon Wallace's achievement: many of those who fought at Stirling Bridge fought also at Bannockburn, and shared the same outrage at the English occupation and humiliation of their country.

The best monuments to Robert's memory are the captivating narrative of Barbour's *The Bruce* and the stirring rhetoric of the

Declaration of Arbroath. In addition, everyone should read and enjoy, without being duped by, the medieval propagandists for the Bruce dynasty: Fordun, Bower and Wyntoun, who hide Robert's faults and mask his true goals to generate a crude and unreconstructed nationalistic fervour. Robert himself made no generalisations on the basis of nationality. During his rebellion against the English king in 1306 it is interesting how highly Robert valued his English knights – Yorkshiremen Christopher Seton and his brothers, and, later, the Northumbrian Sir William Burradon, with whom he fled into the mountains. In his letter to the 'kings prelates and clergy and the inhabitants of Ireland' Robert understands 'our nation' as a pan-Celtic conglomeration, embracing Irish and Scots. His stated concept of nationhood was already archaic, and far removed from the self-contained, homogeneous units that have been understood as nations since the time of the French Revolution. Tempting as it is to portray Robert as a champion of small identities, nations, languages or cultures under threat from the homogenising, destructive forces of globalisation, to do so would be unjust to the Gallovidian and Manx identities which Robert repressed. It is tempting, too, in view of his letter to the Irish, to represent Robert as a champion of Gaelic culture and of the pan-Celtic ideal, yet this was most likely a pose adopted by Robert and Edward Bruce to attract Gaelic support, for their careers showed only superficial commitment to that ideal.

It is, rather, for his leadership of a beleagured people, his revival of the Scottish kingship, his preservation of the Scottish identity in the face of dire external threat and his personal qualities of daring, leadership and determination, that Robert Bruce's memory should be honoured and cherished. However one pictures Robert – on the run from the tracker dogs in Galloway, wading up to his neck in the icy moat at Perth, manfully dispatching Henry de Boun on the day before Bannockburn, or riding at full pelt across the Pennines in his effort to capture Edward II in 1322 – Robert's remarkable adventures will never fail to entertain, intrigue and inspire. Valiant knight, great sea-lord of the *Gaidhealtachd* and triumphant king, his life serves to illustrate that resolute action, determination and perseverance, even in the face of overwhelming odds, can reverse great injustice.

Genealogical tables

Kings of Scotland are shown in dark type. 'Competitors' are those who participated in the Great Cause of 1290–92. Tables 1 and 2 are based on those in Barrow, *Robert Bruce and the Community of the Realm*, with additional material inserted. Table 3 is that given in Duncan, *Scotland: The Making of the Kingdom*. Tables 4 and 5 are based on those in Young, *Robert the Bruce's Rivals*. I have assumed in Table 5 that Emma and Agnes are the same person. Table 6 is based on Séan Duffy's work, 'A new source for the Bruce invasion'; and Table 7 on McDonald, *The Kingdom of the Isles*.

1. Ancestry and children of Robert Bruce (and some family relationships)

Robert, first lord of Annandale (d. 1142)

Robert, second lord of Annandale (d. 1194)

William, third lord of Annandale (d. 1212)

Robert, fourth lord of Annandale (d. 1230)

Robert 'the Noble', fifth lord of Annandale (d. 1295)
(Competitor for the Throne of Scotland, 1290–2)

Duncan of Carrick (d.1250)

Neill earl of Carrick (d.1256)

[an O'Neill of Tyrone?] =

(1) Robert, sixth lord of Annadale (d. 1304) (2) = Eleanor
earl of Carrick in right of his first wife

Adam of Kilconquhar = (1) Marjorie (2) = Countess of Carrick
(d. on crusade, 1270)

(1) Robert, seventh lord of Annandale (2) = Elisabeth de Burgh
earl of Carrick, 1292–1309
Guardian of Scotland, 1298–1300
Robert I, King of Scotland, 1306–29

daughter of the earl of Ulster

Isabella of Mar =

Matilda
= (1) Thomas Issac
= (2) Hugh earl Ross

Margaret
= William earl of Sutherland

John (d. 1326)

David II King of Scotland, 1329–71

Walter the Steward (d. 1317) = Marjorie

Robert Stewart
Robert II
King of Scotland, 1371–90

2. Siblings of Robert Bruce (and their marriages)

Robert Bruce VI
Lord of Annandale

Marjorie, widowed countess of Carrick (2) = (1) Earl of Carrick in right of his wife (d. 1304) (2) = Eleanor

Robert (d. 1329) = (1) Isabel of Mar = (2) Elisabeth de Burgh	Neil (d. 1306)	Edward (d. 1318) = Isabel of Atholl = Isabel of Ross	Thomas (d. 1307)	Alexander (d. 1307)	Isabella = Eric II, King of Norway	Christina = (1) Garnait earl of Mar = (2) Christopher Seton = (3) Alexander Murray	Mary = (1) Neil Campbell = (2) Alexander Fraser	Matilda = Sir Hugh Ross	Unnamed sister = Thomas Randolph the elder

Thomas Randolph earl of Moray, Guardian of Scotland (d. 1333)

This substantially follows Barrow. Both Robert's father and his mother married twice. However, the marriages of some of Robert's sisters are controversial. Penman has the unnamed sister, rather than Christina, marry Garnait earl of Mar, with offspring Donald earl of Mar a nephew of Robert I, and excluding the Randolphs from the royal family.

3. The succession to the Scottish throne

Malcolm IV (1153–65)

William The Lion (1165–1214)

Alexander II (1214–49)

Alexander III (1249–86)

Alexander (d. 1284)

David (d. 1281)

Margaret (d. 1283) = Eric II of Norway

Margaret 'the Maid of Norway' (d. 1296)

Margaret

David I (1124–53) — Earl Henry (d. 1152)

David Earl of Huntingdon (d. 1219)

Ada = Florence III Count of Holland

William I

Florence IV

William II

Florence V Competitor

Margaret

Dervoguilla = John Balliol

John (acc. 1292) (**d. 1314**) **Competitor**

Isabel = Robert Bruce IV

Robert Bruce V Competitor (d. 1295)

Robert Bruce VI Earl of Carrick in right of his wife (d. 1304)

Robert I (**acc. 1306**) (**d. 1329**)

Ada

Henry Hastings

John Hastings Competitor

John (d. 1237)

4. The Comyns of Badenoch
("The Red Comyns")

John I
lord of Badenoch
(d. 1277)

William
(d. 1291)

John II
lord of Badenoch
Guardian of
Scotland 1286
Competitor
(d. 1302)
= Eleanor Balliol
sister of King John Balliol

John III
lord of Badenoch
Guardian of Scotland
1298–1301, 1302–3
(murdered 1306)

John IV
(d. 1314)

Alexander

Robert
(murdered 1306)

John
(d. 1295)

unnamed daughter
= Alexander
MacDougall
of Argyll

John of Argyll
John of Lorne
(d. 1317)

unnamed daughter

unnamed daughter

unnamed daughter

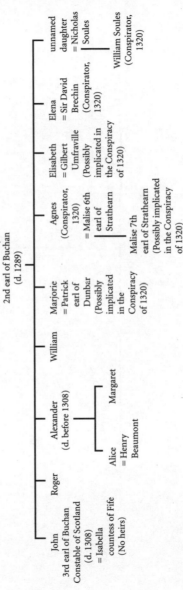

5. The Comyn earls of Buchan ("The Black Comyns")

Alexander Comyn
2nd earl of Buchan
(d. 1289)

John
3rd earl of Buchan
Constable of Scotland
(d. 1308)
= Isabella
countess of Fife
(No heirs)

Roger

Alexander
(d. before 1308)

Alice
= Henry
Beaumont

Margaret

William

Marjorie
= Patrick
earl of
Dunbar
(Possibly
implicated
in the
Conspiracy
of 1320)

Agnes
(Conspirator,
1320)
= Malise 6th
earl of
Strathearn

Malise 7th
earl of Strathearn
(Possibly implicated
in the Conspiracy
of 1320)

Elisabeth
= Gilbert
Umfraville
(Possibly
implicated in
the Conspiracy
of 1320)

Elena
= Sir David
Brechin
(Conspirator,
1320)

**unnamed
daughter**
= Nicholas
Soules

William Soules
(Conspirator,
1320)

6. Possible MacDonald family tree

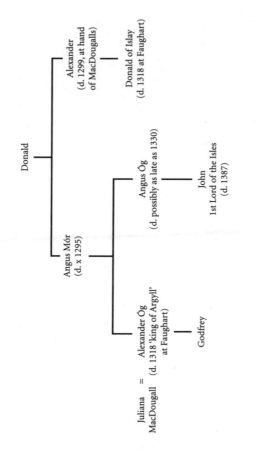

Donald

— Angus Mór (d. x 1295)

— Alexander (d. 1299, at hand of MacDougalls)

— Donald of Islay (d. 1318 at Faughart)

Juliana MacDougall = Alexander Óg (d. 1318 'king of Argyll' at Faughart)

Godfrey

Angus Óg (d. possibly as late as 1330)

John 1st Lord of the Isles (d. 1387)

7. Possible MacDougall family tree

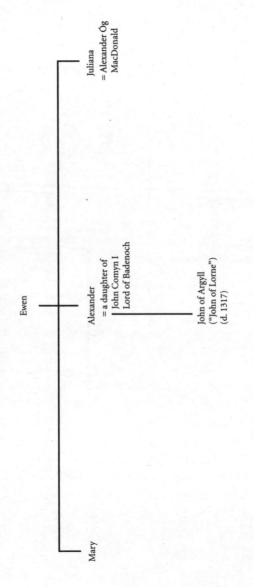

Mary

Ewen

Juliana
= Alexander Óg
MacDonald

Alexander
= a daughter of
John Comyn I
Lord of Badenoch

John of Argyll
("John of Lorne")
(d. 1317)

Notes on sources

Introduction: brushing off the cobwebs

The first chapter of Young, *Robert the Bruce's Rivals* describes the wholesale rewriting of history that occurred to support the cause of the Bruce and Stewart kings against the claims of Edward Balliol and Edward III of England. The Comyns were painted very black indeed by the Brucean propagandists, and an account of Wallace's career was modified to enable favourable comparisons to be made between Robert and Wallace. Quotations in this chapter are from the pro-Bruce partisan chroniclers, Fordun and Bower. The principal milestones in the revision of Robert Bruce are as follows: Barron, *The Scottish War of Independence,* 1934; Barrow, *Robert Bruce,* which first appeared in 1964 and went through four editions, the last of which was in 2005. A.A.M. Duncan edited the collected charters of King Robert in *Regesta Regum Scottorum, The Acts of Robert I.* Duncan also edited and translated *The Bruce* by John Barbour in 1997. The latest biography is by Michael Penman, *Robert the Bruce King of the Scots,* 2014, which is quite incendiary.

1 A man of his time, a man of his place: Scotland in the late thirteenth century

The period is described in the final chapters of Duncan, *Scotland: the Making of the Kingdom* and in the opening chapters of Nicholson, *Scotland: the Later Middle Ages*, and also in the initial chapter of Barrow, *Robert Bruce*. Nicholson is especially strong on medieval economy and society. The Scottish monarchy at this time is described by Duncan in the final chapter of *Scotland: The Making of the Kingdom*, and the concept and process of king-making in *The Kingship of the Scots* by the same author. Gaelic Scotland in this period is explored by McDonald in *The Kingdom of the Isles*; and Irish aspects and resonances by Duffy in 'The Anglo-Norman Era in Scotland' and in *Robert the Bruce's Irish Wars*. I have used Prestwich's examples to illustrate the relative values of commodities: *Edward I,* 'A Note on Money'. The most up-to-date survey of the period is that by Michael Brown, *The Wars of Scotland, 1214–1371*.

2 An inheritance, a grandfather's ambition and a 'coveytous' king (1286–96)

Early family history is covered by Duncan in 'The Bruces of Annandale, 1100-1304'. However, a fuller and more up-to-date treatment is R. Blakely, *The Bruce Family in England and Scotland, 1100-1295*. It is Penman, *Robert the Bruce* who suggests Writtle in Essex as a possible place of Robert's birth. As he points out, Robert's subsequent declaration for the Scots, reported by Guisborough, made in 1297, is less than clear cut. Young, *Robert the Bruce's Rivals* is a valuable study of the powerful Comyn family. The origin of the Bruce claim to the throne is discussed in Duncan, *The Kingship of the Scots*. Duncan is dismissive of Robert Bruce V's claim to have been acknowledged as heir to Alexander II, who in 1238 had no heir of his body. Opinions on Edward I vary markedly: Prestwich defends the English king in his biography *Edward I*, from Barrow's criticisms, set out in *Robert Bruce*. Events following the death of Alexander III are discussed in Barrow, *Robert Bruce* and in Duncan's review of the first edition of that work, 'The community of the realm of Scotland and Robert Bruce'. Nicholson, *Scotland: The Later Middle Ages*, provides a third perspective. Stones is the main authority on the Great Cause, and documents in *Anglo-Scottish Relations* convey a flavour of it. Useful summaries from two different perspectives are given in Prestwich, *Edward I* and Barrow, *Robert Bruce*. The campaign of 1296 and its aftermath are covered in the *Lanercost*, and *Guisborough* chronicles, and the excerpts of popular song are preserved in Peter Langtoft's rhyming chronicle.

3 Resistance and survival in occupied Scotland (1296–1306)

Fisher, *William Wallace* (Birlinn, Edinburgh, 2002) is the leading authority on Wallace himself, though the rebellion is described in Barrow, *Robert Bruce*. The invasion of England is analysed by McNamee, 'William Wallace's Invasion of Northern England in 1297'. The subsequent Edwardian invasions of Scotland are discussed in Prestwich, *Edward I* and in *War Politics and Finance* by the same author. A more recent study however is F. Watson, *Under the Hammer: Edward I and Scotland 1286–1307*. For the MacDougall rebellion, I have used McDonald, *The Kingdom of the Isles*. *Guisborough* and *Lanercost* are the main chronicle sources for the events of 1297–98. The speech to the Annandale knights that *Guisborough* gives Robert cannot be taken as an affirmation that he was born in Scotland. I used Barrow's translation, but adapted it slightly to show the ambivalence that Penman points out. Cressingham's fascinating letters to the English government and king are translated in the second volume of Stevenson, *Documents*. The Battlefields Trust website contains detailed maps and plans of several of the battles connected with Robert Bruce, including: Stirling, Falkirk, Bannockburn and Myton (http://www. battlefieldstrust.com/resource-centre/medieval/).

I have availed of Barrow's translations of the following documents: the letter describing the fracas in the patriot camp at Peebles in 1299; the agreement between Bruce and Edward I; and the letter to Melrose Abbey in 1302. There is some uncertainty as to the precise identity of the MacDonald lord murdered in 1299. This is discussed in McDonald, *The Kingdom of the Isles*. Stones, *Anglo–Scottish Relations* includes a translation of the papal letter 'Scimus Fili'. The idea that Wallace's relationship with the Comyns had been difficult comes from a chronicle tradition, preserved in *Bower,* that he had suppressed the Comyn faction. The episode may belong to 1297–98.

4 'Playing at kings and queens' (1306): Murder, revolution and enthronement

For the coup itself and the coronation the main source is *Guisborough,* interpreted by Barrow, *Robert Bruce*. A radical reinterpretation of John Comyn's murder is offered by Alexander Grant in 'The Death of John Comyn', which leaves open the possibility that Comyn was deliberately assassinated. The evaluation of John Comyn's career is based upon that in Young, *Robert the Bruce's Rivals*. For Robert's escape from Methven to the west, I used Duncan's commentary in (ed.), Barbour, *The Bruce*. The crucial letter of the Berwick correspondent is translated in Stones, *Anglo–Scottish Relations,* No. 34. Duncan's discussion of the rite of king-making in *The Kingship of the Scots* is very revealing. Snatches of English popular song are from Peter Langtoft's chronicle and Wright (ed.), *The Political Songs of England.* Strathearn's predicament is recounted in Neville, 'The Political Allegiance of the Earls of Strathearn during the Wars of Independence'.

5 *'Through the mountains and from isle to isle' (1306–07): Defeat and exile (1306–07)*

The quotation in the title of this chapter is Sir Thomas Gray's description of the fugitive king's western odyssey from his *Scalachronica*. For this chapter I have relied extensively upon Barrow, *Robert Bruce*. The dramatic changes of allegiance in the west are described in McDonald, *The Kingdom of the Isles*. As Duncan points out in his edition of Barbour, *The Bruce,* the murdered Red Comyn, John of Badenoch III, was not John of Argyll's uncle, but his cousin. For Robert's escape from Methven to the west, Duncan's commentary in his edition of Barbour's, *The Bruce* is important. Duncan's views on Robert's intended destination on leaving Dunaverty are given in 'The Scots' Invasion of Ireland, 1315'. The letter to all the kings of Ireland is translated in Barrow, *Robert Bruce*; and for the remarkable 'T' and 'A' letter see Duffy 'The Bruce Brothers and the Irish Sea World, 1306–29', which appears in *Robert the Bruce's Irish Wars*. MacDowall's reward is recorded in *CDS* iv, no. 6. Books IV to VIII of *The Bruce* describe the king's precarious survival in the south-west in 1307. Barbour is also the source for the terrified state of Carrick and Randolph's objections to the king's lack of chivalry in his warfare. Duncan's commentary on *The Bruce* has been followed for the battles of Glentrool and Loudon Hill. The important letter of the Forfar correspondent is translated in Barrow, *Robert Bruce.*

6 *Recovering the kingdom (1307–11)*

This chapter is based on: Barrow, *Robert Bruce*; Duncan (ed.), Barbour, *The Bruce*; and, for developments in England, Haines, *Edward II*. Haines's biography has now been superceded by J.R.S. Phillips, *Edward II*. Higden's famous description of Edward II is from *Polychronicon*. Robert's supposed comparison of Edward II with his father is derived from the *Annales Paulini*. The letter from the earl of Ross, written perhaps in October or November 1307, is a vital source, translated in Barrow, *Robert Bruce*. Further valuable information about events in late 1307 to spring 1308 comes from a badly damaged letter of Duncan of Frendraught to Edward II, which Duncan translates in his commentary to Barbour, *The Bruce*. The 'battle of Inverurie' (or Old Meldrum to give the battle its precise location) is recounted at Duncan (ed.), Barbour, *The Bruce*, Bk. IX; and the 'herschip of Buchan' follows. The special relationship between the Scots and the Flemings is examined in three articles by Reid: 'Trade, Traders and Scottish Independence'; 'The Scots and the Staple Ordinance of 1313; and 'Sea Power and the Anglo-Scottish War 1296-1328'. The campaign against John of Argyll is discussed in McDonald, *The Kingdom of the Isles*. Barrow, *Robert Bruce*, translates John's letter, but I have followed Duncan in dating the letter to after the Battle of Ben Cruachan. The episode of the 'Douglas lardner' is recounted in Duncan (ed.), Barbour, *The Bruce*, Bk V. The sources for the Galloway campaign are *Lanercost*, *Bower* and Barbour, *The Bruce*, Bk. IX. The source for Robert's acquisition of the papal tenth is an article by Easson, 'The Scottish Abbeys and the War of Independence: A Footnote'. The English campaign of 1310–11 is discussed in Haines, *Edward II*, and McNamee, *Wars of the Bruces*. The translation of the Gaelic poem is by Meek, ' "Norsemen and Noble Stewards": The MacSween Poem in the Book of the Dean of Lismore'.

7 The road to Bannockburn (1311–14)

The chief chronicle source for the raiding of England is *Lanercost*. McNamee, *Wars of the Bruces*, analyses the raids into England. Barbour, *The Bruce* is the main source for the capture of the Scottish castles. Galbraith, 'Extracts from the *Historia Aurea* and a French

Brut' reveals the devastating effects of the war on Northumberland. The developing war in the Irish Sea is recorded in Manx chronicle *Chronica Regum Manniae et Insularum*, and in the Anglo-Irish chronicle known as the 'Laud Annals' (contained in the *Chartularies of St Mary's Abbey, Dublin*). Duncan discusses the timing of the arrangements over Stirling Castle in his commentary on Barbour, *The Bruce*, Bk. XI. For the battle of Bannockburn I have relied upon Barrow, *Robert Bruce*, and Duncan's 'Bannockburn Commentary' in his edition of Barbour, *The Bruce*. The main primary sources for the battle are: Duncan (ed.), Barbour, *The Bruce*, Bks. XI, XII and XIII; and the three English chronicles *Lanercost, Vita Edwardi Secundi*, and *Scalachronica*. Even after the publication of the monologues on the battle by Cornell and Brown, debate still rages as to its exact location and the deployments made. The Battlefields Trust website contains detailed maps and plans of the battle: http://www.battlefieldstrust. com/resource-centre/medieval. The polished, possibly official, version of the king's eve-of-battle speech survives in *Bower*.

8 Triumphs and disasters (1314–18): Famine, war and Ireland (1314–18)

Parts of Scotland will have been seriously affected by the widespread animal diseases that occurred in England in the early 1320s, described in Kershaw, 'The Great Famine and Agrarian Crisis in England 1315–1322'. For the raids into England, see Barrow; *Robert Bruce* is perhaps a bit thin on this aspect. Literature on the Irish campaigns is growing. They are discussed in Duncan, 'The Scots' Invasion of Ireland, 1315'; Frame, 'The Bruces in Ireland, 1315–18', and 'The Campaign of the Scots in Munster, 1317'; and Duffy, *Robert the Bruce's Irish Wars*. On the war in the North Sea, in addition to the Reid articles mentioned above, Stevenson, 'The Flemish Dimension of the Auld Alliance' throws light on the complicated relationship between England,

France, Flanders and Scotland. All these aspects are examined in McNamee, *Wars of the Bruces*. Barbour shows interest in raids into England only where chivalric feats of arms are performed; but he is well informed about Ireland and devotes Bk XIV, and parts of XV, XVI and XVIII to events in that theatre of war. The only source suggesting an invitation to Edward is a chronicle fragment, printed in Phillips, 'Documents on the Early Stages of the Bruce Invasions of Ireland, 1315–1316'. The siege of Carlisle is recounted in *Lanercost,* and the anarchic state of Northumberland is described in Scammell, 'Robert I and the North of England', and Miller, *War in the North.* Prestwich analyses the intriguing episodes of the robbery of the cardinals and the Middleton revolt in 'Gilbert de Middleton and the Attack on the Cardinals, 1317' and argues, contrary to my conclusion, that the robbery was *not* orchestrated by King Robert. The raid of 1318, described in *Lanercost,* is analysed in Kershaw, 'The Scots in the West Riding, 1318–19' and McNamee, *Wars of the Bruces.* Sources for the decisive battle of Faughart near Dundalk are the *Annals of Clonmacnoise, Lanercost,* and Barbour *The Bruce,* Bk XVIII.

9 The struggle for peace with honour (1318–23)

Lanercost remains the principal chronicle source for this next phase of the war. The principal secondary works are Penman, *Robert the Bruce,* Barrow, *Robert Bruce* and McNamee, *Wars of the Bruces.* Haines, *Edward II,* covers the important background of English politics, and is also useful for relations between the papacy and the two warring kingdoms. Again, Phillips, *Edward II* is now the authoritative source on English affairs. Barbour shows great interest in the siege of Berwick and in the chivalric feats of the Scottish raid of October 1322. The siege of Berwick is treated in depth in Maddicott, *Thomas of Lancaster* and McNamee, *Wars of the Bruces.* The main chronicle accounts for the raid of 1319 and the battle of Myton are *Vita Edwardi Secundi* and *Lanercost*. For the English invasion of 1322, see Fryde, *The Tyranny and Fall of Edward II*, pp. 129–31. Robert's letter of 1320 to Edward II is translated in Barrow, *Robert Bruce*, and edited and commented on by Duncan, *The Acts of Robert I*. The devastation of the bishopric of Durham early in 1322 is described in the chronicle of Robert of Graystanes, contained in Raine (ed.), *Historiae Dunelmensis Scriptores Tres* and discussed in Scammell, *Robert I and the North of England*. Apart from the stockman's account, most of the financial accounts kept faithfully by Durham Cathedral Priory throughout this period lapse at this point, a circumstance which may be connected with the coming of the Scots. Harclay's appeal for assistance and Edward II's evasive reply is from the *Vita Edwardi Secundi*. Robert's pre-emptive attack on Lancashire and the Western March is described in detail by *Lanercost*. The English invasion of Scotland is described in Barbour, *The Bruce*, Bk XVIII and discussed in Haines, *Edward II* and Fryde, *The Tyrrany and Fall of Edward II*. *Lanercost* provides the narrative of Robert's counterattack. The widespread devastation of Pickering and the East Riding is revealed in McNamee, *Wars of the Bruces*. The Bruce–Harclay treaty is translated in Stones, *Anglo–Scottish Relations*, no. 39; and Robert's letter to Sully in Barrow, *Robert Bruce*.

10 Robert, King of Scots: the governance of Scotland

This chapter relies chiefly upon analyses by Nicholson, *Scotland: The Later Middle Ages* and Barrow's chapter 'Good King Robert' in *Robert Bruce*. However, a more up-to-date summary is provided in Brown, *The Wars of Scotland 1214–1371*. Attempts to deliver papal bulls to Robert in 1317–18 are detailed in the register of the Archbishop of York, William Melton, and recounted in Hill, 'An English Archbishop and the Scottish War of Independence'. We do not have the text of the barons' letter to the cardinals, but Duncan infers its existence from other documents; and as he says in *The Acts of Robert I*, it must have anticipated closely the Declaration of Arbroath. Duncan, *The Nation of Scots and the Declaration of Arbroath* (Historical Association, 1970) was consulted for the Declaration. One of the most entertaining considerations of the document is Brothestone and Ditchburn, ' "1320 and A That": the Declaration of Arbroath and the Remaking of Scottish History', where the modern relevance of the letter is discussed. Antecedents of the Declaration are considered. The letter of the English barons is discussed in Prestwich, *Edward I*; the letter itself was copied into *Guisborough*. The Processus was a legal brief compiled by Baldred Bisset, the chief Scottish lawyer at the papal court in 1301. Many of the materials making up the brief are in *Bower*, vol. vi, and a summary was sent to Edward I by his own lawyers at Avignon, Stones, *Anglo-Scottish Relations*, no. 31. The Scottish arguments are summarised and the English report given in translation in Barrow, *Robert Bruce*. The Remonstrance of the Irish Princes is translated in *Bower*. Cowan discusses the possible meanings of freedom in the Declaration in 'Identity, Freedom and the Declaration of Arbroath'. Penman's article 'A fell coniuracioun' is the first indepth analysis of the Soules conspiracy. The conspiracy reveals the insecurity of the Bruce regime. The main chronicle sources for it are Barbour, *The Bruce*, Bk XIX and *Scalachronica*. The discussion of Robert's relationship with his nobles is abstracted from Barrow, *Robert Bruce*. For Robert's generosity to Moray, see Duncan, *The Acts of Robert I*. The royal administration is discussed briefly in Barrow, *Robert Bruce*, pp. 294-96; and the discussion of Robert's financial arrangements is based upon Nicholson, *Scotland: The Later Middle Ages*.

11 Endgame with England, and death (1323–28)

Barrow, *Robert Bruce*, McNamee, *Wars of the Bruces*, and Nicholson, *Edward III and the Scots* form the basis of this chapter. Two articles by Nicholson, 'A Sequel to Edward Bruce's Invasion of Ireland' and 'The Last Campaign of Robert Bruce', discuss the Irish expeditions of 1327 and 1328 and the Weardale campaign respectively. The main chronicle sources – *Lanercost* and Barbour, *The Bruce*, Bks XIX and XX – are supplemented by a foreigner's point of view in Jehan Le Bel's *Les Vrayes Chroniques*. The part of Le Bel's work which covers the Weardale campaign of 1327 is translated in Duncan (ed.), Barbour, *The Bruce*. The Anglo–Scottish negotiations of 1324 are described in the *Vita Edwardi Secundi*, where it is interesting that Robert demands for the first time the return of the Stone of Scone in expectation of the birth of an heir. Haines, *Edward II* and Fryde, *The Tyranny and Fall of Edward II* describe the overthrow of Edward II and its repercussions for English policy towards Scotland. Philips, *Edward II* now supersedes both. Nicholson, *Edward III and the Scots*, is the best account of this volatile period. Le Bel, Barbour, *Lanercost* and *Scalachronica* all agree that Douglas attacked the English king's camp; Duncan provides all these accounts in his edition of Barbour, *The Bruce*. The possibility of negotiations between the Irish government and Robert in 1327 is considered in McNamee, *Wars of the Bruces*. For the Treaty of Edinburgh–Northampton, I have used Nicholson, *Edward III and the Scots*, which takes account of a trio of articles by Professor Stones in the *Scottish Historical Review* in 1949, 1950 and 1951. The formal quit-claim by which Edward III renounced any claim on Scotland is in Stones, *Anglo–Scottish Relations*. The Barbour passage describing the king's illness is in Barbour, *The Bruce*, Bk XX. On the issue of leprosy versus syphilis, I have consulted Moller-Christensen, and Inkster, 'Cases of Leprosy and Syphilis in the Osteological Collection of the Department of Biomedical Sciences, University of Edinburgh: With a Note on the Skull of Robert the Bruce', and Kaufman and MacLennan, 'Robert the Bruce and Leprosy'. Hamilton, *The Leper King and his Heirs* furnishes the interesting comparison with the twelfth-century leper king of Jerusalem, Baldwin IV. Barrow, *Robert Bruce,* is convinced that the king suffered from leprosy and Penman, *Robert the Bruce*, leaves open that possibility. The paragraph on Bruce's doctors, and the quotation from Maineri is from Caroline Proctor, *Physician to the Bruce*. Financial records, which exist only for the very last years of the reign, are printed in Stuart and Burnett (eds.), *The Exchequer Rolls of Scotland* and contain some details of the royal funeral. Barbour's account of Robert's death-bed speech in *The Bruce*, Bk XX, may be compared with the version in Le Bel (copied into Froissart). Cameron, 'Sir James Douglas, Spain and the Holy Land' and Simpson, 'The Heart of King Robert I: Pious Crusade or Marketing Gambit?' discuss Robert's posthumous crusade and Douglas's exploits in Spain. The interpolation into Barbour's text was borrowed from the allegorical poem by Sir Richard Holland, *The Book of the Howlat*, written *c.* 1448. The Spanish source is the *Gran Cronica De Alfonso XI*, ed. Diego Catalán, Madrid, 1977.

12 The image, the legend and the long shadow of Robert Bruce

Haine, *Edward II* and Maddicott, *Thomas of Lancaster* each describe the popular canonisation of their subjects. The possibility that Edward II survived his reported death in 1327 is reconsidered by Mortimer, 'The Death of Edward II in Berkley Castle'. Part of the report on the exhumation of Robert I was published as 'Extracts from the report made by Henry Jardine'. Little has been written about the exhumation since, except for Kaufman and MacLennan, 'Robert the Bruce and Leprosy'. On the Internet, however, many sites show interest in the present-day whereabouts of Robert's corporeal remains. Penman, *Robert the Bruce*, rather explosively suggests that the tomb and hence the remains are not those of Robert I at all. The subsequent history of Scotland that is given here is based upon Nicholson, *Scotland: The Later Middle Ages* and *Edward III and the Scots*. The reference to Robert in the Union debate is from Szechi (ed.), '*Scotland's Ruine': Lockhart of Carnforth's Memoirs of the Union* (Aberdeen, 1995). The analysis of nineteenth-century attitudes to Bruce and Wallace is based upon that in Morton, *Unionist Nationalism: Governing Urban Scotland, 1830–1860.*

Further reading

About Robert Bruce

Barbour, John (edited and translated by A.A.M. Duncan), *The Bruce* (Canongate Books Ltd, 1997), the verse epic which is the principal narrative source for his life, in the original Scots, with translation on facing pages

Barrow, G.W.S., *Robert Bruce and the Community of the Realm of Scotland* (Edinburgh University Press, 2005), the established scholarly biography

Penman, Michael, *Robert the Bruce: King of the Scots* (Yale University Press, 2014), a revision that challenges some long-accepted notions

About medieval Scotland

Broun D., Finlay R.J., and Lynch M. (eds.), *Image and Identity: The Making and Re-making of Scotland through the Ages* (John Donald, 1998)

Brown, Michael, *The Wars of Scotland, 1214–1371: The New Edinburgh History of Scotland Volume 4* (Edinburgh University Press, 2004)

Ditchburn, D., *Scotland and Europe: The Medieval Kingdom and Its Contacts with Christendom, 1214–1560* (Tuckwell Press, 2001), the European context

Duncan, A.M.M., *Scotland: the Making of the Kingdom (Edinburgh University Press, 1975)*

MacDonald, R.A., *The Kingdom of the Isles: Scotland's Western Seaboard in the Central Middle Ages, c.1000–1336* (Tuckwell, 1997)

Nicholson, R., *Scotland: The Later Middle Ages* (Edinburgh University Press, 1974)

Young, A., *Robert the Bruce's Rivals: The Comyns, 1212–1314* (Tuckwell Press, 1997)

About the battle of Bannockburn

Brown, Michael, *Bannockburn: The Scottish War and the British Isles, 1307–1323* (Edinburgh University Press, 2008)

Cornell, David, *Bannockburn: The Triumph of Robert the Bruce* (Yale University Press, 2009)

Watson, F. and Anderson, M., *The Battle of Bannockburn: A Study for Stirling Council* (Stirling, 2001)

About the English war effort in Scotland

Haines, R.M., *Edward II: Edward of Caernarfon: His Life, His Reign, and Its Aftermath (1284–1330)* (McGill-Queen's University Press, 2003)

Nicholson, R., *Edward III and the Scots* (Oxford University Press, 1965)

Prestwich, M., *Edward I* (Methuen, 1988)

Watson, F., *Under the Hammer* (Tuckwell Press, 1998)

About the Declaration of Arbroath

Duncan, A.M.M., *The Nation of the Scots and the Declaration of Arbroath* (Historical Association, 1970)
Brotherstone, T. and Ditchburn, D. (eds.), *Freedom and Authority: Scotland c. 1050–c. 1650: Historical and Historiographical Essays Presented to Grant G. Simpson* (Tuckwell Press, 2000)

About the wider context of Robert I's wars

Davies, R.R. (ed.), *The British Isles 1100–1500: Comparisons, Contrasts and Connections* (John Donald, 1988)
Duffy, S. (ed), *Robert the Bruce's Irish Wars: the Invasions of Ireland 1306–1329* (Stroud, Tempus Publishing, 2002), a revised itinerary and chronology in Edward Bruce's invasion of Ireland
McNamee, C., *The Wars of the Bruces: Scotland, England and Ireland 1307–1328* (Tuckwell Press, 1997), a survey of the wider implications of the conflict

Bibliography

Printed Sources

The Acts of Robert I King of Scots 1306–1329: Regesta Regum Scottorum, v, ed. A.A.M. Duncan (Edinburgh, 1988)

Anglo-Scottish Relations 1174–1328, E.L.G. Stones (Oxford, 1965)

Annals of Ulster, ii, ed. and transl. W.M. Hennessy and B. MacCarthy (4 vols, Dublin, 1893)

The Annals of Clonmacnoise, ed. and transl. D. Murphy (Dublin, 1896)

Barbour, John, *The Bruce*, ed. and transl. A.A.M. Duncan (Edinburgh, 1997)

The Book of Pluscarden, ii, F.J.H. Skene ed. and transl. (2 vols, The Historians of Scotland, Edinburgh, 1877, 1880)

Calendar of Close Rolls

Calendar of Patent Rolls

Calendar of Documents Relating to Scotland, ed. J. Bain (vols i–iv) (1881–88); Simpson G.C., and Galbraith, J.D. eds. (vol. v, Supplementary, Scottish Record Office, 1988)

Chronica Regum Manniae et Insularum (Douglas, 1924)

The Chronicle of Lanercost, ed. and transl. H. Maxwell (Glasgow, 1913)

The Chronicle of Pierre de Langtoft, ii, ed. and transl. T. Wright (2 vols, Rolls Series: London, 1868)

'Chronicle of Robert of Graystanes' in *Historiae Dunelmensis Scriptores Tres*, ed. J. Raine (Surtees Society, viii, 1839)

The Chronicle of Walter of Guisborough, ed. H. Rothwell (Camden 3rd series, lxxxix, 1957)

Documents Illustrative of the History of Scotland, ed. J. Stevenson (2 vols, Edinburgh, 1870)

Edward I and the Throne of Scotland 1290–1296, ed. E.L.G. Stones and G.G. Simpson (2 vols, Oxford 1978)

The Exchequer Rolls of Scotland, i, J. Stuart and G. Burnett (Edinburgh, 1878)

'Extracts from the Report made by Henry Jardine, Esquire, His Majesty's Remembrancer in Exchequer Relative to the Tomb of King Robert Bruce and the Church of Dunfermline' *Archaeologica Scotica: Transactions of the Society of Antiquaries of Scotland* ii (1822), pp. 435–54

'Extracts from the Historia Aurea and a French Brut', V.H. Galbraith, *English Historical Review* xliii (1928), p. 209

Jacobi Grace, Kilkenniensis, Annales Hiberniae, ed. and transl. R. Butler (Irish Archaeological Society, 1841)

John of Fordun's Chronicle of the Scottish Nation, ii, ed. and transl. W.F. Skene (2 vols, The Historians of Scotland, Edinburgh, 1871 and 1872)

'The Laud Annals' in *Chartularies of St. Mary's Abbey, Dublin*, ii, J.T. Gilbert (2 vols, Rolls Series, Dublin, 1884)

Le Bel, Jean, *Vrayes chroniques*, ed. M. Polain (Brussels, 1863)

'"Norsemen and Noble Stewards": The MacSween Poem in the Book of the Dean of Lismore', D. Meek, *Cambrian Medieval Celtic Studies* xxxiv (1997)

Polychronicon Ranulphi Higden Monachi Cestrensis, ed. J.R. Lumby, viii (9 vols, Rolls Series: London 1865–86)

Rotuli Scotiae, i, (2 vols, Record Commission, 1841)

Scalachronica by Sir Thomas Grey of Heton Knight, ed. and transl. H. Maxwell (Glasgow, 1907)

Scotichronicon by Walter Bower, ed. and transl. D.E.R. Watt and others (9 vols, 1987–98)

'*Scotland's Ruine*': *Lockhart of Carnforth's Memoirs of the Union*, ed. D. Szechi (Aberdeen, 1995)

Vita Edwardi Secundi, ed. and transl N. Denholm Young (London, 1957)

Books and Articles

Barron, E.M., *The Scottish War of Independence* (Inverness, 1934)

Barrow, G.W.S., *Robert Bruce and the Community of the Realm of Scotland* (rd edn, Edinburgh 1988)

Brothestone, T., and Ditchburn, D., '"1320 and A That": the Declaration of Arbroath and the Remaking of Scottish History' in eds T. Brotherstone and D. Ditchburn, *Freedom and Authority: Historical and Historiographical Essays presented to Grant G. Simpson* (East Linton, 2000)

Brown, M., *The Wars of Scotland, 1214–1371: The New Edinburgh History of Scotland*, Volume 4 (Edinburgh University Press, 2004).

—*Bannockburn: The Scottish War and the British Isles, 1307–1323* (Edinburgh University Press, 2008)

Caldwell, D., 'The Monymusk Reliquary: the Breccbennach of St Columba?' in *Proceedings of the Society of Antiquaries of Scotland*, 131 (2001)

—'Scottish Spearmen, 1298–1314: An Answer to Cavalry', *War in History* 19 (2012)

Cameron, S., 'Sir James Douglas, Spain and the Holy Land' in eds T. Brotherstone and D. Ditchburn, *Freedom and Authority: Historical and Historiographical Essays presented to Grant G. Simpson* (East Linton, 2000)

Cornell, D., *Bannockburn: the Triumph of Robert the Bruce* (Yale University Press, 2009)

Cowan E.J., 'Identity, Freedom and the Declaration of Arbroath in Image and Identity' in *The Making and Re-making of Scotland through the Ages*, ed. D. Broun, R.J. Finlay and M. Lynch (Edinburgh, 1998), pp. 38–68, especially pp. 43–49.

Duncan, A.A.M., *Scotland: the Making of the Kingdom* (Edinburgh, 1975)

—*The Kingship of the Scots, 842–1292: Succession and Independence* (Edinburgh, 2003)

—'The Bruces of Annandale, 1100–1304', *Transactions of the Dumfriesshire and Galloway Natural History and Antiquarian Society* lxix (1996) pp. 89–102

—'The community of the realm of Scotland and Robert Bruce', *SHR* xlv (1966), pp. 184–201

—'The Scots' Invasion of Ireland, 1315' in ed. R.R. Davies, *The British Isles 1100–1500* (Edinburgh, 1988), pp. 100–17

—*The Nation of Scots and the Declaration of Arbroath* (Historical Association, 1970)

Duffy, S., *Robert the Bruce's Irish Wars: the Invasions of Ireland 1306–1329* (Stroud, 2002)

—'The Anglo-Norman Era in Scotland: Convergence and Divergence' in eds T.M. Devine and J.F. McMillan, *Celebrating Columba* (Edinburgh, 1999), pp. 15–34

—'The Bruce Brothers and the Irish Sea World, 1306–29', *Cambridge Medieval Celtic Studies* xxi (1991), pp. 55–86

—'The Continuation of Trevet: A New Source for the Bruce Invasion', *Proceedings of the Royal Irish Academy*, 91C (1991), pp. 303–15

Fisher, A., *William Wallace* (Edinburgh, 2002)

Frame, R., 'The Bruces in Ireland, 1315–18' and 'The Campaign of the Scots in Munster, 1317' both in *Ireland and Britain, 1170–1450* (London, 1998), pp. 71–98 and 99–112

Fryde, N., *The Tyranny and Fall of Edward II* (Cambridge, 1979)

Grant, A., 'The Death of John Comyn: What Was Going On?' *Scottish Historical Review* lxxxvi (October 2007), pp. 176–224

Haines, R.M., *Edward II: Edward of Caernarfon: His Life, His Reign, and Its Aftermath (1284–1330)* (McGill-Queen's University Press, 2003)

Hamilton, B., *The Leper King and his Heirs: Baldwin IV and the Crusader Kingdom of Jerusalem* (Cambridge, 2000)

Hill, R., 'An English Archbishop and the Scottish War of Independence', *Innes Review* xxii (1971), pp. 59–71

Kaufman, M.H., and MacLennan, W.J., 'Robert the Bruce and Leprosy', *Proceedings of the Royal College of Physicians Edinburgh* xxx (2000), pp.75–80

Kershaw, I., 'The Great Famine and Agrarian Crisis in England 1315–1322', in ed. R.H. Hilton, *Peasants, Knights and Heretics: Studies in Medieval English Social History.* (Cambridge, 1981)

McDonald, R.A., *The Kingdom of the Isles: Scotland's Western Seaboard in the Central Middle Ages, c.1000–1336* (East Linton, 1997)

McNamee, C., *The Wars of the Bruces: Scotland, England and Ireland 1307–1328* (East Linton, 1997)

—'William Wallace's Invasion of Northern England in 1297', *Northern History* xxvi (1990), pp. 40–58

Maddicott, J.R., *Thomas of Lancaster* (Oxford, 1970)

Miller, E., *War in the North* (Hull, 1960)

Moller-Christensen, V., and Inkster, R.G., 'Cases of Leprosy and Syphilis in the Osteological Collection of the Department of Biomedical Sciences, University of Edinburgh: With a Note on the Skull of Robert the Bruce', *Danish Medical Bulletin* xii (1965), pp. 11–18

Mortimer, I., 'The Death of Edward II in Berkley Castle', *English Historical Review* cxx (2005), pp. 1175–1214

Morton, G., *Unionist Nationalism: Governing Urban Scotland, 1830–1860* (East Linton, 1999)

Neville, C., 'The Political Allegiance of the Earls of Strathearn during the Wars of Independence', *SHR* lxv (1986), pp. 142–46

Nicholson, R., *Edward III and the Scots* (Oxford, 1965)

— *Scotland: the Later Middle Ages* (Edinburgh, 1974)

— 'A Sequel to Edward Bruce's Invasion of Ireland', *SHR* xlii (1963–64) pp. 30–40

— 'The Last Campaign of Robert Bruce', *English Historical Review* lxxvii (1962), pp. 233–46

Oxford Dictionary of National Biography

Pearson, K., 'King Robert the Bruce, 1274–1329. His skull and portraiture', *Biometrika 16* (1924), pp. 252–72

Penman, M., 'A fell coniuracioun agayn Robert the douchty king: the Soules conspiracy of 1318–20', *The Innes Review* vol. 50, no. 1 (1999), pp. 25–7

— *Robert the Bruce: King of the Scots* (Yale University Press, 2014)

— and Stead, M.J., *In the Footsteps of Robert Bruce* (Stroud, 1999)

Phillips, J.R.S., 'Documents on the Early Stages of the Bruce Invasions of Ireland, 1315–1316', *Proceedings of the Royal Irish Academy* lxxix c (1979), pp. 269–70

— *Edward II* (Yale University Press, 2011)

Prestwich, M., *Edward I* (London, 1988)

— *War Politics and Finance (London, 1972)*

—'Gilbert de Middleton and the Attack on the Cardinals, 1317' in T. Reuter, *Warriors and Churchmen in the High Middle Ages: Essays Presented to Karl Leyser* (Hambledon, 1992), pp. 179–94

Proctor, C., 'Physician to the Bruce: Maino de Maineri in Scotland', *Scottish Historical Review* lxxxvi (April 2007), pp. 16–26

Reid, W.S., 'Trade, Traders and Scottish Independence', *Speculum* xxix (1954), pp. 210–22

— 'The Scots and the Staple Ordinance of 1313', *Speculum* xxxiv (1959) pp. 598–610

— 'Sea Power and the Anglo-Scottish War 12960–1328', *The Mariners' Mirror* xlvi (1960), pp. 7–23

Runciman, S., *A History of the Crusades*, iii (London, 1954)

Scammell, J., 'Robert I and the North of England', *English Historical Review* lxxiii (1958), pp. 385–403

Scott, Sir Walter, 'Robert Bruce King of Scotland and the Spider', in *Tales of a Grandfather: Being the History of Scotland* (Edinburgh, 1827–29)

Simpson, G.G., 'The Heart of King Robert I: Pious Crusade or Marketing Gambit?' in ed. B.E. Crawford, *Church, Chronicle and Learning in Medieval and Early Renaissance Scotland* (Edinburgh, 1999), pp. 173–86

Stevenson, A., 'The Flemish Dimension of the Auld Alliance' in G.C. Simpson, *Scotland and the Low Countries 1124–1994* (East Linton, 1996)

Watson, F., *Under the Hammer: Edward I and Scotland 1286–1307* (East Linton, 1998)

— and Anderson, M., *The Battle of Bannockburn: A Study for Stirling Council* (Stirling, 2001)

Young, A., *Robert the Bruce's Rivals: The Comyns, 1212–1314* (East Linton, 1997)

Index

Kings are listed as titled; hence John Balliol is listed as John I, and Robert Bruce as Robert I. Earls who had family names are listed under them, rather than under the name of the earldom. In place-names, references are to historic, rather than modern, counties